FINANCIAL HANDBOOK FOR MAYORS AND CITY MANAGERS

Terry Nichols Clark
G. Edward DeSeve
J. Chester Johnson

Second Edition

For the United States Conference of Mayors

Van Nostrand Reinhold/Council on Municipal Performance Series

VAN NOSTRAND REINHOLD COMPANY
New York

Library of Congress Catalog Card Number: 84-27058
ISBN: 0-442-21775-7

Manufactured in the United States of America

Published by Van Nostrand Reinhold Company Inc.
135 West 50th Street
New York, New York 10020

Van Nostrand Reinhold Company Limited
Molly Millars Lane
Wokingham, Berkshire RG11 2PY, England

Van Nostrand Reinhold
480 Latrobe Street
Melbourne, Victoria 3000, Australia

Macmillan of Canada
Division of Gage Publishing Limited
164 Commander Boulevard
Agincourt, Ontario M1S 3C7, Canada

15 14 13 12 11 10 9 8 7 6 5 4 3 2 1

Library of Congress Cataloging in Publication Data
Clark, Terry N.
Financial handbook for mayors and city managers.

(Van Nostrand Reinhold/Council on Municipal Performance series)
Bibliography: p.
Includes index.
1. Municipal finance—United States. I. DeSeve, G. Edward. II. Johnson, J. Chester. III. United States Conference of Mayors. IV. Title. V. Series.
HJ9145.C53 1985 352.1′0973 84-27058
ISBN 0-442-21775-7

Series Introduction

Financial Handbook for Mayors and City Managers is the second in a series of publications produced by the Council on Municipal Performance (COMP) and published by Van Nostrand Reinhold. The COMP series was introduced with the publication of *Using Performance Measures in Local Government: A Guide to Improving Decisions, Performance and Accountability,* by Paul D. Epstein. Both of these books address municipal problems with a practical approach to implementing and maintaining performance in local government.

COMP is proud to be associated with the series contributing experts who have analyzed the crucial financial problems confronting municipalities and their administrators. The purpose of the series is to educate and inform local officials on methods for improving municipal performance and achieving government excellence.

JOHN TEPPER MARLIN
Series Editor

Van Nostrand Reinhold/Council on Municipal Performance Series

Using Performance Measurement in Local Government, Paul D. Epstein

Financial Handbook for Mayors and City Managers, Terry Nichols Clark, G. Edward DeSeve, and J. Chester Johnson

Foreword

During the 1970s, we saw an increased interest among mayors in financial management issues. This became evident at our Mayors Leadership Institutes (MLIs) which we conduct regularly.

This *Handbook* was prepared to assist mayors to better understand and grapple with their cities' financial problems. Since salient issues differ for each mayor, we chose a handbook format that can stand on its own and thus be consulted by mayors at need.

We have had some of the nation's top experts lead discussions at MLIs and asked three of them to work together on this *Handbook*. They met with city officials and financial institutions to include the best ideas from across the country. We believe that this product of their labors demonstrates the innovative practices mayors have undertaken to meet the complex financial conditions and problems of their cities.

JOHN J. GUNTHER
Executive Director
United States Conference of Mayors

Preface for Mayors

This *Handbook* is for mayors and chief city officials. Prepared for the Mayors Leadership Institute of the U.S. Conference of Mayors, it can be read in its entirety or used as a reference guide. The first pages of Chap. 1 summarize the major themes treated. The checklist in Chap. 11 can be filled out and used as a Mayor's Fact Sheet for individual cities. The Fact Sheet can serve as a major resource for the mayor and city administrators in determining their city's status and identifying the specific problems in need of resolution.

The *Handbook* does not present a "right" way to proceed but rather lists options to review in areas where decisions are necessary. We draw on technical materials but try to minimize technical concerns, instead stressing the critical policy options. To help the reader review problems and solutions, we list specific questions to discuss with local government staff. Further help can be obtained, often without charge, from several groups listed in Chap. 10. Resources in that chapter also include technical analyses and reports.

The *Handbook* reviews some basics in an elementary manner but also summarizes sophisticated financial management tools that will be new to most mayors. Thus, both the mayor with little technical background and the experienced veteran can find the *Handbook* useful.

One of the ways in which a mayor can review financial management options is to discuss them with other mayors who have already resolved related problems. This *Handbook* emerged from many such discussions among mayors. We hope that they will find it useful in addressing the particular needs of their individual cities.

Preface for Local Government Staff and Other "Nonmayors"

In shaping urban policy, city staff and advisors are obviously of critical importance, but since the mayor and council have to "sign off" all major items, we often discuss decisions as if they were largely those of the mayor.

This *Handbook* considers major fiscal policy commitments. It is not a "how to do it" manual on technical issues, although it reviews the best of these, seeks to extract their general policy lessons, and cites many works on them at the end of Chap. 10. The city's public officials play critical roles in filling in details as well as preparing major policy decisions. This *Handbook* should be most helpful concerning the latter. It is meant to bridge technical specialties such as budgeting and auditing, which are sometimes discussed as if they were in conflict with one or another, or in any case separate. If the *Handbook* helps city officials think of these activities as interrelated so that they keep one another informed on general urban policy, it will have achieved one of its major goals.

Acknowledgments

This second edition of *Financial Handbook for Mayors and City Managers* was based on information and materials provided by a number of mayors and cities through Mayors Leadership Institutes and other activities of the United States Conference of Mayors. Appreciation is extended to members of the national advisory group to the project—Mayors Eileen Anderson (Honolulu), Corinne Freeman (St. Petersburg), Arthur Holland (Trenton), Webster Hubbell (Little Rock); Bill Morris (Waukegan), and Pete Wilson (San Diego). The *Handbook,* a project of the Conference's Institute for Urban and Regional Economic Analysis, was prepared under the guidance and leadership of John J. Gunther, Executive Director of the United States Conference of Mayors, with Melvin A. Mister, Director of the Institute, and staff support provided by Jacqueline Aamot, Thomas McClimon, Marta Goldsmith, and Nancy Moore. Consultants for the revised edition included Professor Terry Nichols Clark of the University of Chicago and J. Chester Johnson of Government Finance Associates, Inc. The first edition *A Mayor's Financial Management Handbook* was prepared with assistance from G. Edward DeSeve, Samuel P. Katz, and Public Financial Management, Inc.

Special recognition for significant contributions goes to John Tepper Marlin, Stephen Collins, and Immanuel Ness of the Council on Municipal Performance; Mayors Lucinda Kasperson and Edward G. Crane; and Richard Higgins, William Lucy, Frederick Hayes, Robert D. Fraser, Reid Charles, James L. Chan, and Peter F. Rousmaniere. The index was prepared by Harvard undergraduates David J. Caceres and Michelle Davila, as interns at the Council on Municipal Performance.

Both the first and second editions of the *Handbook* have benefited from the interest and generous support of the Department of Housing and Urban Development's Financial Management Capacity Sharing Program formerly directed by Alan R. Siegel, and assisted by Hartley C. Fitts and Edwin A. Stromberg.

The first edition—prepared by Marta V. Goldsmith and Nancy Moore of the U. S. Conference of Mayors, and by G. Edward DeSeve, Martin S. Dorph, Rodney Johnson, Samuel P. Katz, Christina C. Ward, Eileen C. Lahey, and Norma J. Pettiford of Public Financial Management, Inc.—was issued in 1980 and distributed to many mayors, often via Mayors Leadership Institutes.

Originally a looseleaf volume, the *Handbook* was designed to be updated regularly.

For the second edition, several activities were undertaken. All members of the Conference of Mayors were requested to submit unusual analyses or reports concerning financial management. Materials illustrating specific practices were suggested by dozens of cities. Second, a national advisory group was formed, consisting of Mayors Eileen Anderson of Honolulu, Corinne Freeman of St. Petersburg, Arthur Holland of Trenton, N.J., Webster Hubbell of Little Rock, Bill Morris of Waukegan, Ill., and Pete Wilson of San Diego. They and their staffs reviewed the *Handbook* and suggested additional points to cover. Third, two consultants, Professor Terry Nichols Clark of The University of Chicago and J. Chester Johnson of Government Finance Associates, Inc., reviewed the reports submitted by individual cities and other new materials concerning financial management, especially those from the HUD Financial Management Capacity Sharing Program. Next, they visited 22 cities with (1) particularly interesting practices, or (2) severe fiscal problems. Mayors and their staffs were interviewed about the actual workings of the practices discussed in various documents. In this way, frank assessments of the strengths and weaknesses of many practices emerged, especially as these are viewed from the standpoint of the mayor. Terry Clark then wrote Chaps. 2, 3, and 11 for this volume and revised Chaps. 1, 6, 7, 8, and 9. Chester Johnson wrote Chap. 5 and revised Chap. 4. Tom McClimon of the Conference staff revised Chap. 10 and served as Project Director. Melvin Mister, Director of the Institute for Urban and Regional Economic Analysis of the Conference of Mayors, provided overall direction. John Gunther, Executive Director of the Conference, intervened at critical points to help keep the *Handbook* alive and current. Helpful comments came from Richard Higgins, William Lucy, Frederick O'R. Hayes, Mayor Lucinda Kasperson, Robert D. Fraser, Reid Charles, James L. Chan, Peter F. Rousmaniere, and Mayor Edward G. Crane, Jr.

The first edition was prepared with grant H-5051G and the second edition initiated under Contract Number H-5428-R6, both from the Department of Housing and Urban Development to the Institute for Urban and Regional Economic Analysis of the U.S. Conference of Mayors. Grantees performing such work under government sponsorship are encouraged to express their own judgement freely. Therefore, points of view or opinions stated in this *Handbook* do not represent the official position or policy of the Department of Housing and Urban Development. The *Handbook* has also been supported from other sources, including membership contributions of the U.S. Conference of Mayors. Mayors from cities of all types and sizes contributed their own and staff time to this effort in the hope that it can be useful to other mayors.

Contents

1
Mayoral Leadership and Financial Management

A basic message of this handbook is that mayors have a number of options available in almost every area of financial management. It can be used either as a basic text or as a reference book for problems of a periodic nature. Its major objective is to pose specific questions and then provide possible options and resources that may be resorted to in order to resolve them.

This chapter will begin with a brief overview of subsequent chapters. Its second section outlines the financial functions that are undertaken by a city or county and the financial management activities that *could* be undertaken by a mayor. The third section examines the relationship of the governmental structure to the mayor's role in financial management. It discusses the nature of executive responsibility, the functions of the mayor in the council/manager form of government, the relationship of the mayor to other elected officials responsible for various aspects of financial management, the impact of the intergovernmental structure on the mayor's role, and finally the basic duties that govern the mayor's actions apart from all structural considerations.

I. OVERVIEW

Mayors are being fiscally challenged in all parts of the country. High inflation and low economic growth, tax and expenditure limits, and reduced intergovernmental revenues have generated fiscal crises in many cities. New mayors have come to office committed to more economic management and oversight. This handbook will discuss how specific problems have been resolved in selected cities. Although only a few cities use the more sophisticated methods, considerable financial management expertise has become available. Some methods are costly to implement; many others depend in considerable measure on supportive elected officials. Although city administrators can help the mayors review past practices and implement most new policies, this handbook poses questions and offers options that may well broaden the mayor's outlook.

An inherent problem in most financial management methods is that they are developed more with the staff in mind than the mayor and council. The mayor needs enough information to make decisions but should not be burdened with complicated analyses. Throughout the handbook we review options for developing a city's financial management capabilities. These options should be reviewed within the context of the unique features of the mayor's own city. There is no one right way to manage city finances, but many means are available to help mayors successfully implement policy in their own way. Among the following financial management functions, each of which is discussed in a separate chapter, it is the mayor's responsibility to seek out the easiest and most efficient method. Some are more complex than others, but often the mayor's best approach is to study simple ratios such as debt/taxable property or garbage collected/dollar computed over time or compared to other cities.

Population, Employment, and Citizen Policy Preferences

Several indicators are necessary to help a city assess local population and economic trends. Recent analyses suggest that a focus on migration of households (not just jobs) and on small firms (under 20 employees) is of critical importance for many cities. Past efforts to attract or retain jobs and population have often failed. Strategies in this area should reflect the goals of individual communities and should be based on a realistic appraisal of recent political, economic, and demographic trends. Specific benefits to the city need to be carefully compared to tax abatements and other incentives that developers often urge administrators to extend.

It is important to ascertain citizen priorities before crises occur. Informal procedures include discussion at public meetings and with persons knowledgeable about different neighborhoods. More formal procedures include citizen surveys of organized groups and service recipients, referenda, and reviews of user charges and consumption patterns (such as those for parks or recreation, school enrollment, or housing and migration patterns). Citizen preference data are important to help mayors trade-off demands for services by specific groups while holding taxes down to a reasonable level. Chapter 2 concludes with examples of specific survey items.

Budgeting: Management Reviews, Expenditures, and Cutbacks

The purpose of a budget is to determine what resources can be raised and how to allocate them among service needs. In this regard, the mayor has two primary roles: first, to define the overall level of resources and specific revenues, and second, to create a process allowing both department heads and finance officers to discuss knowledgeably the basic purposes for which budget dollars are intended and the operation levels that will be required.

A clear budget "call" with a detailed budget calendar in a carefully designed format will allow the mayor to communicate his policy on spending levels, operational evaluation, and measurement of achievement to all elements of the government.

The mayor should not depend on one particular budget system since various systems exist that can be helpful in organizing material and activity. The mayor should therefore work with the finance staff to design a system utilizing the most appropriate features of various systems.

Productivity is a continual problem for many cities. It is usually linked to the budget process and financial management. How to approach productivity depends on the styles of individual mayors and the particular needs of their cities. Several options that have worked in cities as diverse as Pittsburgh and San Diego will be reviewed. Cost reduction options, such as contracting, privatization, and use of volunteers are emphasized and each option's advantages and disadvantages briefly discussed.

Debt Management: Impacts of Recent Trends for Cities

Several developments in the 1970s and early 1980s have substantially changed the environment for municipal debt. Market access for cities has grown more difficult as a result of inflation, heightened concerns about credit risk by investors, less demand for tax-exempt securities, and new requirements for disclosure of municipal fiscal practices. These problems have made borrowing more complex and costly. On the positive side, however, several financial instruments have been developed to provide more rapid, flexible, and less costly means for cities to borrow. These include leverage-leases, warrants, and tax-increment financing.

The mayor must have an understanding of how local and state debt affect the borrowing position of a city before considering changes in practices to reduce borrowing costs. Financial advisers can suggest appropriate new financing methods.

Accounting as a Management Tool

After the budget is adopted, the accounting system helps monitor revenue, debt, and expenditure. Most accounting practices are the result of state laws meant to discourage corruption among public officials. Although bond holders also press for such information, the accounting system should not be designed just for outsiders, but to help the mayor manage the city. Valuable data can be obtained from the accounting system on the performance of various services. This information can be matched with expenditures and costs of services by subfunction to help the mayor decide where to increase or curtail service. Administrative problems can be detected and solved by a smooth reporting system. To improve efficiency and reduce costs, underutilized agencies and staff can be merged or eliminated.

Pensions

This handbook poses three basic decision areas concerning pension systems—the benefit level, funding level, and investment strategies. The mayor should be aware of these even if he or she does not directly control them. Chapter 7 outlines how pension systems work.

Integrated Financial Management

In many cities, financial concerns like debt, accounting, and budgeting proceed according to their own independent logic. It is essential for the mayor to make these elements cohere in an integrated financial management picture. This is easily said but never perfectly accomplished. We offer a few checks to show how the elements may be better coordinated to achieve a more coherent financial management.

Checklist and Mayor's Factsheet

The Checklist in Chap. 8 interrelates many of the themes of earlier chapters. It lists problem signals and corresponding countermeasures. In Chap. 9, the Mayor's Factsheet suggests the specific data that may be assembled to see how a city ranks on various indicators.

System Swaps; Who Can Help; Resources

Chapters 9 and 10 list many examples of interesting practices adopted by cities, and the numerous groups available to help mayors in specific areas, many of whose services are free of charge.

II. CITY OR COUNTY FINANCIAL MANAGEMENT FUNCTIONS

The remainder of this chapter will discuss the financial management functions that cities must perform and the mayor's role in implementing them. Subsequent chapters will consider these functions in greater depth. They include financial planning, financial implementation, financial control, money market activity, financial structure and policy, financial disclosure, and pension management.

Financial Planning

Successful financial management requires not only that a city be aware of its financial history but also that it knows its direction and priorities.

Budgeting: Budgeting involves two separate concepts: (1) the budget as a legal document stating how much money is to be spent and for what purposes in the coming fiscal accounting period (usually annual, sometimes biennial, and (2) the budget as a process of planning, negotiating, and allocating governmental resources. The main result of this process is the budget document.

Budgeting can take place on four levels—operating, capital, cash, and performance—as follows:

1. *Operating budget:* The operating budget restricts itself to expenditures (and revenues to raise the required funds) for the coming fiscal period. Decisions concerning choices among competing programs, the size of the programs, and staffing levels are all involved in the operating budget process.
2. *Capital budget:* Capital budget plans are required for projects extending beyond one fiscal period and that result in the construction, acquisition, or improvement of fixed municipal assets or infrastructure: buildings, fire engines, sewer lines, landscaping, street improvements, and similar items. These projects are often financed not out of revenues but from the issuance of debt. Thus, debt planning, debt management, and debt capacity are necessary facets of capital budgeting.
3. *Cash budgeting:* Cash budgeting provides a city with information concerning the timing and level of cash inflows and outflows, given the operating and capital budget spending plans and the corresponding revenue and financial methods. The cash budget allows a city to plan for cash shortages (and borrowings) or surpluses (and investments) and makes changes in spending plans or revenue collection to accommodate cash balances.
4. *Performance budgeting:* Performance budgeting is a new concept now growing in acceptance. It has emerged and re-emerged in a number of new (and not-so-new) budgeting and management concepts: Management By Objectives (MBO), Zero-Based Budgeting (ZBB), and Planned Programmed Budgeting Systems (PPBS). The core concept involves the planning and measurement of program performance and results, as well as financial resources.

Long-Range Financial Planning. Budgeting is frequently approached on an annual basis, but city governments also need to know how a budget may appear in two, three, or five years so that they may take immediate steps to bring about desired future changes in the city's financial or economic outlook. Some of these long-range steps are as follows:

1. *Economic forecasting:* The economic status of a city is a central factor in determining the revenues that can be collected and the level of services that can be provided. For instance, a successful economy can bring increased revenues from property, wage, and sales taxes. High unemployment means increased human services expenditures and perhaps increased police expenditures. By means of economic forecasting and analysis, a city can ascertain the directions its finances may be taking and prepare long-range plans (e.g., investment incentives, employment incentives) to affect that outlook.
2. *Revenue forecasting:* Economic forecasting provides information concerning revenue prospects, particularly of property and business-related taxes. Additional information concerning the long-term prospects of residential property values, nontax revenues, and intergovernmental revenues should also be collected to help identify and address possible revenue surpluses or shortfalls.
3. *Capital planning:* The need for long-term planning for capital construction and purchases is widely recognized. Deterioration of a municipal building must be foreseen at least five years in advance if a new building is to be built by the time the old one ceases to be functional. This simple example indicates the importance of lead time for capital projects.
4. *Policy planning:* Policy planning refers to the use of economic, expenditure, revenue, and capital forecasting to help a city government decide what it wants its economy, expenditures, and revenues to be and how it can act to attain those goals.

Grant Planning. State and Federal legislation offers billions of dollars in grants to local governments. For a city to take advantage of these resources, attention and planning must be given to the status of grant legislation and on-going grant programs, as well as the preparation of grant applications.

Financial Implementation

Once financial matters have been planned and budgeted, the next step is to implement the plans. This process consists of five specific functions—revenue collections, expenditures, grant applications, debt financing, and capital expenditures—as follows:

Revenue Collections. The revenue collection process includes tax collection, both billed (such as property taxes) and self-assessed (wage taxes); fees; fines; licenses and permits; and intergovernmental and interfund receipts.

Operating Expenditures. The two major types of operating expenditures are payroll and purchasing/procurement.

1. *Payroll expenditures:* Payroll expenditures are subject to legal regulations such as civil service and confirmation procedures in addition to the budget process. Once the staff and individual personnel have been selected, however, the payroll process simply continues to generate payroll checks and payments for employee benefits (subject, of course, to changes).
2. *Purchasing and procurement:* Purchasing and procurement refer to the payment for services or products from outside vendors. The process may be subject to bidding by vendors, but the issuance of purchase orders and vouchers or other procedures is governed by law.

Grant Applications. Implementation of grant planning involves completing applications. Some grants are awarded on a competitive basis, some on a formula basis, and others to all eligible governments for the reimbursement of local expenditures. Most applications require a city either to provide the grantor certain necessary information before a grant is awarded or to satisfy postaudit requirements.

Debt Financing. The capital budget is often funded from debt issuance, just as the operating budget is funded from the revenues previously described. Although other considerations may enter the picture, debt financing involves the structuring and issuing of a debt instrument by the city in the most efficient manner and with the lowest possible interest cost.

Capital Expenditures. Once the debt has been issued and sold, the money collected is put to use. Capital purchase and leasing of construction contracts are usually subject to procedures similar to those for operating expenditures. Capital funds can be invested until the cash is actually needed.

Financial Control

A city must receive information about the state of its financial operation and be assured that operations are going according to plan.

Accounting. Accounting is the recognized method by which financial operations are summarized and reported. The cash value of revenues, expenditures, assets, and liabilities are measured, recorded, and reported on a regular basis throughout all levels of the government. Each department usually has personnel assigned to account for its own functional area, and an overall accounting capability usually exists in a central location, such as the city accounting or finance department. The data collected provide managers with all necessary information regarding current and historical levels of operations and compliance with financial regulations.

Legal Compliance. Certain financial operations (such as voucher control or reporting of operations) are required by law. One element of financial control is assuring that all legally required steps are observed.

Grant Administration. Grant money, once received, is subject to the restrictions on its use imposed by the grantors. There are also reporting and operational requirements.

Budgetary Control. Accounting information is often used to assure that budget limits are being met. Each department, fund, activity, or program provides accounting data on its expenditures and revenues. This information is compared to the plan outlined in the budget to assure that the budget is being complied with. Corrective actions, such as purchasing or hiring freezes, are often undertaken if budgetary control operations reveal budget overruns.

Cash Monitoring. Even as budgetary, legal, and accounting controls are being observed, the city must be sure that it has sufficient cash on hand to pay for day-to-day operations. Monitoring cash inflows and outflows for each department or fund also assures that each is operating as expected and helps prevent fraud and embezzlement.

Money Market Activity

Short- and long-term adjustments must be made by a city's financial officers in periods of cash shortages or surplus. These include the following:

Short-Term Borrowing. Unexpected and short-term cash needs may require a city to approach lenders for short-term borrowing, often from a line of credit established with a bank. Both easy access and low interest are important considerations.

Notes. In anticipation of revenues and grants to be received, or bonds to be issued, a city may issue notes. This form of borrowing is usually repaid when the expected funding is received. Its advantage is that it allows the city to begin projects before the anticipated monies are in hand.

Investing. When a city has cash surpluses or is required to put aside money for future needs (such as a debt service sinking fund), the money can be invested. Selecting investments with high yields and advantageous timing is an important part of financial management.

Debt Service. Interest payments and principal repayments are required for notes or long-term debt. In some cases, money to fund these must be set aside periodically. Preparation must be made to meet all obligations as they come due in order to avoid default.

Arbitrage. Since tax-exempt borrowing rates are usually less than the return on some other investment instruments, a city can make money simply by borrowing and reinvesting. Legal limits restrict the use of such arbitrage, but under certain circumstances arbitrage is quite appropriate.

Financial Structure and Policy

The entire organizational and environmental context of city finance requires good management. The mayor should therefore pay attention to the following structural and policy areas to attain the desired goals of efficient financial management:

Population and Economic Base Analysis. National trends have major effects on jobs and population movement within a city. It is useful to monitor these patterns to help adopt specific policies. Monitoring allows the city to secure new revenues, forecast expenditures, and redirect services accordingly. The mayor may be able to shift some trends, but should be informed of the costs to the city in attempting to do so by means of tax abatements and related devices.

Revenue Structure and Planning. A city's economic outlook is closely related to its revenue potential. Just as different types of taxes affect the local economy in different ways, the local revenue base in turn is related to the local economy. For example, tax on wages can act as a disincentive to labor-intensive industry to locate or remain in the area; property taxes can affect decisions to make improvements and development. Conversely, a growing economy will usually coincide with growing revenues. Thus, depending on the state of the local economy, the revenue structure can change. Alterations in types of revenue may be made depending upon the desired economic mix and revenue levels in a city.

Organizational Management. The internal environment and the city organization greatly affect its financial management. The appointive powers of the mayor or council over financial officers, elective financial positions, and formal lines of responsibility, authority and reporting can determine the ability of the mayor's ability to influence financial management. Therefore, it may be necessary to change the city's internal organization before improving financial management.

Budgeting, Accounting and Control Systems. The actual systems and mechanisms in place also affect financial management. An accounting system may be manual, semi-automated, or automated; on a single- or double-entry basis; in conformance or not in conformance with generally accepted accounting principles. Each feature affects the quality of financial information and control.

Financial Disclosure

Disclosure of financial information is a necessary part of city financial activity, for the period just past as well as the current status. This report is used by citizens, investors, and others to evaluate both the city's financial status and the performance of its elected officials.

Debt Issuance Disclosure. When a city undertakes to issue long-term debt, an official statement is usually released, revealing all information and material relevant to the issue and a statement of the city's willingness and ability to repay the debt.

Budget Message. Depending on the structure of the municipal government, an executive (usually the mayor) proposes (or announces, if the mayor alone can legally adopt it) the budget for the coming fiscal period to the legislative body. This message reveals to other government officials and citizens the plans of the city for the coming year.

Rating Agency Presentations. When issuing debt, a factor in the interest rate is an opinion by the independent rating agency concerning the debt and the city's credit worthiness. Most cities therefore try to make special presentations and disclosures to the rating agency in order to attain the highest possible rating and thus reduce interest costs.

Internal Reporting. Adequate reporting within the government is obviously important for officials who need this information to make decisions.

Pensions

Pension benefits for public employees grew considerably through the 1960s and 1970s. Cities that administer pensions have multiple responsibilities. These include actuarial studies, benefit policy, funding, and asset management.

Actuarial Studies. Since a pension is a promise to pay money in a future that is often uncertain, sound financial management requires the availability of critical information. Actuarial studies, even if not legally required, are basic for sound financial management. They allow a city to estimate how much it will have to pay out in the future and how much should be set aside periodically to honor that obligation.

Benefit Policy. A common temptation is to reduce current payroll obligations by deferring costs, i.e., by increasing pension benefits. If pension benefits are not carefully controlled, however, they only contribute to financial problems in the future.

Funding. Money should be set aside in anticipation of future obligations. Doing so assures that the current fiscal period and its taxpayers will bear the burden of the pension obligation—an appropriate measure since the benefit of the city employees' work is being enjoyed in the current period.

Asset Management. The money set aside to meet future obligations should be invested for the most efficient use of city resources. Some cities undertake this task themselves. Others—especially when their assets grow—place the asset management function in the hands of professionals.

III. THE IMPACT OF GOVERNMENTAL STRUCTURE ON THE MAYOR'S ROLE

Chief Executive Officer versus Chairman of the Board

The distinction between "strong" and "weak" mayors has become a common concept, although a better distinction would be one between Chief Executive Officer (CEO) and Chairman of the Board.

The mayor who is a Chief Executive Officer has daily contact with operating departments and divisions and is responsible for the management of all their activities.

In most cities, the mayor serves as the Chairman of the Board. The mayor's primary functions in this case are planning, reviewing, setting policy, and allocating resources and responsibilities. In some cities, the mayor must serve as both Chief Executive Officer and Chairman of the Board.

A mayor functioning as Chairman of the Board must nevertheless be aware of what constitutes proper standards for management. (See Chap. 8, Mayor's Financial Management Checklist.) Any exercise of management prerogatives should be judicious, however, so that the mayor's perspective is not lost, operational authority is not undermined, and policymaking not confused with operational problem solving.

A finance officer reporting either directly or indirectly through the city manager to the mayor should help the latter obtain a comprehensive understanding of the financial management aspects of government. If a management system does not exist to provide this information in an easily comprehensible way, then such a system must be created.

Relationship of the Mayor to Elected and Appointed Financial Officials

In some jurisdictions, several types of elected officials serve and act independently of the city government. These include treasures, auditors, controllers, and county officials.

Treasurer. To protect a jurisdiction's funds and prevent possible collusion between municipal officials, many state laws and city charters provide for an independently elected treasurer. This individual may have another title, but the primary function is the receipt and disbursement of funds.

While respecting the independence of the treasurer's office, the mayor should nonetheless encourage it to utilize the same management and control systems as the rest of the government. General policies of cash management, receivables management, reporting, budgeting, and revenue forecasting should be discussed in detail with the treasurer. If the Chief Executive Officer and the treasurer cannot then work out acceptable procedures and standards, the mayor should seek public support for a policy change.

Auditor. The purpose of an independent auditor is to ascertain whether financial statements fairly present the city's financial position and the results of operations and whether they conform with generally accepted accounting principles (GAAP). A related responsibility is to detect fraud and make sure that funds are expended on the purposes for which they were appropriated.

Some auditors conduct "performance audits" as an extension of the traditional auditor's role to examine not only whether funds were expended appropriately, but also whether the expenditures effectively achieved a stated purpose. The evaluation of performance, however, is ultimately an executive function. The mayor and council should be the judges of the effectiveness of a particular program. To allow independent auditors to take on this function without respect for the responsibilities of management fails in two ways. First, the auditor may duplicate functions already being performed. Second, the executive branch is encouraged to turn over program evaluation to an outside agency.

To deal with such a situation, the mayor can encourage detailed "management letters" from the auditor setting out recommended changes in practices, procedures, and organization based on the review of any agency's financial performance. To eliminate the need for outside performance audits, the mayor should encourage a staff organization to conduct such evaluations on an independent but not adversarial basis.

Controller. In some jurisdictions, the chief financial officer—most often called controller or comptroller—is independently elected. All finance functions except for budget preparation are frequently placed in the controller's hands. This form of organization severely limits the role of the mayor in financial management since it is necessary to negotiate with such independently elected officers in the same way as is described below for county officials.

County Officials. In some jurisdictions, the function described above plus the function of property assessment may be performed by county officials. This situation requires substantial coordination between the mayor and county officials in setting overall city-county policy.

One subject for such coordinating sessions is financial management. This task will become easier for the mayor and county officials if they follow similar procedures and schedules. The mayor and staff should identify city-county disparities that generate potential problems. If the mayor cannot reach agreement with county officials on problems, an outside consultant should be invited to arbitrate differences. Problems should be addressed in more general and procedural, rather than specific, terms.

Intergovernmental Dimensions

Local governments have powers designated by statute or constitutional provison of state and Federal governments. One of the mayor's first tasks is to review these powers if any amendments or modifications are proposed. Financial management is just one of the many functional areas to be addressed in such a review. Various issues should be considered, as follows:

Administrative Consolidation. The independently elected offices described above are often vestiges of former times when separation of powers was more desirable. The mayor should ascertain whether these offices are still required and become acquainted with the specific functions to be performed by each.

Accounting and Auditing Standards. States that prescribe standards in these areas should be encouraged to use accounting and reporting requirements in conformity with the GAAP described in Chap. 6. Although mayors seldom become directly involved in negotiating these standards, they can benefit from the economies, ease of administration, and accountability that are promoted if state and city reporting requirements are in unison.

Investment Restrictions. Although investment restrictions are being liberalized, state laws often limit city investment practices and instruments. The mayor can ask finance officers to determine if state laws unduly restrict the city's return on investment.

Debt Management. Many states still limit municipalities to procedures such as single coupon bonds that they themselves would never be bound by. If a city borrows substantially, a comparison of state laws with the modern practices of such states as Oregon and Hawaii might suggest how to reduce the cost of doing so.

Taxation. Without a flexible tax base that is responsive to inflation and equitably shares the burden of taxes, a jurisdiction's ability to meet expanding service requirements is severely restricted. Modifying the tax structure, however, often requires intercity organization and a careful set of strategies to maintain equity among cities regarding tax effort formulas.

Fund Distribution. The form and timing of state and Federal revenues have severe cash flow implications for a jurisdiction. The mayor should attempt to influence guidelines in state and Federal programs to require that projects are prefunded or that municipalities are reimbursed for them on a timely basis as they perform the services.

Basic Financial Responsibilities

The mayor's involvement is discretionary in many areas of financial management, but several items demand attention, as follows:

Establishing Spending Limits and Priorities. The responsibility for answering the dual questions, "How much government can this city afford?" and "Who will get how much of the pie?," ultimately will wind up on the mayor's desk.

Requiring Modern Accounting, Reporting, and Financial Disclosure Practices. Chapter 6 discusses municipal accounting and reporting in some detail. The impetus to adapt or improve this system must come from the city's leadership.

Economic Base Development. The careful creation of a climate that allows particular businesses to thrive requires leadership by the mayor in ways elaborated in Chap. 2.

Seeking Intergovernmental Revenues. To take maximum advantage of available revenues from other governmental bodies requires careful coordination of line departments with staff units of intergovernmental relations. Successful mayors do careful homework and make a good sales pitch to convince the senior government that their jurisdiction is deserving.

SUMMARY

The mayor has wide latitude in defining the role of the mayor's office in financial management. Factors affecting this role are the organizational and structural arrangements of the jurisdiction as well as the mayor's assessment of what is required. Within limits, the mayor has many options to improve fiscal management in a city. It is primarily up to the mayor to suggest specific directions for public officials in providing better services at lower costs. Each chapter that follows probes a single area. The various problems will come together at the end in the Checklist.

2
Population, Employment, And Citizen Policy Preferences

This chapter encourages cities to monitor population and employment changes. It points up recent variations in the factors affecting employment and population change, including the importance of small firms in the service sector and the interconnections between job and population movements. Five strategies that chief administrators may adopt follow from these changes.

This chapter also outlines procedures for assessing citizen preferences, starting from informal conversations and moving on to voting, patterns of public service use, migration, and citizen surveys. Surveys offer the most direct and precise information on citizen preferences, provided that proper questions and analysis are used. Poorly designed surveys can be misleading. Several uses that cities make of surveys are reviewed, and a list of pointers are presented to help reduce the expense of conducting them.

I. POPULATION AND EMPLOYMENT PATTERNS

To monitor and forecast revenues available to the city government and demands for public services, it is important to assess basic population and employment patterns. To stay within the limits of citizen support for taxes and spending, however, citizen preferences must also be respected.

Population

Population growth and decline are among the most visible signs of change in the socio-economic base. The U.S. Census Bureau completes a full enumeration only every decade, providing data by Census tract and careful breakdowns by income, education, and race, among other social indicators. About every two years, the Census estimates the current population of many cities based on past trends. Because funds for many Federal and state grants are disbursed on a per capita basis, some cities have protested undercounts in lawsuits but have seldom won. Several have even hired the Census or accredited or private firms to do a city population count between decades, but the results have seldom been found beneficial. Since special counts are very expensive, one should be cautious about committing funds for this purpose. The U.S. Department of Labor and some state employment departments often maintain more current data than the Census Bureau.

Changes in the composition of the population (e.g., more elderly, fewer young persons) are also important to monitor; the Fact Sheet in Chap. 11 outlines one way to do so. Such changes are most important when they result in changed service demands, which can be gauged by means of the citizen surveys discussed later in this chapter.

Employment

Many citizens and private groups press for the creation of more jobs, and public officials often seek to increase the number of jobs in their cities. The mayor should assess rapidly changing employment trends in order to make more informative decisions. The Mayor's Fact Sheet in Chap. 11 can help in the task of tabulating city trends.[1] Data are compiled in five-year intervals by the Census of Manufacturers. Summaries for all cities with populations exceeding 25,000 can be found in the U.S. Census *County and City Data Book*. More current data are available every two years from *County Business Patterns*. Some city governments and local firms compile their own estimates of local employment. State agencies often publish census data for smaller cities. From these sources the mayor can prepare basic tables of the number of persons employed in manufacturing, services, and other sectors, and the rate of change occurring in them over time.

Gross and Net Changes in Population and Employment

From 1970 to 1975, the average population change for U.S. central cities was minus 3 percent, but this does not necessarily imply that only 3 percent left the city. Of the 44 percent of residents that moved between 1970 and 1975, half moved to another part of the same city and the other half left the city. Since most of those who left were replaced by new residents, however, the net change was only minus 3 percent. The point is that people move

[1]For a comprehensive ranking of America's 100 largest cities in financial, economic and demographic areas, see John Tepper Marlin and James S. Avery, *The Book of American City Rankings* (New York: Facts on File, 1983), pp. 33-171.

Table 2.1. The Birth and Death Rates of Jobs, 1972-76

Area*	Percent Gain	Percent Loss	Percent Net
Houston	62.7	35.7	27.0
Charlotte	48.0	40.4	7.5
Dayton	36.4	31.4	5.1
Rochester	33.7	29.3	4.5
Boston	37.4	33.7	3.8
Baltimore	36.5	32.9	3.5
Hartford	36.6	35.5	1.1
Worcester	24.6	25.1	−0.5
New Haven	27.0	29.5	−2.6
Greenville	26.9	35.1	−8.4
U.S. Average	37.0	33.7	4.1

(Source: David Birch, MIT Program on Neighborhood and Regional Change)
*Standard Metropolitan Statistical Area.

continuously, far more than implied by net changes. As shown in Table 2.1, the same changes are true of commerce and industry. As old firms are closed, new ones are started. For example, within four years, Dayton lost some 31 percent of its firms but gained over 36 percent, for a net increase of 5 percent. Although most such firms are small, they tend to generate the most new jobs. Of all the net new jobs created from 1969 to 1976, 66 percent were by firms with 20 or fewer employees, and 80 percent by firms with 100 or fewer employees. These dramatic findings about the role of small firms come from recent studies by David Birch at MIT and contradict many established views. They also suggest distinctive strategies for affecting this process that we will consider presently.

Causes of Population and Employment Changes

There are many interrelated causes of urban population and employment changes. One recent study lists 40 causes for declining population, including high crime rates, racial tension, high taxes, and other economic factors.[2] Some of these patterns are well known, but others have been identified only recently. For example, it was generally assumed in the past that people moved to those cities with good job opportunities, often in the manufacturing sector, but in the decade between 1970 and 1980, only five percent of net new

[2]Katherine L. Bradbury, Anthony Downs, and Kenneth A. Small, "Forty Theories of Urban Decline," in Terry Nichols Clark, ed., *Community Development, Symposium Issue of Urban Affairs Papers,* vol. 3, No. 2 (Spring 1981), pp. 13-20.

jobs were in manufacturing and 89 percent were in the service sector. Nevertheless, economic factors still appear to be the most significant causes for net migration or influx into cities. The expansion of industrial capacity as a result of new investments in the southwestern United States and other new centers of growth has redounded negatively against cities in the industrialized Northeast, which are now experiencing serious revenue shortfalls for short-term service delivery and long-term capital projects as a result of a reduction in their tax base.[3] City administrators have limited power in reversing these economic trends. They must either add economic incentives for private sector industry or adjust their revenue forecasting and budget priorities accordingly.

Strategies for Cities

These new patterns suggest that cities should take advantage of the following five strategies:

Monitoring Changes. Population and employment changes should be monitored and studied. Some sources to consult have been previously indicated, and the Fact Sheet in Chap. 11 outlines some specific patterns to track.

Paying Attention to Small Firms. As small firms create most of the new jobs, the mayor should establish a climate where they can prosper. Since every city has distinctive strengths for attracting specific types of firms, however, these should be reviewed with city administrators and local business leaders.

Comparing Costs and Benefits of Strategies. Many cities have given up more in tax abatements and other incentives to individual firms than they get back in revenues. This often happens because no one ever asks how the two are related. Cost/benefit studies of specific economic development projects range from the very simple to the very complex.[4] The mayor should be especially wary of developers and entrepreneurs who seek major economic incentives from the city. Most studies of potential firm location place tax incentives low on the list of factors to be considered. It therefore behooves a mayor to make a methodical and realistic calculation before the city grants a tax abatement.

---

[3]See Marlin and Avery, *op. cit.,* pp. 36-37.

[4]Robert W. Burchall and David Listokin. *The Fiscal Impact Guidebook.* New Brunswick, N.J.: Rutgers University Center for Urban Policy Research, 1978.

Stressing Amenities for Residents as Well as Firms. Each city should consider the assets that make it pleasant (e.g., beaches, museums, shopping plazas, ethnic festivals). These are not frills and may be more important than tax incentives to private industry as a means of retaining or attracting people and jobs. Many cities with populations below 100,000 are now conducting citizen surveys and using consultants to find creative ways to make themselves more attractive.

Considering Public Goods as Well as Specific Benefits. Since many small firms come and go, it is necessary to retain citizens. It is dangerous to grant excessive subsidies for one large firm. All firms and residents can benefit from a sound infrastructure of roads and transportation, efficient basic services, and a reasonable tax burden. If you do favors for one firm, others will have to pay more. Public goods shared by most residents are thus distinctly attractive for cities, even if they have less obvious effects than specific benefits such as tax abatements.

II. CITIZEN POLICY PREFERENCES

One of the most difficult tasks for the mayor is to balance spending pressures from different constituencies. Mayors are usually elected because of their ability to balance these group pressures. Particularly difficult is charting a course between groups demanding specific services and other groups supporting tax reductions.

Informal Pressures

A procedure that most mayors follow instinctively is to hold discussions with council members, organized group leaders, visitors and spokesmen from different neighborhood, and social groups. Although continual contacts of this sort provide a sense of constituency pressures that nothing else can, this grass roots sense can be sharpened by other indicators.

Revealed Preferences: Voting, Usage Patterns

Referenda. Public referenda often reveal citizen preferences for service and tax policies, but if the turnout rate at an election falls below 50 percent, the results may be misleading. Referenda, especially recent votes on statewide tax and expenditure limitations, can serve as useful indicators of citizen concern.

Elections of Candidates with Distinctive Preferences. Elections to the council and other positions usually reflect citizen preferences, but the personal appeal of specific candidates sometimes make it difficult to draw conclusions about citizen preferences on specific policies.

Patterns of Service Use. The support of citizens for general policies such as overall tax rate and service level is hard to ascertain from their customary behavior; one can monitor rates of tardiness and nonpayment of taxes, but these are crude indicators. Demands for specific services are more readily measured by consumption patterns, for example, electricity usage, revenues from public transit and toll roads and bridges, museum receipts, recreation program registration, and library circulation. (Similar performance measures of municipal services are discussed in Chap. 3.)

Migration by Neighborhood and Population Subgroup. It is necessary to investigate the causes of population decline if the rate exceeds that of comparable cities in the same region. This may be a reflection of particular public policies as well as private sector forces. Nearby cities gaining in population should be studied, as well as neighborhood differences within cities. This review should take differences in income, age, and education into account. Movement of private firms into or out of a city is also an indication of its economic vitality.

Positions Taken by Organized Groups. Organized groups may reflect citizen preferences, but it is often difficult to know to what extent leaders speak for their constituencies. If an organization is of sufficient inportance to respond to, fine, but paying too much attention to organized groups while ignoring the more silent majority is not always recommended politically. Nevertheless, group leaders can assist the decision-making process by collecting data from their memberships at their own expense. Even if they tend to slant studies toward policies they favor, if their own position is not overly strong, it may be possible to persuade them to do a study convincing even to skeptics.

Citizen Surveys

Despite the problems here discussed, many cities have conducted surveys of citizen spending preferences. Such surveys usually provide more direct and specific information about citizen preferences than the previous indicators. Like the others, however, they have their strengths and weaknesses. One important example was the Urban Observatory survey jointly conducted by 10 cities in 1970. A key question asked was if the local government should spend "more," "the same," or "less" than at present. Many citizens wanted "more" on most items, as shown in Table 2.2.

There can be great variance between cities and between neighborhoods within cities for tax cuts and service gains. It is the mayor's job to calculate sentiment from diverse constituencies to organize the right balance between taxes and services. Citizen surveys are quite appropriate for this task, but the mayor should be especially careful not to consider the results of such surveys as unequivocally authoritative. They may at times lead to contradictory

Table 2.2. Citizen Preferences in Services and Taxes

	Boston	San Diego
Services		
Public Schools		
Spend More	66%	45%
Spend Same	26	45
Spend Less	2	7
Police Patrolling		
Spend More	70	33
Spend Same	24	61
Spend Less	3	3
Street Lighting		
Spend More	31	34
Spend Same	60	62
Spend Less	5	3
Medical Care for Poor		
Spend More	65	42
Spend Same	26	44
Spend Less	6	8
Low-Cost Housing		
Spend More	68	41
Spend Same	20	38
Spend Less	9	16
Taxes		
Are local taxes		
Too High?	67%	28%
About Right?	22	60
Too Low?	7	6
Not Ascertained	4	6

(*Source: Urban Observatory Survey as summarized in Floyd J. Fowler, Jr.,* Citizen Attitudes Toward Local Government, Services, and Taxes. *Cambridge, Mass.: Ballinger, 1974.*)

conclusions since the same individual may simultaneously state a preference for both increased spending on services and lower taxes. We call this the Paradox of Contradictory Pressures. Obviously, a survey can lead to biased results if it is limited simply to service or tax questions. In the late 1970s, the intensity of feelings on taxes in some cities and states shifted as new tax and expenditure limits were passed. The level of concern varied across cities, of course, but results for Boston in Table 2.2 are consistent with the 2-to-1 vote in favor of Proposition 2 ½ throughout the state of Massachusetts, a proposition that was far more stringent than California's Proposition 13 or similar measures in other states.

What preference then should mayors consider—service questions or tax questions? Both, but to resolve disparate results, the mayor needs to gauge the *intensity* of each preference. In the past, Americans often seemed more intensely concerned about services than taxes. This was in part because the most concerned citizens were often the direct beneficiaries and would attend city council meetings or protest in other ways; nevertheless, they were still few in number compared to all taxpayers. A critical part of the policy process is to assess how strongly service recipients feel. Turnout at public meetings, letters, complaints, or petitions come largely from organized groups. The mayor will have to determine how much to be influenced by these groups, realizing that they can organize support for political candidates and issues. More balanced decisions can be made if the mayor has a sense of the support for a service from the general citizenry as well as from organized supporters. This usually requires a public survey of policy preferences.

A survey can generate results measuring intensity of preference for a representative sample of citizens. One of the most useful methods is to force respondents to *make tradeoffs,* such as between a new bridge or more tennis courts. Alternatively, the *imposition of budget constraints* with budget pie-type formats can also be helpful. These formats ask respondents if the whole budget pie should be enlarged or reduced, while indicating the tax increase necessary to increase the overall size of the pie. Services can then be allocated in pie slices. Since all the slices total 100 percent, this method avoids confusing results of the type found in Table 2.2.

The disadvantage of the budget pie format is the greater complexity involved in administrating it. Some related questionnaire formats also seek to capture budget constraint ideas, although less thoroughly than the budget pie.[5] Neighborhood conditions are likely to affect responses about public services. People who live in ghettos and slums are likely to rate street cleaning as poor

[5]See Terry Nichols Clark, "Can You Cut a Budget Pie?" *Policy and Politics* 3 (December 1974), pp. 3-32 and T. N. Clark, ed., *Citizen Preferences and Urban Public Policy* (Beverly Hills: Sage, 1976).

even if their streets are cleaned as carefully, and as often, as in other neighborhoods.[6]

Uses of Surveys. Cities have dramatically increased their use of surveys. The subjects addressed include the following:

1. *Service Preferences,* as discussed, include evaluation of service quality and tradeoffs among services and taxes.
2. *Identification of problem areas,* to assess their relative importance to citizens.
3. *Reasons for Nonuse of Services* (too distant, inconvenient hours, long wait, etc.) These are good to compare across services and with data on actual use patterns.
4. *Studying Causes of Population Influx or Flight.* Cities losing population have been especially concerned to allocate scarce resources to attract and retain residents.
5. *Polling on New Policies.* Before holding a referendum or making a major decision, such as creating a new transportation system, citizens can be polled for their views.
6. *Surveying Candidates on Issues.* Although polls on specific candidates or highly partisan issues may not be taken by the city government, candidates and parties can conduct their own surveys and make the results known. As Mayor Daley once observed, "good government is good politics." Not only have state and national politicians used polls with great success, but sophisticated candidates in middle-sized cities are also increasingly using them.

Pointers on How to Take Polls:

1. An expert consultant from a local university, survey center, or another city should be available to oversee the process.
2. Volunteers may help administer the survey. Civic groups can help coordinate the effort.
3. Many cities use larger samples than they actually need. About 1,500 respondents are sufficient for most purposes, and as few as 300 can produce useful results. In small-size samples the random variation in responses will be larger and the differences (e.g., between young and old respondents) less statistically significant.
4. Habitual nonvoters can be tapped by a survey and differentiated from

[6]Procedures for dealing with related issues are considered in Harry Hatry et. al., *Efficiency Measurement for Local Government Services* (Washington, D.C.: The Urban Institute, 1978) and Peter H. Rossi, Richard A. Berk, and Bernice Edison, *The Roots of Urban Discontent* (New York: John Wiley, 1976).

voters and organized group members in the analysis. Representative organized group members can thus be compared to the others.

5. *Identical* wording to that used for surveys in other cities, or for previous existing surveys, is desirable to permit comparison.
6. Survey results should be integrated with related information, such as service use levels, neighborhood migration patterns, socio-economic characteristics of respondents, etc.

Examples of Interesting Surveys. Several cities have conducted suggestive surveys. A few examples appear in Tables 2.3, 2.4, 2.5, and 2.6.

Table 2.3. Typical Survey Questions

1. In general, would you rate the St. Petersburg Bus Service AVAILABLE to you and members of your household as Excellent, Good, Fair, or Poor?
2. Would you say the amount of street lighting at night in this neighborhood is about right, too low (need more lighting), or too bright (more lighting than necessary)?
3. Generally speaking, would you rate the St. Petersburg Municipal Library Services as Excellent, Good, Fair or Poor?
4. I am going to read a list of reasons SOME people have given for NOT using libraries more often. Please tell me which, if any, generally are TRUE for you or members of this household?

   Library hard to get to
   Library not open right hours
   Personal health problems prevent my using the library
   Buy my own books and magazines
   Not interested in library
   Too busy to go to library
   Poor staff service at library
   Library does not have books I want.
5. Turning now to neighborhood cleanliness, would you say your neighborhood is USUALLY Very Clean, Fairly Dirty or Very Dirty?
6. In the past 12 months, did the collectors ever miss picking up your trash and garbage on the scheduled pick-up days? (If YES, ASK:) How many times would you say this occurred?
7. Turning now to police protection and public safety, how safe would you feel walking alone in this neighborhood at NIGHT, Very Safe, Reasonably Safe or Not Safe at All? (Repeat for 'DAY').
8. In the past 12 months, did anyone break in or was there strong evidence someone tried to break into your home? (IF 'YES', ASK:) How many times did this occur? Were all incidents reported to St. Petersburg Police? (IF 'NO' ASK:) How many were not reported? What was the main reason for NOT notifying the police?

Source: 1975 St. Petersburg Citizen Survey. Summarized in Harry P. Hatry and Louis H. Blair, "Citizen Surveys for Local Government," in Terry Nichols Clark, ed., Citizen Preferences and Urban Public Policy *(Beverly Hills: Sage Publications, 1976, pp. 129–140).*

Table 2.4. Contacts with City Government

Questions: During the past year, have you contacted anyone in city government or in a city agency about a problem or for any other reason?

[IF YES] What was it that you contacted the city about?

Using the zero to 100 scale, how satisfied were you with the response you received?

Number	Per,entage	Mean Satisfaction	Code	Problem or Other Reason for Contact
363			01	Never contacted city
12	6.9	57.00	02	Maintenance of neighborhood, housing
45	26.2	67.74	03	Police service, crime, etc.
21	12.2	51.66	04	Zoning, building codes, etc.
6	3.5	85.50	05	Fire protection
7	4.1	40.00	08	Parks and recreation
16	9.3	53.12	11	Traffic engineering, streets, sidewalks
2	1.2	50.00	12	Bikes
17	9.9	63.52	13	Garbage
3	1.7	63.33	14	Animal control
2	1.2	70.00	15	Welfare, handicapped services, etc.
35	20.4	68.02	17	Other
3	1.7	100.00	18	Taxes, city budget
3	1.7	81.66	20	Education

NOTE: The numbers listed above will not sum to 509 as each individual respondent was given an opportunity to list up to three reasons why they contacted city government.

(*Source: L. A. Wilson II, Citizen Preferences for Public Expenditures:* A Survey of Opinion in Tempe, Arizona. *Center for Urban Studies, Arizona State University, 1981.*)

Table 2.5A. Investigating Willingness to Pay for Parks and Recreation Programs

City should spend more, less, or same?	Be willing to pay more in taxes?	How much willing to increase taxes?
1. More: 26.2%	1. Yes: 79.5%	*Mean* $30.24 / *Median* $10.00
		No change or reallocate from other program?
	2. No 20.5%	1. No change 34.8% 2. Reallocate 65.2%
2. Same amount: 68.0%		
3. Less: 5.8%	What should city do with money saved?	
	1. Reduce taxes 46.7% 2. Reallocate money to other program 53.3%	

Part A: These are responses to items shown in Part B. *(Source: Same as for Table 2.4.)*

Table 2.5B: Questionnaire

<table>
<tr><th>Spend More</th><th></th><th>Services</th><th></th><th>Spend Less</th></tr>
<tr><td rowspan="7">You have indicated that you would like the City of Tempe to spend more on [SPECIFIED SERVICE]. The next questions are whether you would be willing to pay more in sales taxes in order for the city to spend more on these services.

Now looking at [SPECIFIED SERVICE], would you be willing to pay more in taxes in order to spend more on [SPECIFIED SERVICE]?

1. (Yes)➡ You are currently
1st spending about $_______ in sales tax to support existing services;
2nd+➡ How much would you be willing to increase taxes in order to provide more</td><td>⇦</td><td>LANDSCAPE MAINTENANCE OF MEDIAN STRIPS AND RIGHT-OF-WAYS</td><td>⇨</td><td rowspan="7">You have indicated that you would like to have the City of Tempe spend less money on [SPECIFIED SERVICE]. If the city were to reduce its spending in this area, what should it do with the money saved?

1. Reduce taxes 2. Reallocate the money
⬇
On what services would you like to see this money spent?

1. ____________
2. ____________
3. ____________</td></tr>
<tr><td>⇦</td><td>CRIME PREVENTION AND CONTROL</td><td>⇨</td></tr>
<tr><td>⇦</td><td>EFFORTS TO REDEVELOP THE DOWN-TOWN AREA</td><td>⇨</td></tr>
<tr><td>⇦</td><td>LIBRARY SERVICES</td><td>⇨</td></tr>
<tr><td>⇦</td><td>PARKS AND RECREATION PROGRAMS</td><td>⇨</td></tr>
<tr><td></td><td>PUBLIC TRANSPORTATION</td><td>⇨</td></tr>
<tr><td>⇦</td><td>INSTALLATION OF BIKE PATHS</td><td>⇨</td></tr>
</table>

2. No of the service? ↓ $______ Would you suggest that there be no change in service level if it means increased taxes or would you reallocate money from some other program: 1. No change 2. Reallocate ↓ If the City of Tempe were to take money from some other program, what program should have its funding cut? 1. ______ 2. ______ 3. ______		

Table 2.6. Measures of Effectiveness of Library Services

Objective	Quality Characteristic	Specific Measure	Data Collection Procedure
Overall Citizen Satisfaction	Citizen Satisfaction	1. Percentage of citizens rating library as satisfactory	General citizen survey
	User satisfaction	2. Percentage of clients using city libraries that rate them as satisfactory.	Library user survey or general citizen survey
	Use—Household	3. Percentage of households using (or not using) a public library a minimum number of times, such as 4 times over past 12 months—with reasons for nonuse.	General citzen survey
	Registration—Household	4. Percentage of households with (or without) a valid registration card.	Statistics from public library or general citizen survey
	Use—Visitation	5. Number of visits to library facilities per capita (or per household).	Library counts of number of users with population estimates from city planning department
	Use—Circulation	6. Circulation per capita by type of material—e.g., fiction, nonfiction, records, film—divided between internal and external	External circulation figures, kept by most public libraries. Internal figures, estimated from periodic sampling

Table 2.6. *(Continued)*

Objective	Quality Characteristic	Specific Measure	Data Collection Procedure
Comprehensiveness Timeliness Availability of Holdings	Diversity and currentness of book and periodical holdings	7. Probability of owning (a) books, and (b) periodicals published during given time period (e.g., last 5 years).	Random sample of (a) books published from the *Book Publishing Record* (BPR) or other bibliographic catalog, or (b) citations published in one of common periodical indexes—compared with library holdings
	Availability of book holdings	8. Probability of a user's obtaining (a) a book or (b) a periodical when it is wanted.	Random sample of (a) books or (b) periodicals held and checked against availability in the proper area
	Speed of service	9. Percentage of users who rate speed of service as satisfactory.	Library user survey or general citizen survey
Helpfulness of Staff	Helpfulness—Courtesy of Staff	10. Percentage of persons using library who rate helpfulness and general attitude of staff as satisfactory.	Library user survey or general citizen survey
	Helpfulness—Quality of reference service	11. Percentage of persons using library reference services who rate them as satisfactory.	Library user survey or general citizen survey
Attractiveness of Facility	User satisfaction with comfort crowdedness, noise, etc.	12. Percentage of persons using library who rate comfort, crowdedness, noise, cleanliness, and temperature/ventilation as satisfactory.	Library user survey or general citizen survey

(continued)

Table 2.6. *(Continued)*

Objective	Quality Characteristic	Specific Measure	Data Collection Procedure
	Nonuser satisfaction	13. Percentage of nonusers who cite lack of comfort, crowdedness, noise, cleanliness, or temperature/ventilation as reasons for nonuse.	General citizen survey
Accessibility and convenience	Physical accessibility, convenience	14. Percentage of users rating convenience as satisfactory.	Library user survey or general citizen survey
		15. Percentage of nonuser households who give poor physical accessibility as a reason for nonuse.	General citizen survey
		16. Percentage of citizens who live within 1 specific travel time (such as 15 minutes) of a public library.	Counts from mapping latest census tract population figures against location of facilities with appropriate travel time radius drawn around each facility
	Hours of operation	17. Percentage of users rating hours of operation as satisfactory.	Library user survey or general citizen survey
		18. Percentage of nonuser households who give poor hours as a reason for nonuse.	General citizen survey

(*Source: The Urban Institute*, Performance Measurement: A Guide for Local Elected Officials (*Washington, D.C.: The Urban Institute Press, 1980), p. 12*).

3
Budgeting: Managing Revenues, Expenditures, and (Sometimes) Cutbacks

This chapter begins by outlining general approaches toward budgeting such as program and zero-based budgets and management by objective. Revenue policies that may shape budgeting are reviewed next. Expenditures are considered on the basis of some decision-rules that mayors can apply to evaluate alternatives, such as responding to citizen preferences or making comparisons with other cities. A list of specific budgeting methods is presented, showing particular programs, stating objectives, using demand, workload, efficiency, and effectiveness measures, etc. Finally, cutback management is addressed by outlining a series of alternative strategies such as user charges, privatization, volunteers, and contracting services.

I. FORMULATING A GENERAL POLICY

Establishing General Policies

Major policy shifts typically emerge with the election of new mayors or council members, or a political groundswell such as Proposition 13. Past commitments continue in established programs, however, and these are often resistant to change. General budget policy must thus adapt old programs to meet current priorities. How?

Some cities such as Lincoln, Nebraska issue public statements on such topics as projected future revenues and expenditures and overall shifts in policy (see Table 3.1). Presenting such matters in writing provides citizens, bond investors, and others with a tangible statement of where a city plans to go. The statement can stress general goals (for example, improving parks, public transportation, and sanitation) or itemize financial management procedures. Whether or not a public document is issued, it makes sense for the mayor to establish the major priorities so as to focus efforts on the issues of greatest importance.

Forecasting Revenues and Expenditures

Some cities develop specific multiyear plans for operating and capital budgets and itemize specific services, projects, and changes in staff over two, three, or (in Downers Grove, Illinois) ten years. Even if these plans are not followed, they help to clarify which current policies can or cannot be continued. A common "plan" is simply to continue current policies for the next few years. Trend lines for revenue and expenditure for the preceding few years can be easily projected for a few more years. Adopting this procedure, however, may lead to a large deficit in just a year or two. The mayor will have to find new revenues or cut some expenditures. Because of inflation or other pressures, many cities have been forced to reduce expenditures substantially. The task is made easier if the mayor has a sense of *which* revenues and expenditures for *which* programs are likely to increase most.

If individual revenue sources and program expenditures are reviewed, however, it will become clear that some grow faster than others and often for predictable reasons, such as termination of a federal revenue program or the necessity to replace old motor vehicles. Forecasting revenues and expenditures more realistically through individual sources than by a simple "straight-line" projection can be useful. Many procedures are available to make forecasts with varying degrees of precision and realism.[1]

Elected officials often complain that finance staff are unduly conservative in projecting revenues. One way that some cities have dealt with this tendency is to specify the percentage of accuracy that the finance staff should attain in revenue forecasts. Cities that use this approach usually forecast local revenues with less than three percent error. Alternatively, high, medium, and low estimates can be asked for each revenue source, along with the appropriate justification, rather than one figure.

II. BUDGETING APPROACHES

Many "systems" for budgeting have been suggested, and many, unfortunately, have been "oversold," which in turn has led some observers to overly cynical views. Nevertheless, quite a few cities have now devised their own systems that clearly do work and are useful to consider as options.

[1]See Public Technology, Inc., *Multi-Year Revenue and Expenditure Forecasting* (Washington D.C.: Department of Housing and Urban Development, 1980. Report HUD-401) and David A. Kern, *Municipal Revenue Estimation with a Focus on Sales Tax Revenue* (Chicago, Illinois: "Comparative Study of Community Decision Making," Report No. 92, University of Chicago, 1978).

Line-Item Budget

This traditional format is often complemented by others but is still resorted to for at least parts of a city budget. A simple line-item budget might look something like the following:

Police Department

Police Chief	$38,000
Police Officer	18,000
Clerk	10,000
Total	$66,000

Program Budget

In principle, a program budget shows all costs related to particular programs, such as Traffic Regulation and Investigation, both of which are primarily Police Department programs. A simple example:

Traffic Regulation	$75,000
Investigation	30,000

The program budget should include appropriate amounts for related departments (in this case, Finance, Personnel, and Motor Vehicles) since their support is necessary to generate the program's activities.

Performance Indicators

Sales or profits indicate the performance of private firms. Analogous measures are available for many public services but often demand more effort to collect. For example, use levels of museums, parks, recreation, and bridges can be fairly easily compiled. More complex measures include citizen satisfaction with a particular service—for example, how clean the streets are, and others that we will elaborate on shortly. The point here is simply that performance indicators are necessary for certain types of budgeting systems.

Management by Objective (MBO)

This format consists of stating quantifiable objectives and comparing actual performance against them. For example, one objective of the motor vehicle department may be to reduce costs 10 percent over the next 12 months with no decrease in service level. If objectives are too vague, they can be lost in the shuffle, but if they are too demanding and focused only on limited tasks, other agency activities may be sacrificed to meet the stated objective. Knowing this in advance, many city officials continue to feel that certain objectives help focus energy and improve efficiency. MBO implies the use of a program budget format and performance indicators. Whether such objectives become empty exercises or team-building incentives depends largely on the leadership of the mayor and the city administrative staff.

Zero-Based Budgeting

This form of budgeting was made famous by President Carter. The principle is that every component of a program must be justified. It is contrasted with *incremental budgeting,* in which department chiefs justify, and elected officials examine and approve, only incremental changes from a previous year, taking the rest as given. Some mayors mainly make decisions incrementally, others strive for a zero-based approach, but most use a combination of both. Zero-based budgeting is a stringent ideal, virtually impossible to implement comprehensively. Given the limited time of staff and council, only selected activities can be realistically evaluated. One solution is thus to use a zero-based approach only for functions particularly salient to citizens or for functions that need the most improvement. A zero-based perspective can then be applied to the remaining functions the next year. It is necessary to be specific about the extent of review needed and realistic about the amount of staff time required.

III. REVENUE POLICY

Revenue-Driven Budgeting

Some cities follow revenue-driven budgeting, especially those operating under state tax or revenue limits. The latter may be set, for example, at a 7 percent annual increase. If revenues are thus fixed, budget decisions tend to be driven by this revenue constraint. By contrast, in a pure *expenditure-driven approach,* decisions to provide certain services are made, and then whatever revenues are necessary are raised.

The Revenue Structure

The revenue structure of a city refers to the distinctive configuration of its revenue sources—for example, 40 percent from the property tax, 30 percent from charges and fees, and 30 percent from intergovernmental revenues. What constitutes the most desirable revenue structure has been much debated. The property tax, in particular, was long criticized. One reason was that it was presumably inelastic in that it did not increase revenues as fast as general inflation rates. However, this was no longer true in many cities in the 1970s, since property values grew faster than the rest of the economy. Still, since increased property values only translate into revenues if the city increases the assessed value or the tax rate, many cities have not increased property tax revenues fast enough to keep up with inflation.[2]

Property taxes are disliked by citizens more than any other tax.[3] This seems largely due to its lump-sum, one-time character that makes it highly visible compared to sales taxes. In the past, it was also held to be regressive, taxing the poor for a larger percentage of their income than the rich. This no longer seems to be the case, according to more careful research as well as new circuit-breaker laws in many states that exempt the poor, elderly, and others from some or all property taxes.[4]

Property tax collection rates vary across cities from about 85 to 100 percent. Some strategies to improve tax collection rates are as follows: computerized and more frequent billing and reminders, steeper rebates for

---

[2]The sources of change in property tax revenue may be calculated by

$$TR = r\,(a/m)\,(M_e + M_n)$$

where

- TR = property tax revenues
- r = nominal tax rate
- a/m = ratio of assessed to market value
- M_e = full market value of existing propety as of the last assessment
- M_n = full market value of new property since the last assessment

You can change property tax revenues (TR) by changing any one of the other terms. Consider each at least briefly if you decide that you must raise property tax revenues.

[3]One survey that shows this to be true follows:

"Which do you think is the worst tax—that is the least fair?"

Federal income tax	30
State income tax	11
State sales tax	18
Local property tax	32
Don't know	10
	101%

This question was posed to a national sample of Americans in 1978; similar results emerged from 1973 to 1978. See Advisory Commission on Intergovernmental Relations, *Changing Public Attitudes on Governments and Taxes* (Washington, D.C.: ACIR, Report S-7, 1978), p. 1.

[4]Henry Aaron, *Who Pays the Property Tax?* (Washington, D.C.: Brookings, 1975).

early payment, higher fees for tardiness, more rapid foreclosure and sales of delinquent property (e.g., via a private contractor), and publicizing names of delinquent taxpayers. With rapid inflation and interest rates, fines must be updated regularly or made to float with interest rates if they are not to encourage delinquency. Still, given public dissatisfaction with property taxes, cities are considering other revenue sources, discussed in the cutback management section to come.

Integrated Presentation of Revenues Including Debt

Few city budgets show debt, and intergovernmental revenues are often omitted or mingled with the city's own revenues. State law may require appropriation ordinances to show simply the latter, but the mayor should make a request for an integrated budget presentation somewhere. A simple memo could list local and intergovernmental revenues and planned debt offerings. Debt scheduling is often linked to a capital budget. Higher borrowing costs are leading more cities to prepare *three- or five-year capital budgets,* in part to help set priorities but also to assuage constituents by pointing out that their pet project has also been included in the future budget. Outside investors also press for multiyear capital budgets and can punish cities that fail to prepare them with higher interest rates. Some officials intentionally omit debt from budgeting documents so that specific amouts and timing factors can be adjusted and not be subjected to the full budget process review. City managers and staff may not disclose planned debt issues to elected officicals for similar reasons. The mayor should decide whether or not to delegate this authority to city officers.

IV. EXPENDITURES DECISIONS: HELPFUL RULES AND TOOLS

Some Decision Rules

How should the mayor assess a proposed budget? The following criteria can be used by the mayor's staff for occasional bargaining purposes.

Incremental Growth (or Decline). This forecast suggests that this year's budget is the same as last year's plus or minus a fixed increment, usually the same for all departments. This is a common decision rule, especially for cutback management. The mayor should be convinced that all departments are delivering proper service levels without any reasons for change (as a result of shifts in citizen preferences, revenue sources, etc.). Few cities, however, fully adhere to such incrementalism.

Respond to New Policy Goals. The mayor or elected officials may have campaigned for certain policies with budgetary implications. It may still be useful to present them to staff in general terms and have them propose two or three alternative means of implementation, along with arguments for each.

Respond to New Citizen or User Preferences. Surveys of citizens or service users may define new preference patterns.

Compare Present and Past Personnel and Service Costs. All mayors should encourage their staffs to create simple charts and memos to give an overall perspective for important decisions. For major items, a five- or ten-year expenditure trend line is helpful.[5] Having ten or twenty of these trend lines for different expenditure items can give the mayor a sense of which items will be easiest to implement. Such charts can be more helpful than many tables, especially budget tables that show only two years of expenditures (see Exhibits 1 and 2 in Table 3.1).

Compare Personnel and Service Costs with Those of Other Cities. Percentage changes in wages and overall spending patterns are reasonably easy to compare across cities. Many cities regularly compute such data for ten or so nearby cities. Most of the latter may be chosen for their basic similarity, but a few may be included precisely because they are much more or much less affluent in order to illustrate a range of alternative policies. These comparative data also create a basis for regional discussions among local leaders on such subjects as wage increases or contractors' fees. City officials in the Chicago, Minneapolis, and San Francisco areas have discussed these matters regularly.

Per capita expenditure levels, or per unit levels of service, are also useful to compare but demand closer attention than simple percentage increases. Mayors having difficulty comparing entire police budgets, for example, may still be able to compare subfunctions such as police patrol or dispatching with those of reasonably comparable cities.[6] Mayor Bill Morris of Waukegan, Illinois has used such comparisons on many occasions, especially to help

---

[5]Two useful handbooks that show how to compute basic trends for the past five years or so for cities are *Is Your City Heading for Financial Difficulty?* (Chicago, Illinois: Municipal Finance Officers Association, 1978) and the five volume series, *Evaluating Local Government Financial Condition* (Washington, D.C.: International City Management Association, 1980).

[6]Level and change measures of fiscal strain for cities are compared across cities in Terry Nichols Clark and Lorna Crowley Ferguson, *City Money* (New York: Columbia University Press, 1983). A handbook for city officials on how to compute such measures is Terry Nichols Clark and Earl Ray Hutchison, *Fiscal Strain and Your City* (Chicago, Illinois: Comparative Study of Community Decision-Making, Research Report No. 75, University of Chicago, 1976).

mediate labor disputes. Mayor Morris has prepared charts on large sheets of paper listing cities across the top and items such as hourly salary, paid sick days, and other benefits down the side (see Table 3.2). Such charts have generated information that neither management nor labor had been aware of and several difficult strikes were settled in this way.

Prepare User-Adjusted Measures of Services. Cities differ in their delivery of services, in part because their service users differ; one city, for

Table 3.1. Lincoln, Nebraska Report on Recommended Fiscal Guidelines for General Government Functions 1981-82 to 1986-87

Introduction

Since the scope of City services must exist within the overall revenue limitations of the City, a logical step in the preparation of the City budget is the projection of future revenues, and the establishment of expenditure guidelines which are consistent with projected revenues. Such fiscal planning insures that all legislative constraints are satisfied, that planned uses of City funds are fiscally sound, and that the level of tax effort is known and supported by a majority of the legislative body.

The purpose here is to provide the City Council with a six-year financial plan for those funds used to finance general government functions. These funds include Tax Funds, Revenue Sharing Funds, Street Construction, and Wheel Tax Funds. This plan is prepared over a six-year time frame in order to provide continuity between the Capital Improvement Program and Annual Budget.

Summary of Budget Projections

Financial constraints confronting the City have become increasingly inhibitive. In preparation of the 1981-82 budget, the City must cope with the revenue limitations imposed by the 7% Budget Lid, and an annual inflation rate projected to average 10%. Given these constraints, it has become clear that, without additional taxing authority, the City will not be able to maintain current staffing levels in the coming fiscal year. Moreover, future cutbacks in City services are likely unless additional revenue sources are realized. As long as inflation continues to erode the tax base of the community, hard choices will have to be made as to which programs and services will be provided by City government.

A summary of the revenue and expenditure projections is displayed graphically in Exhibit 1. As shown in this graph, the budget gap between available revenues and the cost of maintaining existing services is projected to total $1.0 million in 1981--82 and increase to $5.5 million by 1986-87. This gap is highlighted in Exhibit 2. It should be noted that a budget gap can only exist "on paper." The City Charter requires that the budget be balanced in terms of revenues and expenditures. Accordingly, the City must in the near future develop strategies to cope with this potential budget gap, that is, seek ways to secure additional revenue and/or effectuate budget cuts.

Table 3.1. *(Continued)*

EXHIBIT 1: Budget Projections: 1981-82 to 1986-87
For Tax, Revenue Sharing, Street Construction, and Wheel Tax Funds

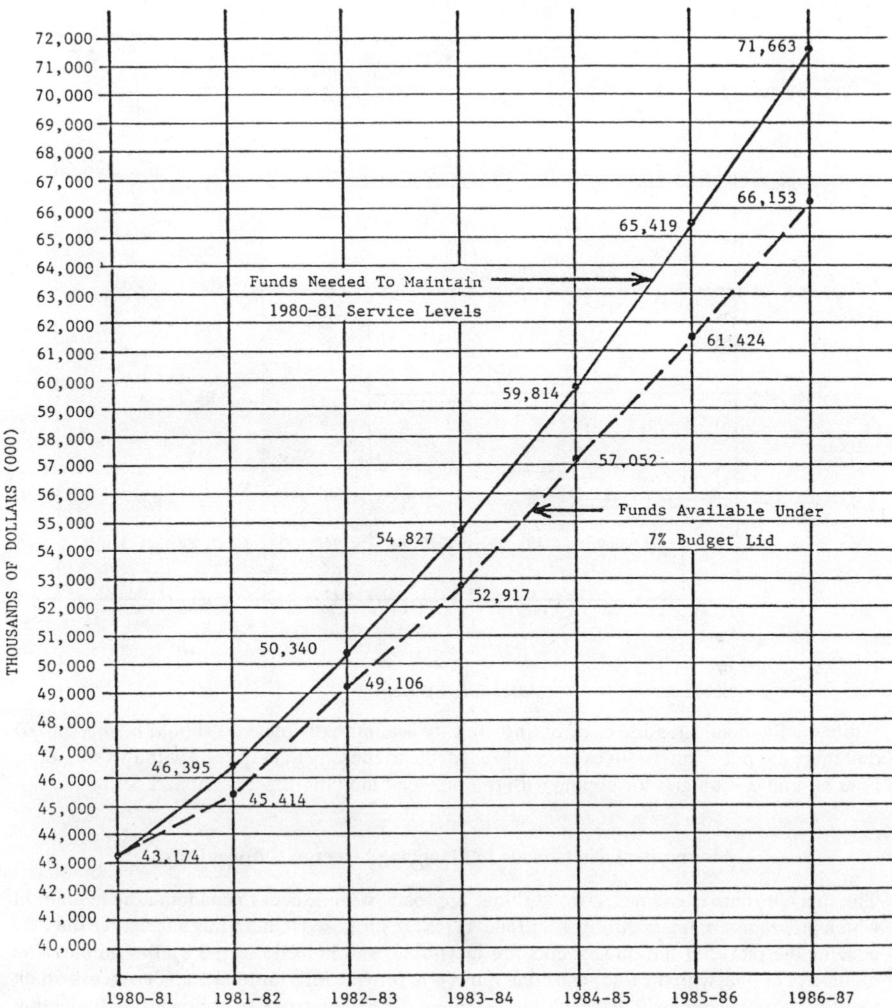

(continued)

Table 3.1. *(Continued)*

EXHIBIT 2: Forecasted Budget Gap in Terms of Maintaining 1980-81 Service Levels

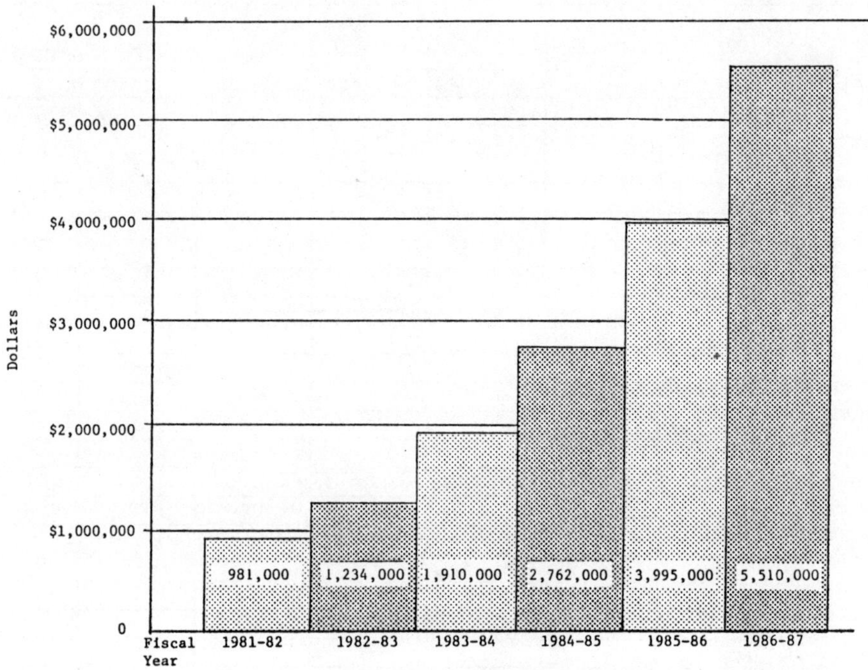

Alternate Strategies

While the financial situation confronting the City is admittedly bleak, it should be recognized that there are policy alternatives currently available to the City to help cope with this situation. Four alternate strategies for coping with the financial limitations are discussed below.

Alternative 1-No Change in Financing Structures, Make Cuts

The first alternative assumes a "do nothing" approach with respect to changing the manner in which programs are financed. No additional taxes are proposed. Under this alternative the City accepts the fact that the budget cuts are inevitable, and indeed desired by the public. The method of coping with the financial constraints is to provide for a rational budget process which identifies service areas which can either be reduced or eliminated. Use of Zero-Base Budgeting techniques is recommended. Asking departments to prepare a Base Level budget at 90% of their current budget will, more than likely, identify the areas of highest priority to the department

Table 3.1. *(Continued)*

head. Requests for funding above the 90% Base should be prioritized and presented so as to identify service level increments and their related costs. This will enable the Mayor and Council to compare the "benefits" of spending (or not spending) above the 90% Base in one department vis-à-vis other departments.

Under this concept, total staffing is projected to be reduced from the current level of 1,608 FTEs to somewhere between 1,535 and 1,560 in 1981-82, and to approximately 1,400 in 1986-87. The *actual* reduction in staffing will depend on salary levels of the positions eliminated.

Alternative 2—Increase Occupation Tax

The second alternative is to increase the Occupation Tax levied on the telephone company and gas company. Currently a tax of 2% on gross receipts is levied on both the telephone and gas companies. An increase of one percentage point to 3% of gross receipts would generate an additional $700,000. This alternative would help soften the impact of the cutbacks since the budget gap would be reduced to roughly $300,000. This tax source is outside the restrictions of the 7% Budget Lid and thus could be increased by local option.

Alternative 3—Increase Wheel Tax

The third alternative proposed is to increase the Wheel Tax by 50%. This increase would generate approximately $475,000 in additional income. By local ordinance, the additional income must be used to finance either street maintenance or street improvements. In the aggregate, however, the additional income could help soften the impacts of the cutbacks since under this alternative the budget gap would be reduced to $500,000. The current fee structure is provided below along with the projected fee structure assuming a 50% increase in rates.

It is perhaps worth noting that Wheel Tax rates have not been adjusted since 1965, although the cost of improving and maintaining the street system has more than doubled over the same period. Consequently, this tax base has been substantially eroded by inflation, resulting in reduced effectiveness with respect to financing street maintenance. This revenue source is also outside the restrictions imposed by the 7% Budget Lid and could be increased by local option.

Alternative 4—Increase Both the Occupation Tax and Wheel Tax

The fourth alternative identified is to increase both the Occupation Tax and Wheel Tax by 50%. Under this alternative, operations would, in the aggregate, not have to be reduced during 1981-82. Some cutbacks would, however, have to be made in subsequent years if, as is assumed here, inflationary increases outpace growth of the City's tax base.

Recommended Strategy

Lacking a clear mandate to exceed the 7% Budget Limitation through other legal tax increases, the alternative recommended for coping with the upcoming financial crunch is Alternative 1—No change in Financing Structure, Make Cuts.

The immediate consequence of this alternative is the elimination of roughly a million dollars

(continued)

Table 3.1. *(Continued)*

worth of City services. Hard choices will have to be made as to which programs are provided by City government and which ones are reduced or eliminated. Despite the above mentioned consequence, this alternative is selected because no tax increases are considered to be appropriate at this time. Even though increases in the Occupation and Wheel Tax are legally possible, it is felt that such increases would violate the spirit and intent of the 7% Budget Lid.

Conclusion

The establishment of fiscal guidelines is proposed in order to provide an overall framework within which budget priorities can be set. Such fiscal planning is the foundation for a fiscally sound and prudent plan relating to the use of City funds. The proposed plan will require reduced services in certain areas. Nevertheless, it is felt that such reductions should be realized in order to minimize the tax burden on City residents. Again, it is important to note that the budget projections do not consider the impact of possible reductions in Federal monies. These reductions may prove significant depending upon the type and magnitude of such cuts.

example, may have more public or private transportation users than another. The service level can be divided by the size of the recipient group, and the resulting ratio compared with that of other cities. For example, dollars spent on elderly recreation programs can be calculated on a per capita basis. Using an analogous but more complex procedure, "Indexes of Staffing" have been computed for cities, showing over- or under-staffing after adjusting for user characteristics such as poverty, taxable property value, crime rate, cost of living, etc.[7]

Compare with Private Sector. Staff salaries and benefits are a major area for private sector comparisons. Many cities now have data comparisons with the private sector compared annually for a dozen or more positions. Useful comparisons can be made on the basis of city, county, state, or national data. Costs for items such as office equipment and motor vehicles are determined primarily by private market forces, but the city should try to obtain discounts for quantity purchases. It is more difficult to compare costs for entire services such as police and fire protection, but the city can obtain bids from private contractors for the support of services such as dispatching or motor vehicle maintenance. Some cities, however, already contract out core functions such as police and fire; San Francisco even contracted out its finance department in the late 1970s.

[7]James L. Chan, Terry Nichols Clark, and Margaret A. Troha, "Organizational Slack in Municipal Governments." *Journal of Urban Affairs* 5 (Spring 1983), pp. 95-108.

Create Budget-Choice Situations for Organized Groups. Active organized groups are often mentioned as sources of pressure for spending in ways that conflict with general citizen preferences. Hearings held for specific user groups may be appropriate if the mayor is in a strong enough position to grant or deny their requests, but doing so is sometimes difficult. Alternatively, the mayor may find it useful to assemble representatives of several organized groups simultaneously and encourage them to discuss ways of sharing budget pie slices. This can be done simply by holding informal meetings with several group leaders or by holding a more structured session where budget priorities are already listed. City councils have used similar devices for difficult situations.[8] The underlying idea is to give participants a sense of the city's overall needs to help moderate their demands. The same approach is applicable to groups in particular neighborhoods or program areas.

Reward Success. The most critical ingredient is encouragement of the staff by the mayor and the council. Promotions, allocating extra staff, new office arrangements, press conferences that publicize staff achievements, all of these can work. Some cities use cash incentives. Although these incentives may be successful, they often prove very expensive if they do not work. The other side of the coin is to accept occasional failures as inevitable. Mayoral staffs in San Diego, Palo Alto, and Sunnyvale, California have commented that council members include many engineers and managers from aerospace and computer firms who expect innovative performance but also tolerate occasional failure.

Budgeting Tools

Many cities have developed tools to help in budgeting. The annual budget is usually the major document that summarizes them. It might be helpful to meet with the mayors of nearby cities to learn of their experiences, as well as with staff or consultants who can help develop additional tools at reasonable cost. Although specific tools are listed here, it is most important to know how to use them properly. If the mayor can work with the city administration in a way that improves services each year, such results are more important than a complex system. The mayor can seldom tell how much improvement there is, however, without specific management tools to measure it. In some

[8]See James G. Coke and Carl M. Moore, "Group Processes for Making Public Expenditure Reduction Decisions," in Herrington J. Bryce, ed., *Managing Fiscal Retrenchment in Cities.* Columbus, Ohio: Academy for Contemporary Problems, 1980, pp. 25-30.

Table 3-2. Driver Salaries and Benefits for Waukegan, IL and Other Nearby Cities

	Waukegan				Joliet				Elgin			
	1979	1980	1981	1982	1979	1980	1981	1982	1979	1980	1981	1982
Salary	9.22					8.46	8.585	8.71	7.70	8.20	8.35	8.45
Pension	0				Co. pay only .25/hr; Emp. .25/hr.				4.5% after 8hrs Ret full 60 day +30¢/hr			
Sick Days	0				—				12 per year			
Personal Days	0				11 personal days				3			
Holidays	7				7 days, 1 floating				6			
Sick Pay	0				Sick for 7 days/collect $115/wk				—			
COLA	Full				Index up .35% re-1¢ if down falls 1¢				None			
Spread Time	13 hrs				40 hr wk; 6 day wk.				Avg 41 hr/wk;ex 55 hr/wk			
Call In	2½ hrs				2 hrs				2 hrs			
Tool Allowance	0				0				0			
Tool Insurance	0				0				0			
Night Mechanics	1.5% 14¢				No night diff/no night work				10¢ hr more for 4 hr (till 9:45)			

Hospital Insurance	Driver	Fm cov. $150. Inc. Co pay 75%;em 25%	Family coverage
Dental	0	50% Co; 50% empl.	0
Eye	0	0	0
Leave of Absence	35 days	No provision for this	Availability for
Straight Runs	70%	No percentage	60% of drivers
Vacation	—	1 yr/1 wk; 2 yr/2wks; 8 yrs/3 wks	1 yr/1 wk; 9 yr/3 wk; 16 yr/4 wk
Missed Time	—	Mand. 1 hr call in over 2 hr/miss out	call in/fill in pick up; lose ½ day pay; habitual 1 day pay
Overtime	1½	Time and ½	
Life Insurance	5,000	20,000 natural; 40, accidental	$2,500
Uniforms	—	$60/year after 6 months	Are Provided
		First time receive warning Second time (60 days) placed bottom of board/2 day Third time 3 days at bottom or termination	

Source: Kathy Burns, *Mayoral Leadership and Financial Management in Waukegan, Illinois.* Chicago: Comparative Study of Community Decision-Making, Research Report #102, University of Chicago, 1981.

cities management systems are imposed from above and subverted from below; in other cities they work well. The involvement of upper and middle managers in assisting with the improvement of services is essential; a new management system cannot succeed without them.[9] Here is a list of tools to consider.

Distinct Programs. About 50 to 100 programs are reasonable for a program budget. Some cities have more, but larger amounts are usually more appropriate for individual administrators than leading officials. The more that programs match actual service delivery units, the easier it is to collect data and monitor activities. Program units should be defined with the participation of the program staff.

Specific Objectives for Programs. The mayor's specific concerns may vary each year. Major cutbacks may be required for one year, productivity in another, business incentives in a third. Each can be specified in stated program objectives. (In many other areas, of course, objectives may be informally understood.) With proper encouragement, the city administrative staff can take pride in surpassing stated objectives.

Demand Measures. Ideally every program should respond to a measured demand. The number of reported fires or users of parks are examples. The important point to remember is that without a demand measure, the service level cannot be evaluated in terms of impact. Lakewood, Colorado lists three or four quantitative demand measures for each of about 100 programs in its annual budget. Several pages from this budget are reproduced in Table 3.3.

Workload Measures. Work completed in units by city departments are called *workload measures.* An example is the lineal feet of pipes installed in the Lakewood, Colorado example.

Efficiency Measures. Workload measures divided by costs are variously termed *efficiency measures* or *cost of service measures.* They are often easy to compute but harder to present in ways that are useful for policy evaluation. The simplest way is to examine data presented over several years; the mayor can than ask for explanations of increases or decreases. The decision rules

[9] See George J. Washnis, ed., *Productivity Improvement Handbook for State and Local Government.* New York: John Wiley, 1980, chs. 1-4.

listed above suggest other ways of asking questions about these data. Sometimes the term "productivity" is used interchangeably with "efficiency" (as in Table 3.3), but later in this chapter we will show how "productivity" takes on a much broader meaning.

Effectiveness Measures. Effectiveness measures are often used to show how fully a community goal has been met. For example, if the goal is to correct all life-threatening situations created by damaged or missing traffic signs and signals within 24 hours, an effectiveness measure would be "percentage of life-threatening traffic signs and signals defects repaired within 24 hours of notification." When, as in this case, the goal is to respond to a varying demand, then the importance of measuring demand to help judge effectiveness becomes clear. For example, if a flooded-cellar crew responded to 90 percent of citizens' service calls in two years, but there were twice as many calls in the second year, it obviously had to do more work in the second year. Sometimes effectiveness is defined quite broadly, for example, as the "degree to which services are responsive to the needs and desires of the community."[10] One of the most common distinctions drawn between efficiency and effectiveness is that efficiency refers to "doing things right" and effectiveness refers to "doing the right things." Actually, effectiveness measures tell if *enough* of the right things are being done to meet public needs and demands.

Show Several Years of Data. It is necessary to clarify the importance of several years of data to interpret any one year.

Textual Rationale for Program and Proposed Changes. A brief explanation, especially of changes, should be included. Ideally, all documents should be sufficiently understandable for the mayor and council members to read on their own, *without* an expert nearby.

Line-Item Format for Personnel and Basic Services. A few cities omit the line-item format altogether, arguing that council members should not pay attention to salaries or equipment costs but instead focus on the larger policy issues. The counter argument is that if these items are not disclosed, the council has no way of checking except by questioning. Large dollar amounts are harder to interpret than a line item of the staff and salaries

[10]Paul D. Epstein, *Using Performance Measurements in Local Government: A Guide to Improving Decisions, Performance, and Accountability.* New York: Van Nostrand Reinhold, 1984.

Table 3.3. Two Pages from Lakewood, CO Annual Budget.

ENVIRONMENT	DRAINAGE SYSTEMS
PROGRAM	DRAINAGE MAINTENANCE
PROGRAM DESCRIPTION	To maintain the City's drainage system including engineering, pipe cleaning, installation and repair of culverts and inlets, and ditch and channel cleaning.

PERFORMANCE OBJECTIVES

1. Maintain 110,000 lineal feet of drainage channels and ditches where legal access is available.
2. Prevent deterioration of substandard drainage facilities by installing 1,100 lineal feet of drainage pipes.
3. Clean 28,000 feet of pipe and grills.

INDICATORS OF PERFORMANCE

	MEASUREMENT	OBJECTIVE	1979 ACTUAL	1980 PROJECTED	1980 REVISED	1981 PROJECTED
DEMAND	Lineal Feet of Channels and Ditches	1	1,260,000	1,260,000	1,261,400	1,261,400
	Lineal Feet of Drainage Pipe	3	96,180	96,180	104,365	104,365
	Lineal Feet of Improved Major Gulches	1	15,800	15,800	15,800	15,800
	Citizen Requests for Drainage Maintenance	1,2,3	258	275	267	253
WORKLOAD	Lineal Feet of Channels and Ditches Cleaned	1	105,818	110,000	115,000	120,000
	Lineal Feet of Pipes Installed, Concrete and Metal	2	36,805	28,000	32,000	35,000
	Lineal Feet of Pipes and Grills Cleaned	3	1,273	1,100	1,400	1,200
PRODUCTIVITY	Average Cost per Foot for Cleaning Channels and Ditches	1	$ 1.24	$ 1.51	$ 1.65	$ 1.44
	Average Cost per Foot for Installing Various Size Drainage Pipes, Concrete and Metal	2	$ 1.74	$ 2.27	$ 2.93	$ 2.47
	Average Cost per Foot for Cleaning Various Size					

EFFECTIVENESS					
% Lineal Feet of Channels and Ditches Cleaned	1	105.8%	72.3%	71.0%	100%
% Lineal Feet of Drainage Pipe Installed	2	147.2%	78.20%	73.0%	100%
% Lineal Feet of Pipes and Grills Cleaned	3	84.9%	100.1%	79.3%	100%
% Change in Citizen Requests for Drainage Maintenance	1,2,3	−6.2%	+6.6%	−3.0%	−5.3%

ANALYSIS

Very little change is anticipated in this program for 1981. Workload indicators are the same as in 1980. Depending upon frost depth in 1981 this program should be able to match or exceed 1980 levels of performance. An estimated 50% of program effort goes into cleaning channels and ditches. 25% of effort goes into cleaning various size drainage pipes. 5% of effort goes into the installation of various size metal and concrete drainage pipes and 20% of program effort goes into miscellaneous areas, such as special projects from the Engineering Division, Water and Sewer excavation repairs for the Lakewood Board of Water & Sewer Commissioners, guardrail replacement and repair. Citizens requests for drainage maintenance has been moved from this category to the demand category.

The lineal footage of drainage pipe is the result of an actual annual inventory that includes the pipe installed by the City and private developers.

RESOURCES

	1979 ACTUAL	1980 BUDGET	1980 REVISED	1981 BUDGET
CATEGORY: PERSONNEL	$192,767	$194,516	$220,737	$220,642
OPERATING/MAINTENANCE SUPPLIES	31,927	22,369	22,369	23,594
CHARGES & SERVICES	40,694	83,774	92,556	92,314
CAPITAL OUTLAY	9,800	14,571	8,162	9,543
TOTAL	$275,188	$315,230	$343,824	$346,093
FUNDS: GENERAL	$275,188	$325,230	$343,824	$346,093
OTHER	0	0	0	0
TOTAL	$275,188	$315,230	$343,824	$346,093

RESOURCE ALLOCATION REQUIREMENTS

DEPARTMENT	PUBLIC WORKS	1979 ACTUAL	1980 BUDGET	1980 REVISED	1981 BUDGET
PROGRAM	DRAINAGE MAINTENANCE	$275,188	$315,230	$343,824	$346,093

POSITIONS	NO. OF POSITIONS 1979 ACTUAL	1980 BUDGET	1980 REVISED	1981 BUDGET	EXPENDITURES 1979 ACTUAL	1980 BUDGET	1980 REVISED	1981 BUDGET	
Maintenance Operations Engineer	.20	.25	.25	.25	$ 6,325	$ 6,500	$7,377	$ 7,375	PERSONNEL
Deputy City Engineer	—	—	—	—	25	—	—	—	
Maintenance Supervisor	.90	.90	.90	.90	18,515	18,023	19,131	20,025	
Principal Civil Engineer	—	.10	.10	.10	391	2,380	1,442	1,250	
Associate Civil Engineer	—	.10	.30	.30	1,937	1,957	3,337	6,376	
Chief of Surveys	—	.05	—	—	165	926	71	—	
Maintenance Crew Leader	.90	.90	.90	.90	16,170	15,161	16,829	16,587	
Engineering Technician IV	—	.10	.05	.15	2,978	1,500	713	1,970	
Engineering Technician III	.10	.05	—	—	791	684	—	—	
Engineering Technician II	.05	.10	—	—	930	1,256	246	—	
Engineering Technician I	—	.10	—	—	87	1,137	112	—	
Administrative Clerk I	.25	.25	.10	.15	2,299	2,378	1,583	1,467	
Clerk III	.20	.20	.10	.20	2,352	1,743	1,456	1,966	
Maintenance Specialist III	1.80	2.25	2.25	2.25	27,842	33,091	36,712	35,721	
Maintenance Specialist II	—	—	—	—	1,423	—	502	—	
Maintenance Specialist I	3.80	2.70	3.60	3.60	55,037	29,951	47,422	46,962	
Maintenance Worker II	3.60	3.60	3.60	3.60	26,334	38,533	38,160	41,548	
Technicians (P)	84 hrs	—	16 hrs	—	290	—	64	—	
Laborer II (P)	7 hrs	2240 hrs	2243 hrs	—	363	7,280	7,852	—	
RETIREMENT					17,389	15,304	17,263	17,869	
INSURANCE					9,878	19,912	19,465	19,546	
OVERTIME					1,246	1,800	1,000	2,000	
TOTAL	11.80	11.65	12.15	12.40	$192,767	$194,516	$220,737	$220,642	

SUPPLIES

CODE	DESCRIPTION OF EXPENDITURE	1979 ACTUAL	1980 BUDGET	1980 REVISED	1981 BUDGET
220	Operating Supplies	$ 687	$ 1,985	$ 1,985	$ 1,674
230	Repair and Maintenance Supplies	31,240	20,384	20,384	21,920
	TOTAL	$31,927	$22,369	$22,369	$23,594

CHARGES & SERVICES

CODE	DESCRIPTION OF EXPENDITURE	1979 ACTUAL	1980 BUDGET	1980 REVISED	1981 BUDGET
310	Professional Services	$ 1,030	$ 2,500	$ 2,500	$ 2,165
330	Transportation	66,794	78,274	86,366	84,281
370	Repair and Maintenance Service	3	—	—	2,668
380	Rentals	49	2,000	3,690	2,000
390	Other Charges and Services	(27,181)	1,000	—	1,200
	TOTAL	$40,694	$83,774	$92,556	$92,314

CAPITAL OUTLAY

CODE	DESCRIPTION OF EXPENDITURE	1979 ACTUAL	1980 BUDGET	1980 REVISED	1981 BUDGET
430	Other Improvements	$ 7,995	$ —	$ —	$ —
440	Machinery and Equipment	1,805	14,571	8,162	9,543
	TOTAL	$ 9,800	$14,571	$ 8,162	$ 9,543

involved. Many cities show the line-items on the budget page after each program (see Table 3.3).

Distinguish Categories of Employees. Authorized positions that are filled and full-time, part-time, or temporary employees who are funded by special grants or revenue sources (e.g., Federally funded) can be reported by department or program. This distinction is especially important for determining the impact of the elimination of special grants or revenue sources (which happened, for example, when Federal CETA public employment funds were eliminated). It also helps the mayor plan and manage transitions and eliminate positions without a disruption of services.

Audit Performance Measures. Periodic audits are essential to verify the accuracy of basic data. They can be costly, however, suggesting a need to audit the few most important items. Detailed unannounced audits can be made of agencies on a rotating basis.

Periodic Simplification. If auditing errors are found in several series, and their data are not being used by staff, they should perhaps be eliminated. Since management systems can grow incrementally, it is suggested that regular simplification procedures be built in.

V. HOW TO IMPROVE PRODUCTIVITY

Improved productivity is a logical solution to the combined pressures for lower taxes and high service levels. When mayors and other local officials refer to their "productivity improvement programs," they are usually not speaking of narrowly focused efforts to increase specific input/output ratios alone but of their extensive efforts to improve services while controlling costs. The term "productive" is here thought of as encompassing both efficiency and effectiveness, a meaning encouraged by the old National Commission on Productivity and other authoritative sources.[11] This is important for mayors to remember, because the specific nature and emphasis of a productivity program should vary in accordance with the specific situation of a community. For example, in a community with a growing population and tax base, where service expansion is inevitable, it may be easier and more "profitable" (in dollar value or service improvements) to increase the efficiency of services than in a community with a declining or stable population and tax base.

[11] *Measuring the Effectiveness of Basic Municipal Services: Initial Report.* Washington, D.C.: ICMA and the Urban Institute, 1974, p. 3.

When a service is expanding, increased efficiency means controlling the cost of that expansion so that unpopular measures such as layoffs of city employees or cutting back needed services need not be taken. In cities that are not expanding, it is often more important to concentrate on improving the overall effectiveness of services by improving their deployment and basic resource allocation. Efficiency improvement can still be a part of these efforts, but it should be undertaken within the context of the city's overall improvement needs and potential. For example, when Phoenix and San Diego began their productivity programs in the early to mid-1970s, they were rapidly growing communities and focused their efforts almost entirely, and quite successfully, on efficiency improvement. Conversely, when Dayton, Ohio, a stable, but not rapidly expanding city, began a major improvement effort at about the same time, it focused on strategic resource allocation and service effectiveness. Both Phoenix and San Diego have since broadened their efforts, and Dayton's program, which continues to be active and successful, includes efficiency objectives that are subservient to broader community goals. Despite the complex nature of productivity improvement, many cities of various types have engaged in it.

Productivity as a Political Program

In cities with major political conflicts, strong unions, and open patronage, productivity is likely to improve only if it is part of a political program. During the 1970s and early 1980s, many cities elected mayors who emphasized productivity (e.g., Flaherty in Pittsburgh, Koch in New York, Green in Philadelphia, and Morris in Waukegan, Illinois). Productivity improvements followed from the general commitment of these mayors to improve services while holding down taxes.

Mayor Peter Flaherty of Pittsburgh was the first of the mayors to institute productivity improvements, and his efforts might well be considered for implementation in other cities. In 1969, Flaherty ran as an independent Democrat against the Democratic establishment and won without any major obligations to municipal employees or organized groups. Pledging his administration to reducing city expenses, both he and his department heads gave up their use of chauffeured limousines to set an example to the public. Major critics included the head of the Teamsters local, who, as a negotiator for many employees and a city council member as well, was concerned with jobs for drivers. Despite a period of strikes in the early years of Flaherty's administration, the mayor prevailed and was able to win on most labor issues during his seven years in office. The mayor and his officials abolished some agencies, consolidated others, transferred many employees, and promoted middle-level managers who adopted the new approach.

Flaherty's approach can succeed when the fundamental problem is political opposition to productivity and employees' resistance to change. As the most glaring problems are solved over time, however, more subtlety becomes necessary. By the late 1970s, Pittsburgh had developed a new approach closer to that of other cities: Productivity via a separate professional staff.

Productivity as a Professional Activity

Productivity functions should be assigned to separate departments and specialized staff as they become an accepted part of government. Many cities have separate productivity agencies, but these are often associated with finance staff because of the importance of fiscal data and budgetary authority to back up recommendations. One common method is to have a budget analyst monitor the finances of one or more departments and conduct reviews for possible productivity improvements. This method is used in San Diego, for example, where it is supplemented by a separate productivity agency with a staff of experts in both engineering and organizational psychology. These experts work together as a team that involves middle managers and workers throughout the review processes. They often spend six months or more on a single agency such as motor vehicle maintenance by studying it thoroughly and considering alternative procedures for improvement. Suggestions often come from the staff of the agency itself. The productivity team prepares detailed recommendations for the department head and central administrative staff. In some cases, the combination of savings and service improvements achieved have been worth about 10 percent of the prior cost of the service.

Involvement of departmental staff in the review has made implementation reasonably simple. Almost all activity takes place among staff; the city manager and mayor only receive reports. Such an incremental nonpolitical approach fits the pattern of productivity adopted by San Diego.[12]

Alternative Organizational Models

Cities encourage productivity in many different ways. The most essential is creating an overall climate to reward productivity while remaining personable.

[12]The Pittsburgh and San Diego programs are presented in *Issues in Financial Management of Local Governments,* U.S. Conference of Mayors, Washington, D.C.: USCM/HUD, 1978. Further discussion of San Diego's program, with case examples on Phoenix, Dayton, and other communities, is in *Using Performance Measurements in Local Governments: A Guide to Improving Decisions, Performance, and Accountability* by Paul D. Epstein (New York: Van Nostrand Reinhold, 1984).

Pittsburgh and San Diego illustrate two of the many ways of adapting productivity to governance. Once leading members of the administrative staff have formulated the general approach, the following specific techniques can reinforce their efforts:

1. *Assigning an official from the finance staff to monitor the finances of each department* and watch for major problems on a continuing basis. The financial officer may also be responsible for determining problem areas and generating a more extensive review (as is the case, for example, in Palo Alto, California).
2. *Using a team to conduct brief reviews (from a few days up to a month) of specific program areas.* This may include a roving team made up of finance staff, engineers, psychiatrists, and social workers (as is the case, for example, in Lincoln, Nebraska; see Sec. IV in Chap. 10) or the team may consist of regular city staff on loan from different departments for a one-year period (as in Dallas). These experts can work in different combinations depending on the issue.
3. *Using a productivity staff for more intensive reviews (over one month) of critical areas.* Although few cities have the professional staff needed for detailed productivity studies, such studies (for example, the one in San Diego) have proven successful.
4. *Fundamental problem reviews.* At the time of a major crisis or inauguration of new state or Federal program, more fundamental priority shifts may become necessary. A committee of outside advisors, department officials, or others can be used to mobilize support (as in Cambridge, for example; see Sec. IV in Chap. 10).

Use of Outside Consultants

Many cities begin productivity programs by seeking help from outside consultants. Various types of management and productivity consultants are available from accounting or management consulting firms to assist in productivity studies. They can be engaged for an inexpensive short-term overview but will sometimes be needed on a long-term basis. Some consultants often remain on city staff for long periods. Local businesses may volunteer part-time assistance (as in Pittsburgh, for motor vehicle fleet maintenance). Faculty or students from local universities can be encouraged to donate their time in work-study or internship programs. State agencies or leagues of cities in some areas have staff that pursue these issues (for example, in Illinois), and it is up to the mayor to involve them.

Reviewing Experiences with Other Cities

Groups of cities can pursue productivity jointly by having their mayors, city managers, and other staff informally meet their counterparts from other cities. Such regional conferences can also enlist the services of specialists in productivity. Localities can improve productivity through employing personnel from pace-setting cities and instituting training programs for their existing staff. The budgeting and performance measurement sections in Chap. 10 review some interesting examples of productivity-related matters.

VI. CUTBACK MANAGEMENT

As more and more cities are forced to make cutbacks in services, new problems have arisen. Although few options appear to be available, the following are some of the more important measures that mayors can take:

Adopt Low-Visibility Revenue-Raising Devices

Low-visibility revenue-raising devices are consistent with the strategy that views visible property taxes as the problem (rather than the more general citizen resistance to taxes and government spending). After property taxes were limited by the adoption of Proposition 13, many California cities found new revenue sources and increased other forms of taxes.

Low-visibility revenue sources include value-added taxes and long-term debt in the form of revenue bonds issued by subordinate special districts (housing authorities, etc.) rather than by city government. Specific fees may also be imposed on certain activities.[13]

User Charges

User charges can be imposed on recipients of specific government services. These charges both reduce consumption of the service by increasing its cost and permit the intensity of preference of the service to be gauged by observing use levels under different charges. The principle of full-cost recovery in the public sector is similar to that for certain unsubsidized services provided by the private sector. Calculating full-cost recovery is sometimes complex; heavy concentration of usage at certain times may lead to a charge schedule including peak-load pricing, such as lower charges for

[13]Many new forms of borrowing are discussed in Chap. 5. Special districts are covered in Annmarie Hauck Walsh, *The Public's Business* (Cambridge, MA: Massachusetts Institute of Technology Press, 1978).

electricity at night.[14] User charges may be imposed selectively to protect the socially disadvantaged. For example, the elderly or poor may be given lower rates, a free day can be declared for museums and swimming pools, or citizens can be given credit cards of varying amounts to spend on municipal services.

Make Visible Efforts to Improve Productivity and Fiscal Management

Productivity improvement is the major means of resolving the apparent conflict between reducing taxes and maintaining services and is thus likely to be stressed as a major policy in itself. Fiscal management can improve the quality of information available for leading officials and thereby improve productivity. More serviceable accounting and budgeting systems, revenue and expenditure forecasts, and a multiyear capital funding program are important, if only to help persuade municipal employees to accept multiyear policies rather than bargain for cash on hand. Monthly or quarterly statements of important revenues and expenditures help monitoring. Clear and meaningful budgets, financial statements, and bond prospectuses can help build support with citizens, investors, and organized group leaders, as can accounting and reporting procedures comparable to those in pace-setting cities. These measures also make room for cross-city and over-time comparisons to assess service costs.

Demonstrating a continual commitment to productivity improvement may be as important as actually improving productivity, since seldom can anyone outside government assess actual productivity changes. Publicizing improvements is thus essential, as is introducing technology that symbolizes efficiency, such as computers. Promulgation of program budgets, performance indicators, cost of service data, and revenue-forecasting models may suggest that top management is in control and improving services.

Privatization

Privatization—i.e., terminating government services and letting the private sector supply them—is more often resorted to than publicized. Some elected officials publicize local "service cutbacks" in an effort to generate more support from the state or Federal government. This was done occasionally

[14]See Selma Mushkin, ed., *Public Prices for Public Products* (Washington, D.C.: The Urban Institute, 1972) and J. Richard Aronson and Eli Schwartz, eds., *Management Policies in Local Government Finance* (Washington, D.C.: Municipal Finance Officers Association and International City Management Association, 1981).

in cities after statewide propety tax referenda passed in California and Massachusetts, the goal often being to encourage citizens or state officials to allocate more funds to needy local governments. Most observers feel that criticizing your own government or services indicates poor leadership except under circumstances where blame can be deferred to another party. In general, it seems better to let privatization take place quietly.

Use Volunteers

Volunteered time is recorded and treated as a contribution to the city (in New Orleans, for example, volunteers work free of charge for some periods and are paid for others). In the wake of Proposition 13, a park that had its budget cut in half promoted an "Adopt-a-Park" program and raised $15,000 from Kaiser Aluminum. Many private firms have facilities and equipment such as swimming pools and trucks that they can donate or lease for a nominal fee to the city for favorable publicity. Banks and commerical firms have talented staff they can loan to the city. Chambers of Commerce and similar organizations have developed networks of information about the availability of such help. Universities can provide faculty and student interns. New York, Pittsburgh, and Waukegan are among the cities that have used volunteers for fiscal management, secretarial support, and other tasks.[15]

Contracting

Contracting is resisted on principle by some leaders concerned with loss of patronage, but the main obstacle usually comes from workers who are trying to save their city jobs. Some leaders may make it a practice to contract with their campaign contributors or generate political benefits in other ways. These political motivations are not inherently more costly; competitive bidding can keep costs of contracts with political supporters reasonable.[16] Contracting has traditionally been limited to new construction, office supplies, and related items. More recently, cities have begun to contract basic services; as much as 80 percent of all services are contracted in some small towns.

Scottsdale, Arizona provides a good example of contracting municipal services. In the Scottsdale area, fire protection is provided to nine municipali-

[15]David Rogers, *The Management of Big Cities* (Beverly Hills: Sage, 1971); Kathy Burns, *Mayoral Leadership and Financial Management in Waukegan, Illinois* (Chicago: Comparative Study of Community Decision-Making, Research Report #102, University of Chicago, 1981).

[16]For a thorough analysis of both the benefits of and constraints on contracting, see John Tepper Marlin, editor, *Contracting Municipal Services: A Guide for Purchase from the Private Sector,* New York: John Wiley & Sons, 1984.

ties and fire districts at significant cost savings by a private firm using regular city staff as part-time employees in various departments. Employees receive a monthly salary plus an hourly fee for answering calls.[17] Lakewood, California and many other Los Angeles area localities regularly contract services. In 1978, San Francisco even contracted out finance department services, albeit with a firm headed by the former city finance director. San Diego set up a nonprofit firm to provide data processing, thus avoiding civil service requirements for highly-paid programmers.[18]

VII. CONCLUSION

This chapter has not presented any single approach or tool as essential or "correct" but rather a list of options for review and consideration. We have mentioned labels and slogans that have become famous, some of them because of their adoption by important political leaders. A similar message is that various budgeting tools, productivity approaches, and cutback management strategies are available. Even if the mayor adopts approaches quietly and incrementally, they can still have a major impact on administrative patterns. Budgeting is the basic fiscal record of the policy perspective.

---

[17]Roger S. Ahlbrandt, Jr. *Municipal Fire Protection Services: Comparison of Alternative Organizational Forms* (Beverly Hills and London: Sage Professional Paper in Administrative and Policy Studies 03-001, 1973).

[18]Barbara J. Nelson, "Purchase of Services," in *Productivity Improvement Handbook for State and Local Government,* edited by George J. Washnis (New York: John Wiley & Sons, 1980); Donald Fisk, Herbert Kiesling, and Thomas Muller, *Private Provision of Public Services* (Washington, D.C.: The Urban Institute, 1978); E. S. Savas, *Privatizing the Public Sector* (Chatham, N.J.: Chatham House, 1982).

4
Debt Management and Policy

Access to the tax-exempt credit markets is a critical resource in the financial management of America's cities. As public capital investment has grown to meet the changing demands and needs of urban society, other pressures for environmental protection, targeted economic development, expanded health care facilities, low-cost housing and mortgage financing, and transportation revitalization have begun to compete with each other in a unique marketplace whose key elements are now engaged in vigorous debate about its own purpose and future.

The diversity of these financing requirements imposes many policy dilemmas for cities, their elected officials, and citizens. The most important questions are as follows:

- How much debt can a jurisdiction afford?
- Is the self-supporting potential of public projects being fully utilized?
- Should taxing powers be pledged and, if so, when? Should bond issues be negotiated or publicly bid?
- How can city policymakers control increased local borrowing?

The mayor's influence on these and other debt-related policy issues is important for ensuring the operation of a fiscally well-managed community. The numerous benefits of a prudent debt policy include the following:

- Maintenance of critical access to the markets
- Stronger credit perception among investors
- Reduced borrowing costs
- Opportunities to carefully broaden use of tax-exempt financing
- Ability to plan both development and operating budgets realistically

To help mayors toward the goal of prudent and sensitive borrowing policies and debt management practices is the purpose of this chapter of the *Handbook.* The objectives are as follows:

- To familiarize mayors with the tax-exempt bond market
- To review the various types of debt instruments and their proper use

- To fully define functions and responsibilities in the debt issuance process
- To explain the debt issuance process and its pitfalls
- To analyze the key issues of debt policy
- To help mayors get help when they need it

I. THE TAX-EXEMPT BOND MARKET

Local government debt issuance laws permit varied applications of the Federal income tax exemption in state and municipal capital raising activities. A complex and changing market totaling more than $220 billion of outstanding debt at any given time serves as the source for satisfying a wide variety of capital needs. During the past decade, changes in both the supply and demand side of this market have considerably altered the way in which cities and other governmental entities sell their debt. Prominent among these changes has been the growth in revenue debt issued by statutory authorities, particularly in the area of public utilities, pollution control, and housing financing. The sharp growth in the bond holdings of casualty companies and other investors with specific income needs has changed debt practices, among them the use of the negotiated sale process and the issuance of larger blocks of term (sinking fund) bonds to satisfy actuarially oriented buyers. Recent economic bumps and shocks moreover, have disrupted the normal course of municipal market trends. The resolution of critical issues regarding distressed cities (New York and Cleveland, for example), refunding of outstanding debt, regulatory oversight, mandatory disclosure, limitations on use of housing bonds, bank underwriting of revenue bonds, and efforts to expand the taxable bond option program will further change municipal debt policies and practices. Chapter 5 contains additional information on trends in the tax-exempt market, including the issuers of debt, purposes of borrowing, and the composition of the market for tax-exempt debt.

Legal Basis

Federal legislation. Since the 1913 enactment of the Federal income tax, interest on state and local debt has been exempt from Federal income taxes (see Sec. 103 of the Internal Revenue Code). Despite periodic attempts to remove this tax-exempt status by legislative and judicial actions, it has survived over the years and has become a key element of both municipal finance and the capital markets. In fact, the scope and types of tax-exempt financing have gradually been broadened over time to include a number of public-purpose uses.

State legislation. State and local debt issuance powers vary widely across the nation. Each state has unique legislation governing the issuance and sale of general obligation bonds by its political subdivisions. These constitutional and statutory provisions affect the manner in which cities issue their debt, varying as to debt limitations, public approval, structure and time of issue, method of sale, basis of award, price, and premium. In addition, cities and other municipal corporations sometimes operate under various forms of state oversight and regulations of debt issuance programs.

Interest income on municipal bonds is usually exempt from income taxes in the state in which the bonds were issued, but taxable when received in other states.

The Issuers

Tax-exempt bonds are issued by state and local governments, school districts, special districts, and statutory authorities. Trends in the amount of debt sold by type of issuer and recent growth in the bond sales of state governments and statutory authorities can be found in Chap. 5.

Uses of Debt

The purposes for state and local government borrowing have changed markedly over time. Whereas loans for education, transportation, water, and sewers represented nearby two-thirds of total bond issues in 1970, they now represent only about one-fifth. Pollution control, hospital, utility, port facilities, and industrial revenue bonds have grown from nearly zero to more than one-third of the total, and refunding bonds have also exhibited substantial growth. In 1978, the mortgage revenue bond concept was extended to provide low interest rates on single-family mortgages.

The Bond Buyers

The overwhelming majority of tax-exempt bonds are held by commercial banks, individuals, and casualty insurance companies. Other holders, growing in their involvement, but still under 10 percent of the total, are businesses, government, savings and loan associations, mutual savings banks, government pension funds, brokers, and dealers.

Investment Bankers and Bond Dealers

Underwriters. Underwriters purchase bonds from the issuer and distribute them to dealers. These purchases may take place through public bidding (competitive sale), private sale (negotiation), or private placement. The underwriters advance the bond proceeds to the issuer; their return is based on their ability to reoffer the bonds to the market at a higher price than they paid for them.

Dealers. The primary (new issue) market is dominated by national and major regional firms, although underwriters often combine efforts to underwrite municipal debt. Of the 450 securities dealers, less than 100 of them underwrite 90 percent of the bonds sold in the new market. The secondary (or resale) market, where securities are bought from other investors rather than the issuer, is twice the size of the new issue market. This activity in the secondary market, however, represents transfers of ownership rather than net increases in the amount of outstanding securities.

The "Red Book," *Directory of Municipal Bond Dealers of the United States,* offers a list of investment bankers and securities dealers engaged in municipal bond underwriting and trading.

II. TYPES OF DEBT

There are a number of types of tax-exempt debt. One major distinction is that between short- and long-term debt. The few variations of short-term borrowing are similar in overall form. There are much sharper distinctions between the major types of long-term debt obligations. They differ markedly in their purposes and use of proceeds as well as in underlying security and source of revenues to make interest and principal payments.

Short-Term Debt

Short-term debt is usually considered to be municipal obligations that mature within one year of being issued. It is typically used to provide temporary or interim financing.

Purpose and Use. Short-term debt may be defined as debt used for the following purposes:

- To provide cash to get an operation or project started
- To provide cash while awaiting improved market conditions for long-term debt issuances
- To provide cash for initial construction work
- To borrow while financial problems are being resolved
- To fund unbudgeted expenses
- To smooth out cash flow fluctuations

Short-term debt usage grew from $4 billion in 1960 to $29.5 billion in 1974 and to $34.4 billion in 1981. Market shifts have changed the demand for short-term instruments. Furthermore, extended use or overuse of short-term debt is often central to the problem of financially distressed cities. In most cases, short-term borrowings should be repaid by the end of a fiscal period.

Instruments

1. *Tax Anticipation Notes (TANs).* Tax anticipation notes are used to cover cash flow shortfalls resulting from a lag in tax collections. The notes are often placed with local banks and secured by the pledge of the anticipated taxes. In order to place TANs, the government should be able to show a reliable cash flow. TANs should be used sparingly, for example, when internal cash management techniques are not sufficient to produce an adequate cash flow and it becomes necessary to borrow temporarily to meet cash needs.
2. *Revenue Anticipation Notes (RANs).* RANs are used to provide cash when intergovernmental grants lag. They are secured by the anticipated Federal or state revenue and repaid upon the receipt of that revenue. The certainty of reimbursement is a critical factor in the use of RANs. Cities should avoid borrowing against revenues that are speculative or uncertain of receipt.
3. *Bond Anticipation Notes (BANs).* BANs are used to provide start-up cash for capital projects or to await a more favorable interest rate on long-term debt. The borrowing is secured by the proceeds of the anticipated future bond sale. BANs may be limited on term or rollover (issuing new BANs rather than the anticipated bonds to repay the old BANs). BANs may be repaid out of current revenues so long as sufficient funds exist.

Long-Term Debt

Long-term debt is used to provide permanent financing for the acquisition, construction, or major renovation of capital assets. It should not be used to provide funds to meet current operating expenses. The term of the issue should not exceed the extimated useful life of the asset being financed, although maturities can be thirty or more years in some cases. The debt can be structured as a term issue, with periodic payments consisting of interest only and the entire principal payable at maturity, or as a serial issue in which the principal is retired systematically over the life of the issue.

General Obligation Bonds

General obligation bonds are issued with the full faith and credit of the issuer standing behind them. Thus, general tax revenues of the issuer are the ultimate source of funds for repayment. Originally, tax-exempt debt was almost exclusively general obligation. Over time, however, there has been a pronounced shift toward the issuance of revenue bonds. (See Revenue Bond section below.) For example, about 30 percent of all long-term debt issued in 1960 was revenue debt; by 1980, this percentage had increased to 70 percent.

Purpose and Use. General obligation bonds may be used for practically any general governmental project or facility—parks, streets, schools, public buildings, etc. These projects are for use by diverse population groups, service to the city's overall economic or social purpose, promotion of the tax base, or other local benefit.

General obligation bonds also may be used as a guarantee for revenue bond projects (such as sewer, water, or airport) when the projects yield community-wide benefits and the use of general obligation financing may reduce interest costs.

Security. General obligation bonds are secured by the "full faith and credit" of the issuer. This pledge indicates that the taxing power and all general revenues of the government that are not legally restricted will be used to pay back the bonds. Furthermore, bondholders are entitled to be paid before the government expends money for any other purpose.

Other Types. Other general obligation types of bonds exist, among them the following: "limited" bonds (secured with a pledge, but the issuer's taxing power is limited to a maximum rate), "special tax" bonds (payable only from special tax yields), and "special assessment" bonds (payable only from assessments on those who benefit directly from the projects).

Limitation on the Use of the Pledge. States may impose constitutional or statutory debt ceilings on the issuance of general obligation bonds, often related to property values or locally generated revenues. Good debt management requires that a mayor be aware of his city's debt limit and available borrowing capacity in planning for future needs.

Approval of the administrative body of the governing unit (the Council) or the voters is often required before general obligation debt can be issued. More than 35 percent of bond referendums are defeated, for reasons such as public opposition to the projects, anti-tax sentiment, or poor voter turnouts.

The bond market may also impose limits on the amount of general obligation debt a municipality can issue. Such factors as annual debt service as a percentage of the general fund budget, the tax structure, age and condition of the city's physical plant, future financing needs, the perceived quality of the city's financial management, and the health and growth of the city's economic and tax base are examined to determine how much borrowing capacity is available to the city. If a city is not deemed creditworthy, it will not be able to issue debt.

Revenue Bonds

Revenue bonds rely on a stream of revenue generated from user charges or the sale of a product generated from the project financed to repay the debt. General obligation debt, in contrast, relies on all revenues of the issuing government. Revenue bonds have become increasingly popular as a means of avoiding the use of the general obligation pledge, shifting facility costs away from taxpayers to users, avoiding voter referenda on bond issuances, circumventing debt ceilings imposed on the issuer, and securing pledges from private interests.

Purpose and Use. Revenue bonds are issued to finance special-purpose facilities that have discrete revenue sources and definable user bases. They are often used to finance the purchase of, and improvements to, energy, sewer and water systems, airports, toll roads, hospitals, pollution control, industrial development, housing, parking and nursing homes.

Revenue debt is used when a charge is appropriate and a project's revenues are sufficiently large and predictable to meet all debt service requirements. This method of financing can circumvent statutory debt limits on tax-supported financing and preserve the general obligation credit.

Security. The issuing governmental unit is obligated to pay for the service of the debt, but only from the specified source of revenue. In order to provide buyers with the necessary measure of security, the user charges are covenanted to be set at a level to return some multiple of debt-service requirements. Furthermore, future revenue bond debt may not be issued against this revenue source unless an agreed-upon multiple debt service is met by user charges. In fact, the flow of funds into and through the project may well be controlled by the "bond indenture" agreement under which the bonds are issued.

An extra measure of security may be offered by the requirement of "reserves"—money put aside or invested to guarantee that funds will be available to meet certain contingencies. These reserves may include a bond reserve, debt service reserve, maintenance reserve, and escrow accounts.

Some revenue bonds may actually combine the pledges of specified revenues and full faith and credit. This double pledge occurs when the municipality guarantees a revenue obligation and is a common arrangement for water, sewer, and airport projects that provide community-wide benefits. The advantages of a guarantee are that it can lower interest costs and relieve pressure on the enterprise activity's debt capacity. It becomes especially justified when a feasibility study has shown that a project should attain self-sufficiency. One disadvantage is that it creates a contingent liability that must be shown on the city's financial statements.

Industrial Development Bonds

Enabling legislation at the state level authorizes municipalities to issue tax-exempt bonds to finance the acquisition or construction of industrial facilities or other physical assets. In some cases these bonds are general obligations of the issuing municipality, but usually they are secured only by the revenues from the lease payments by the private corporation. Thus, they are also often referred to as industrial revenue bonds.

Purpose and Use. The broad purpose of industrial development bonds is to promote local economic development. The facilities built or acquired from the bond proceeds should provide both public and private benefits, including job creation and strengthening of the local tax and economic base. Industrial development bonds originally were used almost exclusively to attract new (or expand or retain existing) industrial facilities. In recent years, however, the uses of such financing have been extended to hospitals, sports facilities, utilities, transportation, pollution control, and industrial parks. Some of these more recent uses have been criticized in certain quarters as an abuse of tax-exempt financing because they impose upon public credit for private purposes, although others argue that they represent only the natural evolution of the market as it gains experience and sophistication.

The proceeds of industrial development bonds can be used only for the construction or acquisition of depreciable property. In most cases, the amount of the financing and the total capital investment made by the private concern during a six-year period covering three years prior and extending to three years after the issue date cannot exceed $10,000,000. This limit is waived for many uses, however, including hospitals, pollution control, port facilities, and other projects with broad public benefits.

Security. Industrial development bonds are issued by cities or industrial development authorities and are secured by any number of arrangements: a lease between the issuer and the private concern that will operate the facility; an installment sales contract for the sale of the facility to a private concern; a mortgage; or other guarantee. In all of these arrangements, the periodic payment made by the private concern (whether it be a lease payment, installment sale payment, or other) is sufficient to cover the issuer's debt service requirements and, in some cases, includes a small additional amount to compensate the issuer for clerical and other handling costs.

Unique Borrowing Vehicles

Some new borrowing vehicles and purposes have been created to take advantage of the expanded public role in the delivery of goods and services, the desire of the private sector to capture the benefits of tax-exempt financing, joint action between governmental units, and the need for special controls for certain distressed credits, including the following:

Resource Recovery. Transactions such as financing a privately-owned plant to burn city wastes and sell steam produced from the waste disposal can be arranged to yield a depreciation tax benefit to an equity owner as well as to reduce sanitation disposal charges and perhaps generate additional revenues to the city.

Mortgage Financing. Tax-exempt bonds are sold by a municipality or authority, and the proceeds are placed under the supervised control of mortgage lenders to make low-interest mortgage loans.

Joint Action Power. A number of governmental units join together to own a power plant that is financed by the issuance of tax-exempt bonds by the consortium.

Municipal Assistance Corporation. A separate municipal entity is established to issue tax-exempt obligations supported by special revenue sources when the city's credit does not allow for debt issuance directly. The proceeds of the bond sale are used for municipal purposes. The most notable example of this arrangement has been in New York City, where a municipal assistance corporation was formed following the city's fiscal problems in 1975.

III. DEBT MANAGEMENT POLICY

Cities have formal policies to deal with a wide range of financial issues, such as balanced budgets, tax rate limitations, and personnel. A number of issues often recur when the use of debt is involved, such as debt limits, the use of the general obligation pledge, the frequency, volume, and structure of debt, and disclosure practices. Mayors can play the leadership role in the development of clear and well-communicated policies governing a city borrowing program. A well-defined policy should provide a road map for future administrations and city officials. A debt management policy should address the following primary issues:

Objectives of Debt Policy

A debt policy should make it possible for the city to optimize a number of related factors, as follows:

Access. The need to issue debt may be sudden, and the decision immediate, or it may be pursuant to a long-term plan. In either case, once the decision has been made, a set of procedures should exist to allow the issuer to go through the steps required for a rapid issuance.

Security. The issuer should be sure that the money borrowed can be repaid, and the pledge will be met. If the debt is not secure, and default occurs, the city's ability to borrow will be greatly damaged if not permanently disabled.

Control of Spending. Every city should be assured that the planned use of debt financing is worthwhile and economical. The availability of funds should not dictate a spending decision.

Ability to Amortize. A debt issuance obligates the issuer to continuing contributions of resources to debt service for the life of the debt. The long-term revenue and expenditure picture of the issuer should be clearly understood before a decision to issue is reached.

Interest Costs. The higher the interest rate, the more an issuer will be required to pay over the life of the bond. All steps must be taken to keep costs to a minimum.

Confidence. An important element in the determination of interest rates and the placement of the debt is the confidence that investors, underwriters, and rating agencies have in the issuer's financial position and management capability. These factors should be maximized in both perception and reality.

Uses of Debt

As indicated in the previous section, any number of types of debt exist for any number of uses. A debt management policy should require that the following conditions be met for each type and use of debt.

General Conditions. The debt should equal in amount the cost of the project, should extend for the useful economic life of the project with benefits being returned over the entire period of repayment, should be related to economic growth or public service objectives, and should be closely linked to the capital and operating budget.

Short-Term Debt. Short-term debt should comply with state and local limitations thereon, should be used only with cognizance of roll-over limitations, and should be avoided except when necessitated by cash flow or other "emergency" situations.

General Obligation Debt. General obligation debt projects should provide local benefits; should not be susceptible to user charges; should provide a benefit to the broad population of the locality; should be in keeping with the issuer's financial infrastructure and tax base growth; and may be used in conjunction with revenue bond projects to get them "off the ground".

Revenue Debt. Revenue debt projects should be special projects with definable uses, should be self-sufficient with a strong and predictable revenue base, should be for a public purpose, should have a segregable income and accounting system, and, in some cases, should be able to take advantage of "unique" opportunities.

Volume and Frequency

Cities and authorities should lay out long-term borrowing plans that will provide for an entry into the market in an orderly and planned manner. Regular issuers should attempt to enter the market at regular intervals, with similarly sized general obligation issues. Steadiness inspires investor confidence.

Interest Costs

States may impose ceilings on interest rates, or local limits may be imposed by legislation or executive decision. Regardless of the existence of such limits, debt management policy should provide guidance as to the acceptability of given interest rates, establish a basis for analyzing performance in the bond market, and formulate plans to lower interest costs.

Structure of Debt

Any number of options are available when structuring debt. These include equal annual debt service payments, equal annual principal payments, wrap-around, declining payments, more than 50-percent retirement within ten years, balloon payments, term versus serial bonds, and various other provisions. An issuer should analyze its own economic, cash, and budget position in choosing among these alternatives for a long-range policy for each individual decision. The bond market is very dynamic, and the most marketable structures vary over time. These important but complex decisions can make the use of a financial advisor very cost-effective.

Disclosure

Guidelines exist for the amount, quality, and format of financial disclosure. The Government Finance Officers Association (GFOA) offers a "Certificate of Conformance" based upon how a city's financial statement presentations conform to generally accepted accounting principles. The GFOA has also issued separate guidelines dealing exclusively with securities offerings (*Disclosure Guidelines for Offerings of Securities by State and Local Governments*). These guidelines have received wide industry acceptance. Compliance with them represents the optimal degree of disclosure pursuant to debt issuance. In determining policy with regard to disclosure, the issuer should be familiar with these guidelines, as well as the capabilities and needs of its own accounting and financial reporting system.

Method of Sale

The issuer may choose whether to sell revenue debt competitively or by negotiated sale. In most states, general obligation debt must be competitively bid. A competitive sale allows underwriters to bid against each other for the purchase of the debt. This type of sale is often required by law because it removes any possibility of favoritism. The issuer sets the terms of the sale and underwriters bid by specifying a rate that represents the effective interest rate to the issuer. A competitive sale will usually result in a lower interest rate or a higher price for the bonds.

In a negotiated sale, the issuer works with an underwriter to determine the structure, timing, and price of debt that the underwriter will purchase. This type of sale is undertaken when complex transactions, uncertain security, or unusual size or purpose may be involved. Because they often involve complex considerations, many revenue bond issues are negotiated.

Basis of Award

The issuer should determine, as a matter of policy, on what basis the decision to sell debt to a particular buyer should be made when an issue is competitively bid. Two currently popular bases for award are the true interest cost (TIC) and the net interest cost (NIC).

The NIC is determined by taking the total interest payments to be made under a debt issue and subtracting from that total the premium offered (or adding the discount). This number is the net dollar interest cost of the issuance. Divide this amount by a weighted total number of bond years over the issue's life. The bond years are determined by the sum of the dollar amount of bonds in each year's maturity multiplied by the number of years each of these dollar amounts is outstanding. The division will yield the NIC. See Table 4.1 for a prototypical example of an NIC calculation.

The TIC represents the interest rate that must be paid on the actual purchase price—face amount plus (or minus) premium (or discount)—in order to yield the bond coupon. In other words, it is the rate at which future interest and principal payments must be discounted to have a present value equal to the bond proceeds. This is a complex financial calculation but can be performed easily by calculator or computer.

The NIC calculation fails to use the concept of "present value," that is, it values interest payments in the distant future the same as interest payments to be made in the near future. As a result, it may yield a higher figure that fails to reflect economic reality. TIC is the recommended basis for award. When different bidders' prices yield different TICs, the bidder with the lowest TIC should be awarded the issue.

Debt Limitations

Debt limits may be established by the state or by voter referendum. As a matter of internal financial planning, a debt management policy should establish debt limits based on financial figures indicative of the issuer's ability to repay future debt. For instance, measures upon which a debt limit should be determined should include debt service as a percentage of general expenditures (should not exceed a certain percentage), gross and net debt per capita, ratio of gross and net debt to full value of taxable property, and the amount of debt to be retired within ten years.

Table 4.1. Prototypical Example Of Net Interest Cost (NIC) Calculation

1. Formula:

$$NIC = \frac{\text{Total Interest Paid} + (-)\ \text{Discount (Premium)}}{\text{Bond Years } (= \text{Bond Amount} \times \text{Bond Life})}$$

2. Example:
$10,000,000 Serial Bond Issue, maturing in equal annual installments over a 10-year period. Coupon of 9 percent on bonds maturing first five years, 10 percent on bonds maturing last five years, sold at a $500,000 discount.

Year	Principal Outstanding	Interest Rate	Interest Paid	Total Bond Years To End of Year
1	$10,000,000	9% on $5,000,000 10% on $5,000,000	$ 950,000	10,000,000
2	9,000,000	9% on $4,000,000 10% on $5,000,000	860,000	19,000,000
3	8,000,000	9% on $3,000,000 10% on $5,000,000	770,000	27,000,000
4	7,000,000	9% on $2,000,000 10% on $5,000,000	680,000	34,000,000
5	6,000,000	9% on $1,000,000 10% on $5,000,000	590,000	40,000,000
6	5,000,000	10%	500,000	45,000,000
7	4,000,000	10%	400,000	49,000,000
8	3,000,000	10%	300,000	52,000,000
9	2,000,000	10%	200,000	54,000,000
10	1,000,000	10%	100,000	55,000,000
			5,350,000	55,000,000

$$NIC = \frac{\$5{,}350{,}000 + \$500{,}000}{55{,}000{,}000} = \frac{5{,}850{,}000}{55{,}000{,}000} = 10.636\%$$

Refundings

An issuer may wish to refund outstanding debt (pay off old debt ahead of time and issue new debt in its place) in order to save on debt service, avoid restrictive agreements pertaining to the old debt, or save because of reduced interest rates. The debt management policy should indicate the circumstances under which refunding should be considered.

Operating Budget

Debt should not be issued without analyzing its effects on the operating budget. Debt means debt service expenditures. Capital projects mean operating and maintenance costs and may mean future construction costs. The future operating costs of capital projects can sometimes exceed their debt service requirements. The operating budget impact should be considered carefully as part of an overall debt service.

Arbitrage

Arbitrage involves taking advantage of different interest rates to make a profit. Since tax-exempt debt is offered at a lower rate than commercial debt, a tax-exempt issuer could simply reinvest debt proceeds into higher interest rate debt and turn a tidy profit. This activity, however, is subject to legal restrictions that are changed periodically and are complex to interpret. Nevertheless, the use of arbitrage, where legal, can reduce costs to the tax-exempt issuer. Debt policy should allow for the use of arbitrage where possible.

Administer Outstanding Debt

After bonds have been sold, the debt must be administered. As a minimum, this involves two types of recordkeeping:

1. Maintaining special detailed records on the debt
2. Maintaining general accounting records

In addition, restrictive covenants, refunding opportunities, and other items should be monitored on an ongoing basis.

IV. STEPS IN DEBT MANAGEMENT[1]

The Decision to Incur Debt

A local government should go through a thorough assessment of each proposed debt issue before actually selling bonds. This assessment should encompass the following broad considerations:

1. The purposes to which the bond proceeds will be applied to make sure the benefits are worth the cost
2. An analysis of all possible ways to fund projects to reach the most desirable financing scheme

[1]This section draws heavily on *A Debt Management Handbook for Small Cities and Other Governmental Units* (Chicago, IL: Government Finance Officers Association, 1978).

3. Determination of whether it will be more advantageous to sell bonds through public bids or by private negotiation (if the latter is legally permissible)

Securing Needed Specialized Services

After deciding that a particular project is necessary and that debt should be incurred, the issuer should secure the services of consulting specialists, including a consulting engineer, financial advisor, and bond counsel. The use of these services and the application of their expertise can save an issuer money by reducing the project cost, interest costs, and other expenses related to the preparation of the official statement and other documents necessary for the issue.

Obtaining Public Support for General Obligation Issues

If general obligation bonds are to be sold, public approval may be required in the form of an affirmative vote. A campaign to develop approval for the bond sale should focus on two general issues:

1. Voter support for the project
2. Voter understanding of the financial features

Design the Bond Issue's Features

Taking advantage of a financial advisor's expertise to structure the issue is an important step. Although local requirements must be met, marketability can be enhanced and costs reduced by structuring the issue to meet current investor preferences. Consideration must be given to the following:

1. The maturity schedule
2. Bond denominations
3. Coupon rates
4. Call/redemption privileges
5. Registration privileges

Draft the Bond Security Agreement

General obligation bonds are backed by the full faith and credit of issuer and do not require a security agreement (also called bond ordinance, bond resolution, or trust indenture) to guarantee resources for repayment. One of the primary responsibilities of the bond counsel is to draft the security agreement. The agreement should cover the following:

1. The use of bond proceeds
2. The use of revenues from the facility
3. Assurances that adequate rates will be charged by the facility to cover operating costs and debt service

Market the Bonds

When an underwriter is selected by private negotiation, the arrangements for marketing the bonds will be undertaken by the underwriter. Marketing of the bonds by public bidding places a greater burden on the issuer. Six major tasks are involved, as follows:

1. Prepare the documents needed to sell the bond issue
2. Obtain a bond rating
3. Choose a selling date
4. Advertise the bonds and accept bids
5. Award the bids and print and deliver the bonds
6. Close the bonds

Credit Agencies and Investors

The success of a debt offering can begin and end with the credit rating. This rating represents an informed and independent judgment of the debt's quality as an investment and thus (in combination with general market conditions) leads directly to the interest rate that must be paid. Standard & Poor's Corporation rates bonds from "AAA" (highest quality—extremely strong capacity to pay principal and interest) through "CCC" (highly speculative), with a "D" rating for bonds in default. A "BBB" rating is considered to be the lowest investment grade rating. Moody's Investors Service, Inc. ratings range from "Aaa" to "C", with "Baa" the lowest investment grade rating. Table 4.2 presents a list of factors that rating agencies (and investors) consider in determining bond ratings and interest rates.

Any debt management policy must address the need to attain the highest possible bond rating. From a public relations standpoint, this involves providing rating services and investors with regularly updated financial data, visiting the rating services and a regional financial center prior to a sale, working to maintain or improve an acceptable rating level, and maintaining good relations with bankers and buyers. Ultimately, however, the quality of

Table 4.2 Factors Considered By Investors And Rating Agencies In Determining Rates

The Amount and Nature of the Debt and Debt Service Requirements:

- Total amount of debt and per capita debt levels
- Purposes for which debt has been created
- Rate at which debt has increased
- Debt repayment schedules and overlapping debt
- Degree of reliance on short-term debt

Economy of the Community and the Region of Which it is a Part:

- Geographical area and past history of growth
- Educational and income characteristics of the population
- Location of area served and general character of future potential
- Sources of economic activity—employers, diversification and dependence
- Maintenance of the economic plant
- Leadership
- Wealth of the community-taxable property, resources, transportation

Social Factors:

- Educational opportunities
- Cultural opportunities
- Recreational facilities
- The community record of handling social unrest
- The housing stock
- Characteristics of the population

Management of the Local Government:

- Overall governmental structure—professionalism vs. balkanization
- Degree to which the government is well-administered
- Organization of financial administration
- Effectiveness of capital planning and programming
- Quality of revenue administration—passive collector of taxes vs. active
- The revenue base—new reliances
- The revenue calender—out of sync
- Reputation for prudent financial management
- Conditions of the physical plant
- Contingent liabilities
- Contingent liabilities
- Sinking fund management

Other Considerations:

- Debt limitations—higher regulatory controls
- Capacity of government to deal with local problems
- Security of deposits—guarantees of banks
- Bondholders remedies—explicit or implied
- Subdivision controls—poorly planned expansions
- General regulatory codes

the bond rating will rest with the quality of the financial, managerial, and socio-economic factors outlined in Table 4.2.

V. THE MAYOR'S ROLE IN DEBT MANAGEMENT

Debt Policy and Management

Chapter 1 of this *Handbook* indicated that the role of the mayor in financial management is one of planning, reviewing, and policy-setting. This statement is no less true in the particular area of debt management. The areas and concerns that should be addressed by the mayor are as follows:

1. Providing leadership in developing specific policies on debt issuance and management
2. Goal setting for the capital budget
3. Setting limits on capital spending
4. Ranking spending alternatives
5. Demanding information about the impact of the use of debt on the operating budget
6. Limiting the use of short-term debt
7. Knowing the city's brokers and the local bond market
8. Taking leadership in marketing and investor relations
9. Assuming leadership in selling the city's bond program to the public

Getting Assistance

It is not the mayor's job to oversee every decision and activity in the city's debt management department. Rather, it is the mayor's duty to assure that the members of specific departments are capable of making intelligent and prudent decisions. This goal can be accomplished by taking a few simple steps.

First, it is necessary to hire good, experienced, people. This is not as self-obvious a statement as it first appears. Key financial positions should not be filled with politically motivated appointments. The qualifications for good financial people are analytic competence, experience, and the ability to reach reasoned, independent judgments. Second, to the extent a city is a regular issuer of debt, in-house capacity to structure and conduct debt issuances should be developed. This will allow a city to make decisions based on its own priorities rather than rely exclusively on the outside advice of an underwriter. Last, a clear debt management overview and policy should be prepared so that financial personnel are aware of the allowable limits of their decisions and will be guided by a single, city-wide policy.

A city usually works with outside bond counsels, underwriters, financial advisors, and accountants in preparing to issue debt. These participants in the financial process should be selected as carefully as possible. A selection process free of political influence should be established. Suitable criteria should be specified for selecting professionals. Furthermore, after selection has taken place and negotiation has begun, the city should guarantee its bargaining position by hiring or retaining the expertise of a financial advisor to be the city's advocate in dealing with underwriters.

Presiding Officer

Debt management policy, perhaps more than any other city function, requires the careful and thorough oversight of the mayor. This is not to say that the mayor must review every decision, but, as indicated above, the mayor should assure the integrity and prudence of the finance process. This level of involvement is necessitated by the fact that the mayor's signature will appear on the bond prospectus and offering. Untruthful statements and improvident decisions can lead to legal action against the signer. To avoid legal consequences, a mayor must show that *due diligence* has been exercised in the review of the bond issuance process.

5
Debt Management: Impacts of Recent Trends for Cities

This chapter sets forth relevant factors affecting the debt management activities of urban governments and resulting from recent trends in the general credit markets, including the emergence of new alternative mechanisms for financing capital and operating requirements.

A number of new vehicles for short- and long-term borrowing that may save a city substantial amounts are outlined here. One way to consider these issues is to invite one or more banks or financial consultants to review current and planned borrowing practices and to ask for specific bids using alternative financing vehicles. Consideration of the appropriate options listed in the last part of this chapter may be requested along with any other vehicles that the consultants may suggest.

I. GENERAL MARKET ENVIRONMENT

Decreased Relative Demand For General Obligation Financing

A fundamental shift in tax-exempt bond financing occurred in the 1970s in the nature of the security pledged for the repayment of debt. This shift is continuing to the present. Historically, such a pledge has been a "general obligation" promise to repay the debt at maturity, backed by the "full faith and credit" of the particular state or municipality. In the last fifteen years, however, as investors and analysts grew more concerned about the quality of credit, the limited obligation security, or revenue bond, has become increasingly important. As shown in Table 5.1, the proportion of new issues between general obligation and revenue bonds has been reversed in the past decade and a half.

As a result of this shift, many activities (such as industrial development, housing, hospital construction, and public power) that have traditionally been financed by the private sector are now funded through bonds issued by

Table 5.1. Proportion of Revenue and General Obligation Bonds Sold in New Issue Municipal Bond Market: 1970-1983*

Year	Total Volume (billions)	Percent Revenue Bond	Percent General Obligation
1970	$18.083	33.7	66.3
1971	24.929	34.9	65.1
1972	23.692	39.7	60.3
1973	23.821	44.6	55.4
1974	23.560	42.4	57.6
1975	30.699	48.0	52.0
1976	35.416	49.8	51.2
1977	46.706	61.3	38.7
1978	48.352	63.4	36.6
1979	43.317	71.2	28.8
1980	47.133	65.3	34.7
1981	46.134	69.7	30.3
1982	77.179	69.8	30.2
1983	83.348	72.9	27.1

Source: The Bond Buyer.

special-purpose entities. This development has altered the direction of the tax-exempt market from providing construction capital for public works programs to governmental entities acting as financial intermediaries. Perhaps more important, most debt of state and local governments, having direct recourse to the public treasury, can no longer be considered an obligation of the taxpayer.

Several forces have worked to alter the composition of state and local debt. First, capital spending by state and local governments has lagged behind inflation in recent years. During the 20-year period 1963-1983, the implicit GNP price deflator (1972 = 100 per cent) rose from 71.67 to 215.63, or 201 percent. From 1968 to 1983, tax-exempt borrowing for schools and water and sewerage expenses rose only 85 and 136 percent, respectively, as shown in Table 5.2. During that same period, spending on highways, bridges, and tunnels declined 31 percent. According to the Bureau of Census, gross capital formation by state and local governments dropped by 29 percent in constant dollar terms between 1970 and 1982. As a result, public works investment fell from 4.1 percent of gross national product in 1965 to 2.0 percent in 1982.

One important cause for augmented borrowing in the tax-exempt market has been the tendency of increasing standards of living to raise expectations

Table 5.2. Tax-Exempt Borrowing By Purpose in Billions of Dollars: 1968-1983*

	1968	1970	1972	1974	1976	1978	1979	1980	1981	1982	1983
School	$ 4.7	$ 5.0	$ 5.3	$ 4.9	$ 5.1	$ 6.2	$ 4.9	$ 4.8	$ 4.4	$ 6.6	$ 8.7
Water and Sewer	1.9	2.3	2.8	2.1	3.3	4.5	3.7	3.5	2.5	4.6	4.5
Highway Bridge and Tunnel	1.6	1.4	2.1	1.0	1.6	1.9	0.9	1.1	1.1	1.1	1.1
Gas and Electric	NA	NA	NA	1.5	4.5	6.0	4.7	4.8	7.4	9.5	11.3
Hospital	NA	NA	NA	1.3	2.7	3.1	3.5	3.6	5.2	9.7	9.9
State and Municipal Housing Finance	NA	NA	NA	NA	NA	NA	12.0	14.3	6.8	15.7	18.0
Industrial	1.6	0.05	0.5	0.3	0.4	0.6	1.3	1.5	2.2	3.5	4.5
Pollution Control	NA	NA	NA	2.2	2.7	3.5	2.9	2.9	4.7	6.6	5.3
Other	6.6	8.9	12.2	9.5	13.6	20.4	8.2	10.7	11.9	20.0	20.0
Total	$16.3	$17.8	$22.9	$22.8	$33.9	$46.2	$42.2	$47.1	$46.1	$77.2	$83.3

**Source: The Bond Buyer's Municipal Finance Statistics, 1977-1983.*

of the role of government in fulfilling social welfare goals. Leading examples of the new commitments of state and local government include the need to provide adequate housing, to upgrade facilities and opportunities for health treatment, and to foster higher education. Revenue bonds, which are most often used for financing these purposes, historically have been the favorite means of surmounting a variety of constraints on governmental action and for entering new frontiers of public needs. Often it has been easier for state legislatures to allow for the creation of a special district or authority with new bonding authority and have it do the financing for a general unit of government rather than to try to amend restrictive constitutional and/or statutory limitations.

According to data compiled by *The Bond Buyer,* long-term municipal financing rose from 1972 by 105 percent, from $22.9 billion to $47.1 billion; by 1983, the volume of municipal financing reached $81.2 billion, or a 72 percent increase from 1980. As a result, taxpayers have been faced with increasing debt-service charges for governmental services as more financing has been effected at higher costs.

As a result of these factors, the proportion of new issues sold by traditional units of governments—states, counties, municipalities, and school districts—has declined, while the volume of debt raised by special districts and statutory authorities has increased. As shown in Table 5.3, which is based upon material prepared by the Bureau of Census, the proportion of debt sold by traditional governmental units, consisting of states, counties, municipalities, and school districts, has fallen from 69 percent of all issues in 1970 to 59 percent in 1975, and to 43 percent in 1982.

Table 5.3 Percentage Composition of New Bond Sales as Classified by Type of Issuer: 1970-1982*

Type of Issuer	1970	1975	1980	1981	1982
State	23.0	24.2	11.0	11.1	10.7
Special district and Statuory Authority	30.8	40.7	55.8	57.7	57.0
Municipalities, counties, townships, and school districts	46.2	35.1	33.2	31.2	32.3
Total	100%	100%	100%	100%	100%

**Source:* U.S. Department of Commerce, Bureau of the Census, *Statistical Abstract of the United States, 1984.*

Increased Interest Rates and Market Volatility

Over the past two decades, interest rates, as measured by The Bond Buyer Index, have been increasing. The Bond Buyer Index of 20 general obligation bonds was in the 3 percent range in the mid-1960s, increased to a high of 7.67 percent in 1975, and a record high of 13.44 percent in 1982. The Index at the end of 1983 was at 9.76 percent.

Accompanying the rise in the level of interest rates has been an increase in market volatility. During 1961, the range between the low and high yield on The Bond Buyer Index was 3.26 to 3.55 percent, a spread of 29 basis points, or 8.9 percent. During 1971, the range was 4.97 to 6.23 percent, a spread of 126 basis points, or 25.3 percent; and in 1982, the range was 9.25 to 13.44 percent, for 419 basis points, or 45.3 percent. The primary cause for the increased level and volatility of interest rates has been the absolute impact of, and the enlarged uncertainty caused by, inflation.

Change in Composition of Investors

As interest rates have risen, bond prices have, of course, fallen, thereby depressing the portfolio values of large institutional holders of fixed income securities, such as commercial banks. To lessen the effect of such losses, banks have been reducing the relative position of tax-exempt securities in their portfolios. Between 1970 and 1983, according to data developed by the Federal Deposit Insurance Corporation, obligations of states and subdivisions fell from 11.7 percent of total bank assets to 7.8 percent. As a result, banks held 34.1 percent of total outstanding state and local securities in 1983 as opposed to 43.5 percent of the total in 1979 and 48.6 percent in 1970. As Table 5.4 indicates, insurance companies and mutual funds have been com-

Table 5.4. Holders of State and Local Government Debt: 1970-1983*

	1983	1980	1975	1970
		Billions of Dollars		
Total state and local government:				
Debt outstanding	$468.6	$336.1	$223.8	$144.4
Long-term	371.7	296.7	198.6	131.1
Short-term	13.0	15.8	18.6	13.3
Nonfin. corporate business	13.0	15.8	18.6	13.3
(Pollution control and small issue industrial development bonds)	83.8	23.6	6.7	—
		Percent of Total		
Held by:				
Households	34.1%	22.1%	30.4%	31.9%
Nonfin. corporate business	0.9	1.0	2.0	1.5
State and local government, general fund	1.8	1.9	2.2	1.6
Commercial banks	34.1	44.4	46.0	48.6
Savings and loan associations	0.2	0.4	0.7	0.1
Mutual savings banks	0.5	0.7	0.7	0.1
Life insurance companies	2.3	2.0	2.0	2.3
Other insurance companies	18.8	24.1	14.9	11.8
State and local government, retirement funds	0.6	1.2	0.8	1.4
Brokers and dealers	0.3	0.3	0.3	0.6
Mutual funds	6.4	1.9	—	—

**Source:* Federal Reserve Board.

pensating for the commercial banks' diminished participation in the tax-exempt market. Insurance companies have raised their participation from 14.1 percent in 1970 to 21.1 percent in 1983, and mutual funds have raised their participation from no holdings in 1975 to 6.4 percent of the holdings in 1983.

Adjustments In Maturity Structure

Another result of the decline in bond prices has been a requirement by investors for shorter maturities. Whereas 50-year revenue bonds were once commonplace, increasingly the longest maturity is only 30 years, if even this level of maturity can be achieved. In general, as a result, many urban governments have begun to adopt more rapid retirement schedules, thereby reducing the average life on bond issues. Many urban governments have consequently experienced an increase in the provision of debt service as larger repayments of principal have been added to higher interest costs.

Increased Sensitivity to Credit Quality

Recent serious credit crises have increased the sensitivity among the rating agencies, underwriters, and institutional investors regarding the credit quality for securities sold in the tax-exempt market. For example, the default by the New York State Urban Development Corporation, the moratorium (deferred payment) of New York City obligations in the middle 1970s and the highly publicized defaults by the City of Cleveland and the Washington Public Power Supply System have created greater financial disclosure requirements and have caused the rating agencies, underwriters, and purchasers to become increasingly skeptical about credit representations made by state and local issuers of securities. Standard & Poor's Corporation established guidelines in 1981 for improving financial reporting standards and practices by state and local governments; these guidelines were expected to be followed by an issuer in providing financial information to the agency.

It should also be emphasized that in unsettled credit markets, investors and underwriters respond more directly to credit differences among securities, resulting in greater-than-normal spreads in interest costs in credit quality.

These substantial alterations in the credit market have increased pressures on urban issuers to develop considerable flexibility in their debt management. Thus, all cities should begin to consider their technical capacities to take advantage of new opportunities and to meet the new and more complex challenges in the tax-exempt market.

Bond Insurance/Credit Supports

In recent years, there has been a substantial increase in the use of municipal bond insurance. The two firms that currently provide insurance are American Municipal Bond Assurance Corporation (AMBAC) and Municipal Bond Insurance Association (MBIA). Both AMBAC and MBIA will insure only those new issues that meet their standards of investment grade. Standard & Poor's Corporation automatically assigns its AAA rating to insured bonds, whereas Moody's Investors Service, Inc., does not take the insurance into account when assigning a rating. The use of insurance can lower interest costs, but the savings should be greater than the insurance premium to make it worthwhile to the issuer.

In addition to bond insurance, another emerging and similar credit support has been the use of bank lines and letters of credit. In certain circumstances, the municipal borrower has found it cost-effective to supplement its credit with that of a financial institution. In effect, the borrower can rely on a secondary source of funds to add to its own to secure indebtedness, or the borrower can fully replace its payment on the securities with that of the financial institution. Like municipal bond insurance, the cost of the additional credit support must be weighed against the expected lower debt service costs.

In sum, complexity of debt management for municipalities has significantly increased for several reasons: volatility of the public markets, credit concerns of institutional and individual investors, and enlarged disclosure requirements, among others. Many cities have already responded meaningfully to the new demands, but these issues must constantly be addressed.

One favorable development has been the inclination of several urban governments to develop comprehensive financing programs. We next present some key elements to include in such a program for a city.

II. EFFECTS OF CAPITAL BUDGET ON DEBT MANAGEMENT

For many years, municipal analysts have emphasized the significant relationship between a government's capital budget operations and the credit worthiness of the government's securities. The importance of this relationship has been reflected in the credit ratings assigned to the debt obligations and the reception afforded securities in the credit markets.

It is especially informative to review comments offered by Moody's Investors Service, Inc., on this subject:

> Most local governments, however, have recurring needs for improvement and consequently must plan for those needs. Even having no plan is, in a sense, planning—to a municipal bond analyst, it is a plan to meet the problem hit or miss, instead of systematically. The annual preparation of such programs, comprising appropriations for the next year and estimates or projections for the next five years, has been standard practice for well run local governments for nearly a generation now. . . . It (capital improvement program) should be comprehensive in scope of projects covered. It should show not only the amount to be spent but also the source of funds—how much from current budget contributions (taxes, etc.), how much from Federal and state grants, how much from capital fund balances carried forward, how much from the sale of new bonds.[1]

Many other credit analysts have stressed that careful capital planning and orderly debt execution are essential for meeting the physical needs of a community. Development of a coordinated approach toward the capital

---

[1]*Pitfalls in Issuing Municipal Bonds,* Moody's Investors Service, Inc., 1982.

budget and debt management programs can improve the credit posture and marketability of debt obligations for many issuers of tax-exempt securities. Important features of coordinating capital budget activities with proper debt management will now be discussed.

Examination of Recent Financing for Capital Facilities by the Public Sector

Each type of infrastructure is reviewed here according to the source and amount of public financing assigned to it. Several key findings from this information will become apparent. For example, the possibility of identifying the infrastructure categories receiving significant, modest, or minimal attention helps quantify underfunding, if any, for each important infrastructure category. To illustrate the recent capital planning distinction between new initiatives and capital maintenance, data should differentiate between new construction and replacement/alteration expenditures. Review of programs used in the past but unavailable for the future established the context for future funding sources. The organization of the capital planning and financing delivery system should also be considered.

Assessment of Capital Requirements for Public Infrastructure

The next phase of the analysis would consist of an appraisal of the principal infrastructure needs at the present time. Key difficulties would be reflected in such measurements as frequency and size of infrastructure failures, frequency and size of necessary repairs, etc. An analysis should be made to determine the size of the physical plant and its current age and to estimate the rehabilitation/alteration cycle of existing facilities. Large unfunded capital programs would receive special attention, with emphasis given to cases in which the proposed expenditure program appears especially inadequate. Any large shift in financing responsibilities from previous trends should be identified.

Implications for Debt Management Practices

To evaluate the marketability of governmental securities in light of the information presented in the above review, the relationship between the government's financing capacity and its capital requirements would be projected. Justifiable estimates could then be made on the impact of the government's prospective debt issuance on the future marketability of the municipalities' general obligation and revenue bonds. Future debt issuance affects financing capacity in two ways that are especially important for municipalities in the changing market conditions. First, from a strictly market perspective, the volume of long-term debt that a government is required to sell annually affects the reception that the government can expect from the long-term credit markets. Second, the amount of bond financing for the future will influence the size of the government's debt load, a key index of a government's credit quality. Essentially, debt load reflects the relationship between the size of a government's debt and the available resources to repay it. A high debt load represents a relatively poorer ability to repay. A stabilization or reduction in debt load can often be achieved only by establishing alternative funding sources for certain infrastructure categories.

Development of Options for Financing Capital Requirements

Based on completion of the foregoing, a series of possible financing alternatives would then be explored. Alternative financing vehicles applicable to each category would be compared. A decision on the most favorable forms of financing would involve a combination of several factors. For example, the relative interest cost of each method must be appraised, which will require a review of recent market response to each. The ability to provide coordinated debt management and capital planning would also have to be weighed. Special problems of certain debt instruments (e.g., required debt service coverage ratios, purpose, restrictions, and various limitations on the amount of debt that can be issued) would affect the ultimate decisions.

III. ALTERNATIVE FINANCING MECHANISMS

In light of the adverse effects of general market trends for state and local government securities, cities need to give special attention to methods for improving their ability to tap additional sources of funds not considered in the past. The following discussion offers some exploratory approaches to debt management practices. Many are very new and have been used in only a limited number of cases to date, but their potentials are important.

Principal Financing Advantages of Self-Supporting Capital Projects

Many urban governments have been especially attracted to financing certain capital projects through use of fees and charges when their own taxable base, against which prospective financings would be supported, has been declining. The advantages of a self-supporting feature to finance capital improvements stem from overall debt considerations as well as from more specific concerns that operations be conducted on a fully self-sustaining basis. With respect to these two goals, the following significant advantages are achieved:

1. *The city can conserve its general-purpose revenues (e.g., property taxes, assessments, etc.) for projects that either cannot be expected to produce revenue or cannot produce revenue in amounts sufficient to make the activity self-supporting.* Faced with increasing demands for major infrastructure improvements and the erosion of the real purchasing power, cities have found that financing of capital projects on a self-supporting basis provides funding for a major area of demand for revenues, leaving the government with greater flexibility to finance other general-purpose government activities with general-purpose monies.
2. *Use of self-supporting projects increases the government's financing capacity.* Self-supporting projects not only relieve the urban government of a major source of demand for its general obligation debt, they also create a new market for the government issuers by attracting investors who prefer self-supporting securities to general obligation bonds.
3. *Self-supporting debt issues, if well structured, offer the possibility of receiving a strong investment grade rating—in some cases, more favorable than the government's own general obligation bond rating.* There are numerous examples of revenue bond ratings significantly higher than the related urban government's general obligation ratings.
4. *This approach provides the means to insure that various operations are conducted on a fully self-supporting basis.* Because of contractual obligations involved in pledging that the self-supporting nature of projects will be maintained for as long as any debt is outstanding, public officials would be less vulnerable to political pressures regarding the amount and frequency of enterprise rate increases. Furthermore, this approach typically requires not only full costing of service to all customers, public and private, taxable and tax-exempt, but also equitable sharing of these costs, based on the costs of servicing various types of customers.

New Credit Instruments

A number of new credit instruments have been created or expanded. In addition to the applicability of securities supported by fees and charges, which appear especially appropriate at this time for urban governments, other new types of securities can be cited, although the appropriateness of each described here must be evaluated by each urban government. These instruments include tax-exempt commercial paper, option put bonds, floating rate securities, municipal leasing, and warrants, among others. Each is discussed below.

Option Put Bonds

This structure has involved the issuance of long-term debt (e.g., 30 years), primarily for housing and public power purposes. It has been adopted by a number of cities and counties, including the Brevard County Housing Finance Authority in Florida and the City of Baltimore, Maryland. As part of the transaction and to limit exposure to long-term investments, which have become less popular with purchasers of tax-exempt debt recently, investors have the option to return the purchased bonds to the issuer at the price of par (100 percent on the face amount of the bond) at the end of a specific period (usually 5 to 20 years) from the sale date, and every year thereafter. The source of money to meet the tender is a letter of credit from a commercial bank, which usually charges an annual fee based on the outstanding amount of principal. Market participants state that this arrangement has saved issuers as many as 200 to 300 basis points in interest costs for an issue.

Certain Conditions of Purchase. Holders of option put bonds have the option of tendering to the trustee all or any part of the option bonds held. Often, however, there are conditions upon the purchase, including the following:

1. The option bonds will not be purchased if the bonds are in default at the time they are tendered.
2. The purchase price of tendered option bonds can be payable solely from drawing upon the letter of credit.

Arrangements with a Bank. A bank provides a letter of credit under which it is obligated to honor drafts by the trustee to purchase option bonds on behalf of the government. The letter of credit is an irrevocable obligation of the bank to pay to the trustee such amounts as are necessary to complete the purchase on behalf of the government of all option bonds tendered to the trustee for which sufficient moneys are otherwise unavailable.

Reimbursement Agreement. The government's obligations to the bank under the reimbursement agreement are usually limited in recourse to the following:

1. Upon making advances under the letter of credit, the bank will receive a security interest in the government's right to receive option bonds to be purchased with funds provided under the letter of credit. The security interest may be retained by the bank in satisfaction of the government's obligation to reimburse the bank or may be sold by the bank to meet the obligation.
2. As compensation for providing the letter of credit, the bank will receive, so long as any option bonds remain outstanding, a commission that represents an amount of the option bonds outstanding.

Tax-exempt Commercial Paper

In the corporate sector, where this credit instrument was developed, commercial paper was originally sold by merchandising entities to finance seasonal borrowing requirements. Commercial paper is an extremely short-term obligation expected to be self-liquidating. Normally issued by a broker for a nominal fee (one-eighth to one-quarter of 1 percent of the amount of principal sold, depending on the size of the program), tax-exempt commercial paper frequently carries and interest rate well below the cost of a publicly sold note of similar maturity, even taking into account the fees involved. In addition to the broker's fee, the issuer must pay a fee to a bank for a back-up line of credit to be used to repay the commercial paper in the event the paper cannot be "rolled over" at maturity. The cost of the bank line of credit is often less than one-half of 1 percent of the unused portion of the back-up line. Officials in cities—which have been major beneficiaries and users of tax-exempt commercial paper—have concurred with the ability to achieve substantial cost savings through this structure.

For the governmental entity with true seasonal borrowing needs, especially those self-liquidating within 180 days, tax-exempt commercial paper may be a way to reduce borrowing costs because of the huge demand for this type of debt.

Advantages of Issuing Commercial Paper. The most significant advantage is the government's ability to obtain funds at generally lower rates than notes would offer. A second advantage, however, is that the issuance of commercial paper complements the borrower's image in the financial community. Through repeated offering of the issuer's paper, institutional and corporate portfolio managers gain a knowledge and appreciation of the borrower's credit stature, which can benefit the sale of long-term debt. Third, the reliability and ease of obtaining funds through the commercial paper market has been outstanding. Even under the most adverse conditions, the market has been viable and reliable source of funds. Once the initial legal and documentary work has been done, the outstanding amount of paper can be increased or decreased, often only by a telephone call.

Interest Rate Comparison: Notes vs. Paper. Lower interest rates for commercial paper are virtually guaranteed because most financial institutions structure their basic taxable lending rates on the basis of a premium over commercial paper rates or even higher yielding short-term certificates of deposit.

Interest cost savings may be maximized through careful maturity management, that is, the appropriate selection of long or short maturities to take advantage of changing money market trends.

Description of the Notes. Tax-exempt commercial paper notes are interest-bearing obligation, the rate of interest being computed for the actual number of days on a 365-day basis. They are purchased and redeemed in Federal funds through a designated issuing and paying agent.

The commercial paper note is an interest-bearing certificate drawn to the order of bearer for a stated maturity date. Most maturities are concentrated in the 60- to 90-day area.

The Marketing Program. The marketing program for a tax-exempt commercial paper program would include the following: Offering brochures would be prepared and circulated to potential investors. Offerings would be posted for maturity ranges from 1 to 270 days for same-day delivery. Rates would be adjusted periodially to reflect general market movement as well as the management of note maturity patterns to conform to the government's borrowing needs and market judgement. The sales effort would be directed to corporate portfolios, short-term tax-exempt funds, casualty insurance companies and regional and small bank portfolios. The commercial paper ratings from the credit services will help to broaden distribution by identifying the quality of the credit in terms familiar to managers of these funds.

Size of the Program. If the government agrees that tax-exempt commercial paper is a cheaper means of borrowing than notes, then theoretically it should do all of its short-term borrowing through paper. Practically speaking, however, the government may be absorbing the market risk of interest rate increases which could offset an attractive differential. Therefore, it is important to pursue initially a limited borrowing program sufficient to provide market depth, spread out fixed costs of issuance, and allow the dealer to develop investor interest which presumably will continue to grow.

Issuing Procedure. The government would deal with a specific firm, one that was presumably also active in the tax-exempt note trading market and that would maintain a close working relationship with the government's representative in negotiating mutually satisfactory terms for each borrowing.

After the program has been structured for the first issuance, the steps in a typical commercial paper transaction are as follows:

1. The government notifies the broker's representative by telephone of impending cash needs, four or five days prior to the day funds are actually needed.
2. The interest rate, maturity date, and denominations are determined by mutual agreement, taking into consideration the government's needs and the state of the market.
3. The dollar amounts, interest rates, and maturity dates are finalized, and payment instruction verified.
4. The agency instructs the issuing agent bank (usually prior to 1:00 P.M. on the day before the actual borrowing date) to issue the agreed-upon notes and deliver the notes to the broker against payment in Federal funds either by check or wire.
5. After the transaction is completed, the government is to receive a written confirmation of the agreed-upon terms.
6. At maturity, the notes are presented to the paying agent bank for payment in Federal funds. Additional borrowings may be negotiated by repeating the procedures outlined above.

Internal Organization. The financing arrangements being suggested here would require a partial reorganization of the urban government's approach toward its capital financing activities. Programs that conceivably could be developed for the urban government can involve complex debt management matters, especially in the area of establishing adequate financial controls. For example, should the urban government pursue the issuance of tax-exempt commercial paper with maturities as short as 30 days, it will need the capacity to make considered, consistent decisions on a timely basis. The ability of the government to make immediate, knowledgeable judgments would require either the development of considerable internal capacity or the employment of outside advice on these matters.

Floating Rates

Unlike standard notes or bonds, where the interest rate is fixed for the life of the obligation, a floating-rate security has an interest rate that is adjusted periodically in accordance with changes in a base or benchmark rate.

A variable or floating rate can be used to attract investors during times of uncertainty over interest rates. Investors have become increasingly hesitant to lock in their investments at a set interest rate because of possible deterioration in the market value of their notes or bonds and the expectation of higher interest rates in the future. A floating rate serves as a hedge against possible value lost from higher interest rates.

A security's rate may be reset for varying time periods according to each security's provisions, but the periods usually vary from quarterly to annually, although adjustments might be made every time the benchmark rate changes. The interest rate may be tied to any one of several different rates. For example, the interest rate on certain floating-rate securities is based on which is lower: 80 percent of three month Treasury bill rate or 70 percent of the 20-year Treasury bond rate. With the floating-rate arrangement, if interest rates decline, the value of the notes will not appreciably improve; conversely, if interest rates rise, the value of the notes should not automatically decline.

Leasing for Municipal Governments

Everyone is familiar with the general procedures of leasing arrangements. An individual corporation or other entity purchases a capital facility and, in turn, meets the capital costs of this facility under lease arrangements whereby a second party makes rental payments for its use. For municipal purposes, two main considerations should determine the usefulness of leasing as a financing tool. If voters are not likely to approve new bond sales or change existing debt limits, leasing might serve as an alternative. Second, leasing of capital facilities may involve lower costs, taking into account the reduced issuance expenses accruing from a lease and related benefits.

The following material sets forth the key factors that should be considered by a municipality with respect to the use of leasing as a source of capital funding.

Background. A lease is an obligation of the municipality to acquire property that can be continuously in force over a period of years. It may thus contain an interest component on the unpaid balance of the purchase price that is exempt from Federal income taxation, similar to a municipal bond.

Expressed purely as a percentage rate, that rate is frequently higher for a lease than for a bond. However, a lease usually has no additional expenses over and above the interest rate charged. Bonds, however, must amortize the cost of legal fees, printing costs, the cost of ratings, etc. If the total cost of financing is below $250,000 to $500,000, the traditional rule of thumb has been to lease. The more rapid payback on the shorter term lease often results in a lower total expenditure.

For local governments that have reached their debt limit, leasing becomes a means to provide new or additional equipment or facilities. Lease payments usually do not apply to the debt ceiling since the legal repayment period is frequently one year or less.

Equipment Financing. Although the tax-exempt lease can be used to purchase real or personal property, its most frequent use has been for equipment financing transactions. In a typical transaction, the manufacturer of equipment leases property to a municipality pursuant to a lease agreement in which the municipality will pay rent from annual budget appropriations during the lease term. Once all rent payments have been made, the municipality may acquire the property for a nominal price, often the unpaid balance of the purchase price.

Government As Lessee. As a lessee, the government also gains substantial financial benefits. Aside from leasing, the only methods of acquiring assets are from current operating revenues, intergovernmental grants, or sale of bond issues. Current trends in tax limitation legislation, double-digit inflation, uncertain aid programs, difficulty in passing bond referenda, and demands for spending that usually exceed revenues frequently make the outright purchase options uncertain in many circumstances. Another benefit of leasing is that the terms of the lease tend to parallel the asset life.

Budget Implications. The lease itself consists of a current obligation of the municipality that is payable out of budget appropriations over a period of years. The tax-exempt lease is usually structured with an option to purchase or as a conditional sale agreement. Each periodic payment, while constituting "rent" for the use of the property leased, will also constitute the payment of principal and interest on the outstanding principal balance of the purchase price of the property.

Fiscal Funding. An important legal consideration for a government acting as lessee frequently involves the "fiscal funding clause" in lease purchase agreements. This clause makes the lease a one-year contract with automatic renewal, a significant arrangement for two reasons: (1) the lease should not apply to the debt ceiling and consequently voter approval is not required, and (2) the risk of cancellation increases the lease rent/interest rate.

Certain Other Considerations. Tax-exempt lease financing is permitted in some states but not in others. In some states, a tax-exempt lease may constitute an invalid borrowing, one in violation of legal debt limits and debt-incurrence procedures. At the very least, the lease should stipulate that rent payments are subject to annual appropriation so as to avoid any implication of binding future legislative bodies to continue making rental payments. This arrangement is in contrast to long-term bonds, which frequently bind these bodies to continue making payments of principal and interest during the term of the bonds.

Leverage Lease Financing. Like a normal lease, a leveraged lease transaction involves the use of debt and equity capital, with the equity contributor receiving several tax benefits. Leveraged leasing can substantially reduce the cost of money on projects in which the lessee is not a tax-exempt entity. In such transactions, a special authority issues tax-exempt revenue bonds for up to 90 percent of the cost of the project, with the remainder provided by a tax-paying party. The latter, in turn, is benefited principally by being able to use accelerated depreciation on the entire capital project and the investment tax credit. In general, when the effects of these tax benefits are factored in, the cost of money to the issuing government in a leveraged lease transaction will be less than the cost of general obligation debt by 50 to 500 basis points, depending on the tax benefits available, because the overall interest rate will be reduced by the tax savings.

Tax-exempt financings structured as leveraged leases have not been widely used, but the provisions of the Economic Recovery Tax Act of 1981 can make tax-exempt leveraged leasing quite advantageous, as follows:

1. *Economics of Leveraged Leases.* The purpose of a leveraged lease is to transfer tax benefits associated with the ownership of plant and equipment from the actual user to a third party, usually the person or entity providing the financing. This arrangement is advantageous when the user pays taxes at a materially lower rate than the latter because of operating losses or tax credits. Under these circumstances, the cost of financing facilities can be effectively reduced because the investment tax credits and depreciation associated with them have a greater economic value for the person or entity providing the financing than they do for the person or entity using them.

   One could assume that the benefits of a leveraged lease would be maximized in the case of political subdivisions because they are exempt from tax and, consequently, the tax benefits of ownership are of no value to them. The investment tax credit is not available for property leased to a political subdivision, however, and one of the significant tax benefits otherwise available therefore, disappears in a leveraged lease to a political subdivision.[2] In addition, with the exception of "qualified mass-commuting vehicles,"[3] property not eligible for the investment tax credit is also not eligible for the new, liberalized requirements for leveraged leases. Thus, as a practical matter, the leveraged lease structure will not work for property that will be used by the political subdivision itself.

There is, however, a way to structure financings that would avoid the limitations just described, although the circumstances under which such a structure might work are probably fairly limited. In 1981, the United States Court of Claims, in the case of Xerox Corporation vs. U.S. Government, held that if a corporation uses property to provide a service to a political subdivision, that property is eligible for the investment tax credit. The property in question consisted of copying machines provided to the United States government. The utility of this financing structure seems limited since political subdivisions can seldom obtain the use of facilities they need through a legitimate service arrangement. Nevertheless, there may be some circumstances in which this approach will work, and its economic advantages to the political subdivision can be substantial because tax benefits that would be useless otherwise take on real significance because they can be transferred for value.

2. *Leveraged Lease Requirements.* In the past, the Internal Revenue Service has used a number of very stringent criteria to determine whether a leveraged lease was a lease for tax purposes.[4] The Economic Recovery Tax Act of 1981 has eliminated virtually all of the Service's criteria and, in effect, allows taxpayers to sell tax benefits associated with the acquisition or construction of new plant and equipment, although the

[2]Since this limitation also applies to tax-exempt organizations, a lease to a nonprofit corporation would not avoid the problem.

[3]A qualified mass-commuting vehicle is defined as a bus, subway car, rail car or similar equipment which is leased to a government owned mass transit system and which is used by such a system in providing mass commuting services. Information on this form of leasing is found in Section 168 (f)(8)(D)(iii) of the Internal Revenue Code. A leveraged lease financing has been utilized by New York's Metropolitan Authority for the purchase of buses and railcars.

[4]These included the requirements that the lessee not be able to utilize the property for its entire economic useful life, that any option given to the lessee to acquire the property at the end of the lease term be at the then fair market value of the property, that the lessor be able to establish that the lease would be profitable without regard to the tax benefits, and that the lessor at all times maintain an equity investment in the property equal to at least 20 percent of its cost.

property of state and local governments is generally excluded from full advantage of the benefits. A lessor will be treated as the owner of property, with all the attendant tax benefits, so long as certain requirements are met.[5]

3. *Example of Tax-Exempt Leveraged Lease.* Although the documentation for a leveraged lease and the analysis of its economic benefits are quite complex, the general structure can be outlined in relatively simple terms. We will use as an example the financing of a $10-million pollution-control project.

   The pollution-control authority (the "Authority") would issue $10 million of tax-exempt obligations and loan the proceeds to the company constructing the facilities. After the construction is completed, the company would sell the facilities (but could retain title to them) to the lessor (in most cases, a bank or a leasing company) for $1 million in cash, and the lessor would assume the company's obligation to repay the loan from the Authority. (Alternatively, the lessor could issue a note for $9 million with terms identical to those of the company's obligation to the Authority). The $1 million in cash, which is the lessor's required 10-percent investment, would be used to retire an equivalent amount of the tax-exempt obligations.[6] The company would then immediately lease back the facility at a rental rate that would reflect a financing cost below the interest rate on the tax-exempt obligations because of the tax benefits obtained by the lessor in the transaction. The lease would be for a period equal to 90 percent of the useful life of the facilities, and the termination date of the lease would also be the last maturity date for the

[5]These requirements are as follows:

1. The lessor must be a corporation (other than a subchapter of a corporation or a personal holding company), a partnership consisting of such corporations, or a grantor trust with respect to which the grantor and all beneficiaries are either corporations or a partnership consisting of such corporations.
2. The lessor, at the time the property is first placed in service under the lease and at all times during the term of the lease, must have a minimum investment of not less than 10 percent of the adjusted basis of the property (as opposed to 20 percent of the property's *cost* under the Service's former rules).
3. The term of the lease (including any extensions) cannot exceed the greater of 90 percent of the useful life of the property or 150 percent of the present class life of the property.
4. As discussed above, the property must either be eligible for the investment tax credit or be a qualified mass commuting vehicle.
5. The parties must agree to characterize the relationship as a lease.

If the foregoing requirements are met, the lessor will be treated as the owner of the property and the lessee will be treated as the lessee and "no other factors shall be taken into account."

[6]The lessor would recoup its equity investment in relatively short order as a result of the investment tax credit.

tax-exempt obligations. At the end of the lease, the company would buy the facilities for a nominal amount.

4. *Qualified Mass-Commuting Vehicles.* As noted earlier, the new leveraged leasing rules apply to qualified mass-commuting vehicles even if they are leased to a political subdivision and are consequently not eligible for the investment tax credit. The only requirement is that they be financed, in whole or in part, with the proceeds of tax-exempt obligations. The transaction might be structured in the same general fashion as the pollution control financing described above, although the results would not be as favorable because there would be no investment tax credit. In addition, there may be many variations on this financing structure depending on factors such as the use of federal grants to assist in financing vehicles.[7]

Warrant Bonds

Traditionally associated with common stocks, warrants to purchase bonds were first issued at the end of 1980 in conjunction with a bond sale by the Kingdom of Sweden. The first sale of a tax-exempt bond with warrants was by the Municipal Assistance Corporation (MAC) for New York City in 1981.

A warrant typically entitles the holder to purchase an additional amount of bonds at a fixed price for a number of years. Because warrants pay no interest, they have no intrinsic value unless the market price of the security rises above the price at which additional bonds may be purchased through exercise of the warrant option. The lack of intrinsic value does not, however, imply a lack of market price because certain investors have been willing to pay for the right to an option, which means that the buyer anticipates higher bond prices (and lower interest rates) over the period that the warrant is exercisable. In effect, two series of securities are sold, with the second series being invoked only at the time a warrant on the first series is exercised. Each warrant entitles the holder of the first series bond to purchase the second series bond with an identical coupon. The warrants in MAC's case could be exercised monthly at any time prior to the expiration date, or through January 18, 1983.

From the issuer's standpoint, the willingness of certain investors to purchase this option provides an opportunity to reduce the cost of borrowing,

[7]Since the above sections on leasing were written, the Tax Reform Act of 1984 and subsequent U.S. Treasury rulings have sharply curtailed the direct and (through leasing) indirect use by tax exempt entities of accelerated depreciation and investment tax credit. Consult tax attorney for the latest rulings.

with the MAC issue probably having carried an interest rate one-half point lower than would otherwise have prevailed. Although MAC's total debt service costs will, of course, be higher than otherwise if interest rates drop sufficiently to prompt holders to exercise the warrants, it has been estimated that on this particular sale, MAC saved about $11.0 million, compared with issues not utilizing warrants, over the life of the $100-million issue through the use of warrants.

Zero Coupon and Original Issue Discount Bonds

Municipalities have found it cost-effective, under certain circumstances, to issue securities that have below-market interest return or no current interest return at all attached to the bonds. Through this mechanism, municipalities have sold debt at a reduced cost to the borrower. In effect, the bond is sold at a price that falls well below its par value or stated value.

There are several principal advantages to an investor who is willing to pay a lower price in order to take advantage of these aspects. First of all, the securities can benefit from the ruling of the Internal Revenue Service that the capital gain from bonds that are issued at a discount from the stated value will be treated as tax-exempt income. In addition, the investor enjoys no reinvestment risk as the investor does with traditional coupon bonds. For zero coupon bonds, an additional attractive feature to certain investors is the ability to delay the receipt of the payment of principal and interest on the security until the bonds actually mature. A final feature for the investor involves the ability to purchase a rather large amount of securities for a small purchase price.

A number of governments have utilized deep discount and zero coupon bonds, including the Ocean County Utilities Authority, New Jersey; the Commonwealth of Massachusetts; and the City of Tampa, Florida. The most important advantage to an issuer utilizing deep discount or zero coupon bonds is the interest cost savings resulting from the investor whose particular tax or investment program can be met most effectively through the use of this particular financing form. An additional advantage to an issuer involves the postponement of interest payments. With a capital construction project, it is important to note that with deep discount or zero coupon bonds, interest payments are reduced or eliminated during the construction period, and thus the initial financing amounts will be lower since the interest cost will not have to be capitalized into the bond issue.

6
Municipal Accounting: Making It Work For You Too

The purpose of this chapter is to acquaint readers with the basics of accounting for governmental units. General accounting principles are explained and the reasons for their adoption discussed. Understanding basic accounting principles places the mayor in a better position to use accounting and financial data for more creative decision making.

The main source of the principles outlined below is the National Council on Governmental Accounting's (NCGA) *Governmental Accounting and Financial Reporting Principles,* published in 1979. This statement is a modest revision of the NCGA's 1968 *Governmental Accounting, Auditing, and Financial Reporting* (GAAFR), the authoritative statement on application of generally accepted accounting principles to state and local governments. Each major section of this chapter considers one of the twelve basic NCGA Principles.

A glossary of basic municipal accounting terms is included at the end of the chapter.

I. MAKING THE SYSTEM WORK FOR YOU TOO

Accounting systems serve two masters: (1) the mayor and administrative staff, and (2) others outside the city, especially banks and investors. Finance staff feel pressures from their professional associations and investors to follow procedures responsive to outsiders. An accounting system can help the mayor in many ways, but it takes interest on the part of the mayor or other top staff to make it responsive to the mayor as well as to outsiders. Two important uses for the mayor are management control and cost of service information.

Management Control

After the budget has been adopted, the accounting system can help administrative officials control departments and subagencies to observe their budgets.

To this end, the accounting system should be broken down into separate units that are meaningful for administrative control. For example, the city might have an intergovernmental revenue fund that reports revenues received from intergovernmental grants and disbursements for various purposes. Such a fund will not be meaningful for administrative control in most cities, however, since the money is spent in many different departments. The mayor needs smaller categories, closer to the actual uses of the money, to supervise management of the funds. To help assess whether the accounting system is doing its part in administrative control, the mayor can review the system with department officials, asking them if and how they use it for their internal management purposes. If they say they keep their own records and consider the city-wide system too general or too late in its reports (common in many cities), then the accounting system is not performing its administrative control function, and the mayor's finance director and outside consultants should review ways to make the system more serviceable.

Cost of Services

To assess costs of services, financial data must be made available for all costs related to that service. This was discussed in the budgeting chapter, which pointed out that service costs can be presented for general categories such as total police expenditures or broken down to accommodate programs such as dispatching or maintenance of police motor vehicles. Between 50 and 100 such "cost centers" are desirable for most cities, although departmental staff can use smaller units.The accounting system as a whole should be no more complex than necessary, but still flexible enough to permit the occasional need for a more detailed analysis.

Other Uses. The accounting system also generates the financial information necessary for other purposes, including forecasting revenues and expenditures, cash flow management, and monitoring specific activities such as capital construction. Banks and bond rating agencies consider accounting systems important indicators of overall fiscal management. The more a city meets national standards in this area, the more favorable the interest rate will be when borrowing or selling bonds.

Current Developments in Accounting and Reporting Standards

Since the New York fiscal crisis in 1975, there have been numerous discussions concerning the institutional framework needed for setting standards on municipal accounting and reporting. Bills have been introduced into Congress to regulate municipal reporting by a Federal institute. Most state and local organizations have opposed such Federal pressures and sought to strengthen their own standard-setting framework. The National Council on Governmental Accounting has been the official body for many years. From 1979 to 1981, the Department of Housing and Urban Development (HUD) supported a major project of the National Council on Government Accounting to establish a conceptual framework for government accounting and reporting. The project sought to link accounting information to specific uses and thus to help make financial reporting more useful to citizens, managers, and elected officials, among others.[1]

In the early 1980s, extended discussions were held among municipal and state finance officers, the Financial Accounting Foundation, the American Institute of CPAs, city managers, mayors, and their counterparts at the state and county levels concerning the creation of a new organizational structure in this area. A Government Accounting Standards Board (GASB) has been formed, succeeding the National Council on Governmental Accounting (NCGA) as the body promulgating Generally Accepted Accounting Principles (GAAP) for state and local governments in the United States. It operates under the auspices of the Financial Accounting Foundation, whose Board of Trustees will be expanded to include public sector representation. The U.S. Conference of Mayors and other Public Interest Groups participated in deliberations concerning the formation of the GASB.

The GASB is expected to affect municipal governments in several significant ways. GASB standards are intended to improve the quality of municipal reporting. In accounting and reporting, more importance will probably be attached to uniform national standards than to local fiscal laws and regulations. GASB standards are more likely to be accepted and supported by the American Institute of CPAs and the financial community than were NCGA standards. Compliance with GASB standards should therefore improve the credibility of a city's external financial reporting. Still, this increased discipline by uniform national standards is not costless. Any change in financial reporting procedures generates change-over costs for cities. The intended benefits are the facilitation of cross-city comparisons of service costs for the mayor's staff and lower interest costs as a result of greater investor confidence. Extensive due-process procedures including public hearings and exposure drafts of statements on standards will allow interested mayors to bring a mayoral perspective to GASB deliberations.

[1]Allan R. Drebin, James L. Chan, and Lorna Crowley Ferguson, *Objectives of Accounting and Financial Reporting for Governmental Units* (Chicago: National Council on Governmental Accounting, 1981).

II. ACCOUNTING AND REPORTING CAPABILITIES

A municipal accounting and reporting system should make it possible to accomplish two goals:

1. A full and fair presentation of the financial position and operations of the governmental unit
2. A demonstrated compliance with the financial aspects of legal contractual provisions and various regulatory requirements

Generally Accepted Accounting Principles

Generally Accepted Accounting Principles (GAAP) represent the agreed upon body of rules to be applied in accounting. The organizations and documents that most accountants agree define GAAP for governmental units are the following:

1. American Institute of Certified Public Accountants (AICPA), *Audit of State and Local Governmental Units*
2. National Council on Governmental Accounting (NCGA), *Governmental Accounting, Auditing and Financial Reporting,* partially revised by *Governmental Accounting and Financial Reporting Principles*

Full and Fair Presentation of Financial Position

By adhering to the standards of GAAP, a number of purposes are served, as follows:

1. A set of financial measurements is applied that accountants agree comes closest to presenting the true fiscal position of a city.
2. A degree of comparability among financial reports of different cities, states, and other governmental units is assured, as well as comparability of the same unit over different periods of time.
3. A major step is taken toward incorporating the unique legal and contractual environment of governmental units.

Demonstrated Legal Compliance

Government financial operations, just as government itself, are based on legal provisions. Constitutional, statutory, contractual, grant, and administrative authority all limit and define how certain financial activities are to be accomplished. GAAP incorporated into its body of working principles such concepts as the legislative budget and appropriation process, restricted use of certain revenues, special revenue measures, and other unique factors. Thus, GAAP by its very nature helps a governmental unit demonstrate compliance with the legal limitations and restrictions under which it exists.

Conflicting GAAP and Legal Provisions

It is, however, entirely possible that specific legal provisions may conflict with GAAP. For example, in some jurisdictions, cash-basis accounting may be mandated for general fund accounting in conflict with GAAP's modified accrual method. In such cases, it is essential that there be both GAAP reporting and legal compliance reporting. This may require only additional tables or narrative, although in some extreme cases it may be necessary to publish an entirely separate report. One of the future objectives of municipal accounting is to reduce and eliminate such conflicts. This can be accomplished only by a concerted effort of both accountants and government officials to change laws that hinder or prevent the introduction of GAAP into the accounting system of governmental units.

GFOA Certificate of Conformance

Not every governmental unit's accounting system is in conformity with GAAP. For this reason, the Government Finance Officers Association (GFOA) has long promoted the "Certificate of Conformance in Financial Reporting Program" as a tool to improve the quality of application of existing standards. The certificate program is concerned with a city's comprehensive annual financial report, stressing uniformity in accordance with GAAP in order to improve report clarity and increase user understanding. The awarding of the certificate to a city's financial report is considered a testament to the quality of that city's accounting and reporting system.

How to Account

Accounting transactions are recorded in "ledgers." The "general ledger" is the book, file, or device that contains the accounts needed to reflect, in summary and in detail, the financial position and the results of financial operations of the governmental unit. Within the general ledger are the "control accounts," in which are recorded the transactions to a number of identical or related accounts. For example, the taxes receivable account is a control account supported by the individual balances in the individual taxpayers' accounts. The control account is, in turn, supported by "subsidiary ledgers," in which the separate subsidiary accounts are recorded.

Thus, when a financial transaction takes place, such as a citizen paying his property taxes, the following recordings of the transaction (called "posting") occur: First the payment is posted to the subsidiary ledger in that taxpayer's individual account, and then the payment is posted to the taxes receivable and property tax revenue control accounts in the general ledger. In this way, the accounting information of the governmental unit is recorded in ledgers and accounts that offer summary and detail information.

III. THE FUND ACCOUNTING SYSTEM

The entire city is *not* the basic accounting entity of a municipal accounting and reporting system. In this, it presents a sharp contrast to commercial or business enterprises, where the entire business or firm *is* the basic unit. Rather, the basic entity of governmental accounting is the *fund*. The fund has a number of distinct characteristics, as follows:

- A fiscal and accounting entity
- With a self-balancing set of accounts
- Recording cash and other financial resources, together with all related liabilities and residual balances and changes therein
- Which are segregated for the purpose of carrying on specific activities or attaining certain objectives in accordance with special regulations, restrictions, and limitations

The "Separate Pocket" Concept

Simply put, the concept is based on the idea of a city's financial system being a collection of separate pockets. Money and resources are placed in or taken out of certain pockets based upon the sources and intended uses thereof, in conformance with legal requirements.

Fund Balance

Each fund is a self-balancing set of accounts. To the extent that total revenues exceed total expenditures in a given fund, that amount is represented by a "fund balance." A negative fund balance means that cumulative expenditures exceed cumulative revenues in that fund. Note that many governmental units are subject to laws requiring negative fund balances to be erased by increased revenues in subsequent periods.

IV. TYPES OF FUNDS

The three major categories of funds—Governmental Funds, Proprietary Funds, and Fiduciary Funds—are distinguished primarily by the nature of the activity accounted for although this concept does not require that each new or different activity be accounted for in its own fund.

Governmental Funds

Governmental Funds (also called "source and disposition" or "expendable" funds) are those through which most governmental functions are financed. These funds account for the use, acquisition, and balances, of expendable governmental resources. The measurement focus is on determination of and changes in financial position. These funds include the General, Special Revenue, Capital Projects, Debt Service, and Special Assessment Funds. The basic purposes of these various funds are as follows:

General Fund. *To account for activities that are financed out of city general revenues through the appropriation process.* Most, and in many cases all, tax revenues are accounted for in the General Fund, as well as some nontax revenues, reimbursements, and grants. This fund is usually the largest fund and accounts for most basic city services and departments. For example, though they are vastly different activities, fire, recreation, and sanitation are usually accounted for in the General Fund. The building of a firehouse, however, would be accounted for in a different fund from that financing fire protection services. It would probably be financed out of a bond sale and would be subject to an entirely different set of legal and administrative requirements.

Special Revenue Funds. *To account for the proceeds or specific revenue sources that are legally restricted to expenditures for specific purposes.* One example of a special revenue fund would be a gasoline tax earmarked for local road repairs only.

Capital Projects Fund. *To account for financial resources to be used for the acquisition or construction of capital facilities* (other than those financed by proprietary funds, special assessment funds, and trust funds). Note that the bonds that may be used to finance the project are not accounted for here.

Debt Service Funds. *To account for the accumulation of resources for, and the payment of, general long-term debt principal and interest.*

Special Assessment Funds. *To account for the financing of improvements or services that benefit the properties against which special assessments are levied.* For instance, a sewer installation paid for by a special charge to the benefited neighborhood could be accounted for in a special assessment fund.

Proprietary Funds

Proprietary Funds (also called "commercial type" or "nonexpendable" funds) are used to account for a government's activities or organizations that parallel private sector activities. For instance, a municipal water plant that depends on user charges is similar to a privately owned water utility. Thus, just as it is with a private sector firm, the measurement focus is upon the determination of net income, financial position, and changes in financial position. These funds included Enterprise and Internal Service Funds, as follows:

Enterprise Funds. *To account for operations where the city has decided to run the operation like a private enterprise.* Enterprise funds are used when all costs (including depreciation) are met by user charges, or when the city has decided that the determination of revenue earned, or income, is justified.

Internal Service Funds. *To account for the provision of goods or services by one department to other departments of the governmental unit on a cost-recovery basis.* For instance, a city motor pool to which other departments make a contribution could be accounted for by an internal service fund.

Fiduciary Funds

Fiduciary Funds are used to account for assets held by a governmental unit in a trustee or agency capacity. One example would be a bequest left to the city to maintain a park. These funds include Trust and Agency Funds. Expendable Trust Funds account for monies being held that may be totally expended and are accounted for in the same manner as governmental funds. Nonexpendable Trust Funds, not surprisingly, are funds in which the principal amount may not be expended and are accounted for in the same way as Proprietary Funds. Agency Funds are purely custodial and thus do not require measurement of the results of operation.

Timing

For the most part, each of these funds would be accounted for on an annual fiscal-period basis. The Capital Project Funds and the Special Assessment

Funds are project-oriented, however, and may extend over two or three years, with their status being periodically reported.

General Fixed Assets and Long-Term Liabilities

The Governmental Funds and the Expendable Trust Funds are based on the idea that the resources within the fund are to be used up—expended—within a fiscal period (new revenues are then raised to finance the next year's operations). This measurement principle precludes accounting for fixed assets and long-term liabilities. Fixed assets and long-term liabilities are not expendable funds. They continue long beyond a single fiscal period and do not require an appropriation or expenditure every accounting period. Thus, two account groups are used to establish control of the governmental unit's fixed assets and unmatured principal of long-term debt (other than those assets and debt accounted for in Proprietary or Nonexpendable Trust Funds). These two accounts (General Fixed Assets and General Long-Term Debt Account Groups) are *not* funds, merely accounting records.

Keeping the Number of Funds to a Minimum

Generally speaking, a municipal accounting system should strive to maintain the minimum number of funds. Every new governmental activity or organization does not require a new fund. Additional funds or types of funds are unnecessarily complex and can lead to inefficient financial administration.

V. FIXED ASSETS AND LONG-TERM LIABILITIES

As indicated above, general fixed assets are accounted for in the general fixed-asset group of accounts. Fixed assets relating to Proprietary Funds and Nonexpendable Trust Funds should be accounted for through these funds.

Similarly, long-term liabilities are accounted for in the general long-term-debt account group. Certain long-term liabilities, however, are accounted for in Proprietary Funds, Special Assessment Funds, or Nonexpendable Trust Funds.

Nonexpendable Resources

The purpose of governmental funds is to reflect changes in financial position as represented by revenues (sources) and expenditures (uses) of financial resources. General fixed assets and long-term liabilities are not accounted for in governmental funds because they do not represent financial resources available for expenditure. Rather, the expenditure was made at the time the assets were acquired.

Valuation of Fixed Assets

Fixed assets should be accounted for at cost, or if actual cost is unknown, estimated cost. Donated fixed assets should be accounted for at the estimated true value of the assets.

VI. DEPRECIATION OF FIXED ASSETS

Depreciation is given different accounting treatments depending upon the particular fund or account. These distinctions are explained below.

No Depreciation in Governmental Funds

Depreciation of fixed assets should not be accounted for in governmental type funds. Depreciation allocates the cost of a fixed asset over its life. This allocation attempts to represent the degree to which the assets are used up in each of the periods of its life. Depreciation is an important tool for income determination because it allows the cost of an asset to be deducted from the revenue that the asset produces within a given accounting period.

In governmental funds, however, income determination is not essential; rather, one seeks to measure changes in financial position. The actual resources used in acquiring the asset were disbursed at the time of purchase. In later periods, no more governmental resources are expended. The accounting convention of depreciation reflects that actual use of a resource in the given period, but it does not represent a true reduction in the fund's cash position.

Depreciation Accumulated in Asset Account Group

Accumulated depreciation may be recorded in the general fixed-asset account group. Doing so does not violate any measurement principle. Account groups are not concerned with changes in financial position but are simply accounting devices to keep track of fixed assets. Thus, accounting for accumulated depreciation in the fixed-asset account group further aids the governmental unit in keeping an accurate inventory of the remaining life of its assets.

Use of Depreciation for Cost Accounting

Depreciation also may be recorded in cost accounting systems within a governmental unit. Doing so can be a valuable tool for the determination of the total cost of a particular governmental service. For instance, sanitation collection requires the use of expendable resources (for salaries and other expenditures) and general fixed assets (sanitation trucks). Governmental funds do not reflect the latter portion of cost. A cost accounting system, however, can combine these two factors in order to determine the "true" cost, and depreciation is an important part of that calculation.

Accounting for Depreciation in Proprietary and Nonexpendable Trust Funds

Those funds for which income determination is the underlying principle of measurement should account for depreciation in order to determine income correctly. Thus, Proprietary Funds and Nonexpendable Trust Funds should account for depreciation.

VII. ACCRUAL BASIS IN GOVERNMENTAL ACCOUNTING

Bases of Accounting

When speaking of a "basis" of accounting, one is referring to *when* revenues, expenditures, expenses and transfers are recognized. The two predominant bases of accounting are the "accrual basis" and the "cash basis."

The Accrual Basis and Proprietary Funds

Under the accrual basis of accounting, revenues should be recognized in the period in which they are earned (when the consumer becomes obligated to pay for the service provided) and become measurable; expenses should be recognized when incurred, if measurable. Proprietary funds, concerned with the measurements of income and costs, should use the accrual basis of accounting.

The Accrual Basis and Governmental Funds

The accrual basis of accounting is preferred by most accountants, although problems are encountered when one attempts to apply that basis to governmental funds. Certain revenues can be accrued, such as when taxpayers are obligated to pay certain amounts when the tax is levied (although a reasonable allowance should be made for estimated uncollectible taxes). Some revenues, however, such as permits and fees, simply are not measurable or recordable until the cash is collected, for the governmental unit has no idea in advance of how much might be collected. Thus some revenues cannot be accrued when levied.

Another instance of nonaccrual in government accounting occurs when accounting for long-term debt. Although a liability exists on long-term debt from the date of issuance, the liability is not recognized in the debt service fund until the period before payment is due (for only at that point must resources be used to meet that liability).

The Modified Accrual Basis

Given the above problems, and the fact that revenue and expenditure measurement in government may be susceptible to unique legal situations or structural difficulties that make it impossible to accrue all revenues, the "modified accrual" basis of accounting is used.The modified accrual basis requires that those revenues that are measurable and available for expenditure be accrued and that those revenues that cannot be accrued by accounted for when received (such as income and gross receipts, taxes and permits, fees and fines). Other special treatments under the modified accrual method include the debt service treatment described above. Inventory items, when not significant, may be recorded as expenditures, and insurance payments extending over many periods may be recorded as expenditures in the period paid.

VIII. BUDGETING, BUDGETARY CONTROL, AND BUDGETARY REPORTING

Budgeting is an essential planning, control, and evaluation tool of governments. Unlike those of the private sector, revenues are seldom determined by the demand for the services provided. Both revenues and expenditures are determined by budget decisions. These decisions include levels of service, allocations of resources among departments and programs, and revenue measures. In most governmental units, the budget is the legal basis for government operations, and budget decisions have the force of law.

System Should Provide Basis for Budgetary Control

Since budget decisions do have the force of law, it is necessary that governmental units establish a system that will assure that the law is complied with; the budget must be met. It will be simplest and most efficient if the unit's accounting system measures revenues and expenditures in a manner conducive to budgetary control.

Thus, an important element is added to the accounting system: "budgetary accounting." Simply, this involves the integration of budget decisions and estimates into the accounting records for each fiscal period. In this way, as accounting data concerning the receipt and disbursement of resources, is collected it can be compared with the budget decision to assure compliance.

The integration of budgetary accounts into a GAAP-based accounting system may not be easy since budgets are usually defined in form and operation by law. The charter, laws, or by-laws may prescribe the method and accounts that the governmental unit must use to budget. Thus, a governmental unit may be required to budget by department or program rather than by fund. Or, given such new budget techniques as zero-based budgeting, the budget may take the form of "decision packages." In order to integrate budget decisions into the accounting system, it may be necessary to convert a budget-by-department into a budget-by-fund.

Conversely, a budget-by-fund may not tell a manager much about a particular department or activity. Any one department may draw resources from more than one fund. Thus, the information needed to judge whether a department head is meeting his budget may not be available in one place under the fund structure. Good budgetary control therefore requires that the accounting system be prepared not only to measure the changes in financial position by applying GAAP but also to measure the flows of resources in accordance with the budget structure. Only then can budgetary control be assured.

Appropriate Statements Should Include Budgetary Comparisons

Integration of the budgetary accounts into the accounting system provides managers with an ongoing basis of control comparison. Similarly, when interim and annual financial reports are prepared, comparisons of actual activity to budget are needed. Budgetary comparison in interim reports facilitate legislative oversight and budgetary revisions.

IX. TRANSFER, REVENUE, EXPENDITURE, AND EXPENSE ACCOUNT CLASSIFICATION

The Interfund Transaction Concept

At times, financial resources originally accounted for in one fund are to be expended in another. Moving these resources from one fund to the other so that they may be properly accounted for is known as an "interfund transaction."

For example, a water and sewer fund might be charged for computer services supplied out of a general fund appropriation.

Quasi-External Transactions are Accounted for as Revenues or Expenditures

Transactions that would be considered revenues or expenditures to the governmental unit if they involved organizations external to the governmental unit are considered "quasi-external transactions." Such transaction are recorded as an expenditure to the fund receiving the service and a revenue to the fund providing the service. The net effect of this transaction on the governmental unit as a whole is nil; the revenue and expenditure net to zero for the entire governmental unit.

Reimbursements are Accounted for as Expenditures

When one fund makes an expenditure that is properly applicable to another fund, the payment that settles the account is called a "reimbursement." The reimbursing fund accounts for the transaction as an expenditure, and the reimbursed fund simply removes the expenditure from its accounts.

Transfers are not Expenditures or Revenues

All interfund transactions except quasi-external transactions, reimbursements, advances, or loans are considered "transfers." Transfers are not recorded as expenditures or revenues. Any nonroutine transfers of resources between funds are called "residual equity transfers" and are accounted for by adding or subtracting from fund balances of the respective funds. All other interfund transfers that are routine and legally authorized (such as transfer from the General Fund to the Debt Service Fund to make the required contribution to paying off long-term debt) are called "operating transfers." Operating transfers are accounted for as "other sources" (or uses) of financing in the respective funds/accounts.

Long-Term Debt Issue Proceeds are not Revenues

Proceeds of long-term debt issues are accounted for as "other financing sources". They increase the city's cash position but are not treated as revenues. Annual debt service requirements, however, are shown as an expenditure against revenues for the period in which the payment is actually made.

Revenue Classification

The primary classification of governmental fund revenues is by fund and source. Typical sources are taxes, licenses, permits, fines, and intergovernmental revenues. It is also possible to account for revenues by department or organization if management control so requires.

Expenditure Classification

Expenditures should be classified according to a number of dimensions. The primary expenditure classifications are by fund, by program or function (e.g., public safety), organizational unit (e.g., police department), by activity (e.g., criminal investigations), by character (e.g., current expenditures versus capital outlays, debt service, or intergovernmental) and by object (e.g., salaries).

X. SOME QUESTIONS TO ASK ABOUT THE ACCOUNTING SYSTEM

Mayors should review the following specific questions with their finance staff to gain a better sense of how the municipal accounting system works. The mayor can use these as introductory questions for a more general discussion of the accounting system with its major users, asking them how satisfied they are with it and comparing it with those of other cities. The mayor can also go over these same issues with chief executives of other cities.

1. How is the adopted budget entered into the accounting system? By fund, department, program? Is it on-line in a computer? Who has access to it? How fast is access? How long does it take for a department official to obtain a statement of expenditures to date for his department. Do department officials find the system accessible? How often do they use it?
2. What delays are experienced in recording expenditures by the department? By the central accounting staff?
3. How are expenditures monitored at the department level? At the accounting department level? Which items authorized in the budget are checked with the department official? With the chief administrative officer? With the mayor? How about items *not* included in the budget?
4. Who monitors the cash flows and balances of the city? (The mayor should review the processes for the previous two years.)

5. How does the accounting system handle a drop in revenues of 10 percent below the amount budgeted for the fiscal year? Is the budget statement revised? How large have such revisions been in the previous two years? If there were such revisions, was the mayor consulted? What information was the mayor given to document the situation?
6. How are costs of service data presented? Are they reported to the mayor and the council routinely as part of the budget? If not, are they used to compare alternative service delivery modes by departmental staff? When and how? The mayor should pursue one or two examples, such as the cost of a police foot patrol for four hours compared to four hours of safety inspections by a firefighter. Which items, if any, are included in these computations: pension contributions? a share of the administrative staff of the police department? of the general city administration? of motor vehicle maintenance? of dispatchers? How does the cost of recently hired staff compare to that of the most senior staff?
7. Has anyone audited these sources of data to ascertain how accurate the time reports of staff were? How much error did the audit disclose in the police compared to the fire department?
8. How much data for questions 6 and 7 came from the standard accounting system? Were special tabulating necessary? Would it be useful to generate more such costs of service data from the accounting system?

XI. COMMON TERMINOLOGY AND CLASSIFICATION

A governmental unit's accounting system has three basic elements: the budget, the accounts, and the financial reports. In order that the system as a whole be understandable, it is essential that a common terminology and classification scheme be maintained and used consistently. (See Glossary at end of chapter.)

XII. INTERIM AND ANNUAL FINANCIAL REPORTS

Interim Financial Reports

Interim financial reports are primarily prepared for use by management. They may be produced monthly, quarterly, or upon request. The key to interim reporting is a comparison of actual financial operations to budgetary estimates and limits. This information allows managers to plan for the remainder of the year, to evaluate past performances, and to seek changes in the budget as may be appropriate.

The Level of Reporting in the Annual Financial Report

Every governmental unit should prepare and publish a comprehensive annual financial report (CAFR). This report is necessary not only as a managerial tool but as a means of accountability to the public, to investors, and to prospective investors. Two major levels of reporting in the CAFR are envisioned, as follows:

General Purpose Financial Statements (GPFS) by Fund Type and Account Group. Not every user of a governmental unit's financial statements requires a great deal of detail. In fact, a citizen who simply wishes to know how the government spends his money doesn't wish to see statements describing each and every fund. In fact, that level of detail confuses rather than enlightens. The GPFS need go no further than briefly listing financial results by fund type (there are only eight fund types) and in combined total. (The actual content of these statements will be discussed later.) A governmental unit may choose to publish its GPFS separately as a ready summary of financial operations.

Combining Statements by Fund Types and Individual Fund Statements. These statements present the financial results of the governmental unit in greater detail than the GPFS. They can reflect the financial operations within fund types and within each and every fund or account group.

The Nature of the Statements to be Presented

In private industry, two basic financial statements must be presented: the balance sheet and the income statement (with a statement of changes in retained earnings). The governmental parallels to these statements form the core of governmental financial reporting. The difference that often makes governmental statements bulky and confusing is that the private sector reports on only one accounting entity—the firm. Governments have as many entities as they have funds and must prepare a set of statements for each. Moveover, government financial reports combine these fund statements in almost innumerable combinations.

The balance sheet of a municipality is very similar to the balance sheet of a commercial firm. Each fund shows its assets, its liabilities, and resulting fund balance. It should be remembered that governmental funds do not account for (and the balance sheet will not reflect) general fixed assets and long-term liabilities. CAFR should show balance sheets by fund, by fund type (combining funds), and for the governmental unit as a whole (by combining fund types).

Statements of revenues, expenditures, and changes in fund balance are the governmental parallel to corporate income statements. Here, the operations of the fund for the past accounting period will be revealed. Furthermore, funds for which budgets have been adopted should show comparisons of actual results to budget. The individual statements of revenues, expenditures, and changes in fund balance are also combined by fund type and for the governmental unit as a whole.

The Structure of the Comprehensive Annual Financial Report (CAFR)

The CAFR of a government unit should be structured as follows:

1. Introduction Section
   (Table of contents, letter of transmittal, and other material deemed appropriate by management)
2. Financial Section
   a. Auditor's Report
   b. General Purpose Financial Statements
      (1) Combined balance sheet for all fund types and account groups. (See Example 1.)
      (2) Combined statement of revenues, expenditures and changes in fund balances for all governmental fund balances. (See Example 2.)
      (3) Combined statements of revenues, expenditures, and changes in fund balances (budget and actual) for General and Special Revenue fund types and similar governmental fund types for which annual budgets have been legally adopted (See Example 3.)
      (4) Combined statement of revenues, expenses, and changes in retaining earnings for all Proprietary Fund types. (See Example 4.)
      (5) Combined statements of changes in financial position for all Proprietary Fund types. (See Example 5.)
      (6) Notes to financial statements.
      (7) Trust Fund operations may be reported in (2), (4), and (5) above, or separately.
   c. Combining Statements and Individual Fund and Account Group Statements and Schedules.
      (1) Combining statements (balance sheet and statement of revenues, expenditures, and changes in fund balance) by

fund type whenever a governmental unit has more than one fund of a given type. (See Examples 6 and 7.)

(2) Individual fund and account group statements (balance sheet and statement of revenue, expenditure, and changes in fund balance) whenever a governmental unit has only one fund of a given type and for account groups and/or whenever necessary to present prior year and budgetary comparisons. (See Example 8.)

(3) Schedules
   (a) Schedules to demonstrate legal and contractual compliance.
   (b) Schedules to bring together information spread throughout various statements (e.g., accounts receivable and cash receipts and disbursements).
   (c) Schedules to present greater detail (e.g., department or program expenditure data).

3. Statistical Tables

Tables presenting information such as 10-year budget comparisons, tax levels, collectors, property valuation, debt levels, margins, debt service, demographics, and miscellaneous other data.

EXAMPLE 1
(Page 1 of 2)

Name Of Governmental Unit

Combined Balance Sheet — All Fund Types and Account Groups

December 31, 19X2

	Governmental Fund Types				Proprietary Fund Types		Fiduciary Fund Type	Account Groups		Totals (Memorandum Only)	
ASSETS	General	Special Revenue	Debt Service	Capital Projects	Special Assessment	Enterprise	Internal Service	Trust and Agency	General Fixed Assets	General Long-Term Debt	December 31, 19X2	December 31, 19X1
Cash	$258,500	$101,385	$ 43,834	$ 431,600	$232,185	$ 257,036	$ 29,700	$ 216,701	$ —	$ —	$ 1,570,941	$ 1,258,909
Cash with fiscal agent	—	—	102,000	—	—	—	—	—	—	—	102,000	—
Investments, at cost or amortized cost	65,000	37,200	160,990	—	—	—	—	1,239,260	—	—	1,502,450	1,974,354
Receivables (net of allowances for uncollectibles):												
Taxes	58,300	2,500	3,829	—	—	—	—	580,000	—	—	644,629	255,400
Accounts	8,300	3,300	—	100	—	29,130	—	—	—	—	40,830	32,600
Special assessments	—	—	—	—	646,035	—	—	—	—	—	646,035	462,035
Notes	—	—	—	—	—	2,350	—	—	—	—	2,350	1,250
Loans	—	—	—	—	—	—	—	35,000	—	—	35,000	40,000
Accrued interest	50	25	1,557	—	350	650	—	2,666	—	—	5,298	3,340
Due from other funds	2,000	—	—	—	—	2,000	12,000	11,189	—	—	27,189	17,499
Due from other governments	30,000	75,260	—	640,000	—	—	—	—	—	—	745,260	101,400
Advances to Internal Service Funds	65,000	—	—	—	—	—	—	—	—	—	65,000	75,000
Inventory of supplies, at cost	7,200	5,190	—	—	—	23,030	40,000	—	—	—	75,420	70,900
Prepaid expenses	—	—	—	—	—	1,200	—	—	—	—	1,200	900
Restricted assets:												
Cash	—	—	—	—	—	113,559	—	—	—	—	113,559	272,968
Investments, at cost or amortized cost	—	—	—	—	—	176,800	—	—	—	—	176,800	143,800
Land	—	—	—	—	—	211,100	20,000	—	1,259,500	—	1,490,600	1,456,100
Buildings	—	—	—	—	—	447,700	60,000	—	2,855,500	—	3,363,200	2,836,700
Accumulated depreciation	—	—	—	—	—	(90,718)	(4,500)	—	—	—	(95,218)	(83,500)
Improvements other than buildings	—	—	—	—	—	3,887,901	15,000	—	1,036,750	—	4,939,651	3,922,200
Accumulated depreciation	—	—	—	—	—	(348,944)	(3,000)	—	—	—	(351,944)	(283,750)
Machinery and equipment	—	—	—	—	—	1,841,145	25,000	—	452,500	—	2,318,645	1,924,100
Accumulated depreciation	—	—	—	—	—	(201,138)	(9,400)	—	—	—	(210,538)	(141,900)
Construction in progress	—	—	—	—	—	22,713	—	—	1,722,250	—	1,744,963	1,359,606
Amount available in Debt Service Funds	—	—	—	—	—	—	—	—	—	210,210	210,210	284,813
Amount to be provided for retirement of general long-term debt	—	—	—	—	—	—	—	—	—	1,889,790	1,889,790	1,075,187
Total Assets	$494,350	$224,860	$312,210	$1,071,700	$878,570	$6,375,514	$184,800	$2,084,816	$7,326,500	$2,100,000	$21,053,320	$17,059,911

(Continued)

EXAMPLE 1
(Page 2 of 2)

Name Of Governmental Unit
Combined Balance Sheet — All Fund Types and Account Groups, Continued

LIABILITIES AND FUND EQUITY	Governmental Fund Types					Proprietary Fund Types		Fiduciary Fund Type	Account Groups		Totals (Memorandum Only)	
	General	Special Revenue	Debt Service	Capital Projects	Special Assessment	Enterprise	Internal Service	Trust and Agency	General Fixed Assets	General Long-Term Debt	December 31, 19X2	December 31, 19X1
Liabilities:												
Vouchers payable	$118,261	$ 33,850	$ —	$ 29,000	$ 20,600	$ 131,071	$ 15,000	$ 3,350	$ —	$ —	$ 351,132	$ 223,412
Contracts payable	57,600	18,300	—	69,000	50,000	8,347	—	—	—	—	203,247	1,326,511
Judgments payable	—	2,000	—	22,600	11,200	—	—	—	—	—	35,800	32,400
Accrued liabilities	—	—	—	—	10,700	16,870	—	4,700	—	—	32,270	27,417
Payable from restricted assets:												
Construction contracts	—	—	—	—	—	17,760	—	—	—	—	17,760	—
Fiscal agent	—	—	—	—	—	139	—	—	—	—	139	—
Accrued interest	—	—	—	—	—	32,305	—	—	—	—	32,305	67,150
Revenue bonds	—	—	—	—	—	48,000	—	—	—	—	48,000	52,000
Deposits	—	—	—	—	—	63,000	—	—	—	—	63,000	55,000
Due to other taxing units	—	—	—	—	—	—	—	680,800	—	—	680,800	200,000
Due to other funds	24,189	2,000	—	1,000	—	—	—	—	—	—	27,189	17,499
Due to student groups	—	—	—	—	—	—	—	1,850	—	—	1,850	1,600
Deferred revenue	15,000	—	—	—	—	—	—	—	—	—	15,000	3,000
Advance from General Fund	—	—	—	—	—	—	65,000	—	—	—	65,000	75,000
Matured bonds payable	—	—	100,000	—	—	—	—	—	—	—	100,000	—
Matured interest payable	—	—	2,000	—	—	—	—	—	—	—	2,000	—
General obligation bonds payable	—	—	—	—	—	700,000	—	—	—	2,100,000	2,800,000	2,110,000
Revenue bonds payable	—	—	—	—	—	1,798,000	—	—	—	—	1,798,000	1,846,000
Special assessment bonds payable	—	—	—	—	555,000	—	—	—	—	—	555,000	420,000
Total Liabilities	215,050	56,150	102,000	121,600	647,500	2,815,492	80,000	690,700	—	2,100,000	6,828,492	6,456,989
Fund Equity:												
Contributed capital	—	—	—	—	—	1,392,666	95,000	—	—	—	1,487,666	815,000
Investment in general fixed assets	—	—	—	—	—	—	—	—	7,326,500	—	7,326,500	5,299,600
Retained earnings:												
Reserved for revenue bond retirement	—	—	—	—	—	129,155	—	—	—	—	129,155	96,975
Unreserved	—	—	—	—	—	2,038,201	9,800	—	—	—	2,048,001	1,998,119
Fund balances:												
Reserved for encumbrances	38,000	46,500	—	941,500	185,000	—	—	—	—	—	1,211,000	410,050
Reserved for inventory of supplies	7,200	5,190	—	—	—	—	—	—	—	—	12,390	10,890
Reserved for advance to Internal Service Funds	65,000	—	—	—	—	—	—	—	—	—	65,000	75,000
Reserved for loans	—	—	—	—	—	—	—	50,050	—	—	50,050	45,100
Reserved for endowments	—	—	—	—	—	—	—	134,000	—	—	134,000	94,000
Reserved for employees' retirement system	—	—	—	—	—	—	—	1,426,201	—	—	1,426,201	1,276,150
Unreserved:												
Designated for debt service	—	—	210,210	—	46,070	—	—	—	—	—	256,280	325,888
Designated for subsequent years expenditures	50,000	—	—	—	—	—	—	—	—	—	50,000	50,000
Undesignated	119,100	117,020	—	8,600	—	—	—	(216,135)	—	—	28,585	106,150
Total Fund Equity	279,300	168,710	210,210	950,100	231,070	3,560,022	104,800	1,394,116	7,326,500	—	14,224,828	10,602,922
Total Liabilities and Fund Equity	$494,350	$224,860	$312,210	$1,071,700	$878,570	$6,375,514	$184,800	$2,084,816	$7,326,500	$2,100,000	$21,053,320	$17,059,911

The notes to the financial statements are an integral part of this statement.

EXAMPLE 2

Name Of Governmental Unit

Combined Statement of Revenues, Expenditures, and Changes in Fund Balances — All Governmental Fund Types and Expendable Trust Funds For the Fiscal Year Ended December 31, 19X2

	Governmental Fund Types					Fiduciary Fund Type	Totals (Memorandum Only) Year Ended	
	General	Special Revenue	Debt Service	Capital Projects	Special Assessment	Expendable Trust	December 31, 19X2	December 31, 19X1
Revenues:								
Taxes	$ 881,300	$ 189,300	$ 79,177	$ —	$ —	$ —	$1,149,777	$1,137,900
Special assessments levied	—	—	—	—	240,000	—	240,000	250,400
Licenses and permits	103,000	—	—	—	—	—	103,000	96,500
Intergovernmental revenues	186,500	831,100	41,500	1,250,000	—	—	2,309,100	1,258,800
Charges for services	91,000	79,100	—	—	—	—	170,100	160,400
Fines and forfeits	33,200	—	—	—	—	—	33,200	26,300
Miscellaneous revenues	19,500	71,625	7,140	3,750	29,095	200	131,310	111,500
Total Revenues	1,314,500	1,171,125	127,817	1,253,750	269,095	200	4,136,487	3,041,800
Expenditures:								
Current:								
General government	121,805	—	—	—	—	—	121,805	134,200
Public safety	258,395	480,000	—	—	—	—	738,395	671,300
Highways and streets	85,400	417,000	—	—	—	—	502,400	408,700
Sanitation	56,250	—	—	—	—	—	56,250	44,100
Health	44,500	—	—	—	—	—	44,500	36,600
Welfare	46,800	—	—	—	—	—	46,800	41,400
Culture and recreation	40,900	256,450	—	—	—	—	297,350	286,400
Education	509,150	—	—	—	—	2,420	511,570	512,000
Capital outlay	—	—	—	1,625,500	313,100	—	1,938,600	803,000
Debt service:								
Principal retirement	—	—	60,000	—	—	—	60,000	52,100
Interest and fiscal charges	—	—	40,420	—	28,000	—	68,420	50,000
Total Expenditures	1,163,200	1,153,450	100,420	1,625,500	341,100	2,420	4,386,090	3,039,800
Excess of Revenues over (under) Expenditures	151,300	17,675	27,397	(371,750)	(72,005)	(2,220)	(249,603)	2,000
Other Financing Sources (Uses):								
Proceeds of general obligation bonds	—	—	—	900,000	—	—	900,000	—
Operating transfers in	—	—	—	64,500	10,000	2,530	77,030	89,120
Operating transfers out	(74,500)	—	—	—	—	—	(74,500)	(87,000)
Total Other Financing Sources (Uses)	(74,500)	—	—	964,500	10,000	2,530	902,530	2,120
Excess of Revenues and Other Sources over (under) Expenditures and Other Uses	76,800	17,675	27,397	592,750	(62,005)	310	652,927	4,120
Fund Balances — January 1	202,500	151,035	182,813	357,350	293,075	26,555	1,213,328	1,209,208
Fund Balances — December 31	$ 279,300	$ 168,710	$ 210,210	$ 950,100	$231,070	$ 26,865	$1,866,255	$1,213,328

The notes to the financial statements are an integral part of this statement.

EXAMPLE 3

Name Of Governmental Unit

Combined Statement of Revenues, Expenditures, and Changes in Fund Balances—Budget and Actual— General and Special Revenue Fund Types For the Fiscal Year Ended December 31, 19X2

	General Fund			Special Revenue Funds			Totals (Memorandum Only)		
	Budget	Actual	Variance - Favorable (Unfavorable)	Budget	Actual	Variance - Favorable (Unfavorable)	Budget	Actual	Variance - Favorable (Unfavorable)
Revenues:									
Taxes	$ 882,500	$ 881,300	$ (1,200)	$ 189,500	$ 189,300	$ (200)	$1,072,000	$1,070,600	$ (1,400)
Licenses and permits	125,500	103,000	(22,500)	—	—	—	125,500	103,000	(22,500)
Intergovernmental revenues	200,000	186,500	(13,500)	837,600	831,100	(6,500)	1,037,600	1,017,600	(20,000)
Charges for services	90,000	91,000	1,000	78,000	79,100	1,100	168,000	170,100	2,100
Fines and forfeits	32,500	33,200	700	—	—	—	32,500	33,200	700
Miscellaneous revenues	19,500	19,500	—	81,475	71,625	(9,850)	100,975	91,125	(9,850)
Total Revenues	1,350,000	1,314,500	(35,500)	1,186,575	1,171,125	(15,450)	2,536,575	2,485,625	(50,950)
Expenditures:									
Current:									
General government	129,000	121,805	7,195	—	—	—	129,000	121,805	7,195
Public safety	277,300	258,395	18,905	494,500	480,000	14,500	771,800	738,395	33,405
Highways and streets	84,500	85,400	(900)	436,000	417,000	19,000	520,500	502,400	18,100
Sanitation	50,000	56,250	(6,250)	—	—	—	50,000	56,250	(6,250)
Health	47,750	44,500	3,250	—	—	—	47,750	44,500	3,250
Welfare	51,000	46,800	4,200	—	—	—	51,000	46,800	4,200
Culture and recreation	44,500	40,900	3,600	272,000	256,450	15,550	316,500	297,350	19,150
Education	541,450	509,150	32,300	—	—	—	541,450	509,150	32,300
Total Expenditures	1,225,500	1,163,200	62,300	1,202,500	1,153,450	49,050	2,428,000	2,316,650	111,350
Excess of Revenues over (under) Expenditures	124,500	151,300	26,800	(15,925)	17,675	33,600	108,575	168,975	60,400
Other Financing Sources (Uses):									
Operating transfers out	(74,500)	(74,500)	—	—	—	—	(74,500)	(74,500)	—
Excess of Revenues over (under) Expenditures and Other Uses	50,000	76,800	26,800	(15,925)	17,675	33,600	34,075	94,475	60,400
Fund Balances — January 1	202,500	202,500	—	151,035	151,035	—	353,535	353,535	—
Fund Balances — December 31	$ 252,500	$ 279,300	$26,800	$ 135,110	$ 168,710	$33,600	$ 387,610	$ 448,010	$ 60,400

The notes to the financial statements are an integral part of this statement.

EXAMPLE 4

Name Of Governmental Unit

Combined Statement of Revenues, Expenses, and Changes in Retained Earnings/Fund Balances — All Proprietary Fund Types and Similar Trust Funds

For the Fiscal Year Ended December 31, 19X2

	Proprietary Fund Types		Fiduciary Fund Type		Totals (Memorandum Only)	
					Year Ended	
	Enterprise	Internal Service	Nonexpendable Trust	Pension Trust	December 31, 19X2	December 31, 19X1
Operating Revenues:						
Charges for services	$ 672,150	$ 88,000	$ —	$ —	$ 760,150	$ 686,563
Interest	—	—	2,480	28,460	30,940	26,118
Contributions	—	—	—	160,686	160,686	144,670
Gifts	—	—	45,000	—	45,000	—
Total Operating Revenues	672,150	88,000	47,480	189,146	996,776	857,351
Operating Expenses:						
Personal services	247,450	32,500	—	—	279,950	250,418
Contractual services	75,330	400	—	—	75,730	68,214
Supplies	20,310	1,900	—	—	22,210	17,329
Materials	50,940	44,000	—	—	94,940	87,644
Heat, light, and power	26,050	1,500	—	—	27,550	22,975
Depreciation	144,100	4,450	—	—	148,550	133,210
Benefit payments	—	—	—	21,000	21,000	12,000
Refunds	—	—	—	25,745	25,745	13,243
Total Operating Expenses	564,180	84,750	—	46,745	695,675	605,033
Operating Income	107,970	3,250	47,480	142,401	301,101	252,318
Nonoperating Revenues (Expenses):						
Operating grants	55,000	—	—	—	55,000	50,000
Interest revenue	3,830	—	—	—	3,830	3,200
Rent	5,000	—	—	—	5,000	5,000
Interest expense and fiscal charges	(92,988)	—	—	—	(92,988)	(102,408)
Total Nonoperating Revenues (Expenses)	(29,158)	—	—	—	(29,158)	(44,208)
Income before Operating Transfers	78,812	3,250	47,480	142,401	271,943	208,110
Operating Transers In (Out)	—	—	(2,530)	—	(2,530)	(2,120)
Net Income	78,812	3,250	44,950	142,401	269,413	205,990
Retained Earnings/Fund Balances - January 1	2,088,544	6,550	139,100	1,040,800	3,274,994	3,069,004
Retained Earnings/Fund Balances - December 31	$2,167,356	$ 9,800	$184,050	$1,183,201	$3,544,407	$3,274,994

The notes to the financial statements are an integral part of this statement.

EXAMPLE 5

Name Of Governmental Unit

Combined Statement of Changes in Financial Position — All Proprietary Fund Types and Similar Trust Funds

For the Fiscal Year Ended December 31, 19X2

	Proprietary Fund Types		Fiduciary Fund Type		Totals (Memorandum Only)	
	Enterprise	Internal Service	Non-expendable Trust	Pension Trust	December 31, 19X2	December 31, 19X1
Sources of Working Capital						
Operations:						
Net income	$ 78,812	$ 3,250	$44,950	$142,401	$ 269,413	$ 205,990
Items not requiring (providing) working capital						
Depreciation	144,100	4,450	—	—	148,550	133,210
Working Capital Provided by Operations	222,912	7,700	44,950	142,401	417,963	339,200
Cash from revenue bond construction account	127,883	—	—	—	127,883	743,800
Contributions	672,666	—	—	—	672,666	—
Total Sources of Working Capital	1,023,461	7,700	44,950	142,401	1,218,512	1,083,000
Uses of Working Capital						
Acquisition of property, plant, and equipment	324,453	7,000	—	—	331,453	842,812
Retirement of general obligation bonds	50,000	—	—	—	50,000	50,000
Retirement of revenue bonds payable	52,000	—	—	—	52,000	48,000
Repayment of advance from General Fund	—	10,000	—	—	10,000	10,000
Net decrease in other current liabilities payable from restricted assets	8,946	—	—	—	8,946	4,318
Net increase in other restricted assets	1,624	—	—	—	1,624	414
Total Uses of Working Capital	437,023	17,000	—	—	454,023	955,544
Net Increase (Decrease) in Working Capital	$ 586,438	$ (9,300)	$44,950	$142,401	$ 764,489	$ 127,456
Elements of Net Increase (Decrease) in Working Capital:						
Cash	$ 119,276	$(20,300)	$ 4,310	$ 20,121	$ 123,407	$ 796,412
Investments	—	—	45,640	118,341	163,981	(84,286)
Receivables (net of allowances for uncollectibles)	(5,570)	—	(5,000)	—	(10,570)	2,396
Due from other funds	(6,000)	(8,000)	—	2,189	(11,811)	(4,923)
Inventory of supplies	11,250	14,000	—	—	25,250	(3,414)
Prepaid expenses	460	—	—	—	460	520
Vouchers payable	(72,471)	5,000	—	—	(67,471)	(42,427)
Contracts payable	551,653	—	—	1,750	553,403	(525,400)
Accrued liabilities	(12,160)	—	—	—	(12,160)	(11,422)
Net Increase (Decrease) in Working Capital	$ 586,438	$ (9,300)	$44,950	$142,401	$ 764,489	$ 127,456

The notes to the financial statements are an integral part of this statement.

EXAMPLE 6
Name Of Governmental Unit

Combining Balance Sheet — All Special Revenue Funds

December 31, 19X2

ASSETS	Parks	State Gasoline Tax	Motor Vehicle License	Parking Meter	Juvenile Rehabilitation	Totals December 31, 19X2	Totals December 31, 19X1
Cash	$39,525	$22,460	$ 5,420	$16,260	$17,720	$101,385	$ 91,459
Investments, at cost	16,200	—	—	15,000	6,000	37,200	25,000
Receivables:							
Taxes receivable - delinquent (net of allowance for uncollectibles of $500)	2,500	—	—	—	—	2,500	—
Accounts receivable (net of allowance for uncollectibles of $800)	3,300	—	—	—	—	3,300	2,700
Accrued interest	25	—	—	—	—	25	—
Due from state government	—	47,250	28,010	—	—	75,260	62,400
Inventory of supplies, at cost	1,100	990	702	1,066	1,332	5,190	5,190
Total Assets	$62,650	$70,700	$34,132	$32,326	$25,052	$224,860	$186,749
LIABILITIES AND FUND BALANCES							
Liabilities:							
Vouchers payable	$10,000	$11,220	$ 4,260	$ 3,220	$ 5,150	$ 33,850	$ 23,414
Contracts payable	12,500	4,000	—	1,800	—	18,300	12,300
Judgments payable	2,000	—	—	—	—	2,000	—
Due to General Fund	2,000	—	—	—	—	2,000	—
Total Liabilities	26,500	15,220	4,260	5,020	5,150	56,150	35,714
Fund Balances:							
Reserved for encumbrances	14,000	16,500	10,000	500	5,500	46,500	12,550
Reserved for inventory of supplies	1,100	990	702	1,066	1,332	5,190	5,190
Unreserved	21,050	37,990	19,170	25,740	13,070	117,020	133,295
Total Fund Balances	36,150	55,480	29,872	27,306	19,902	168,710	151,035
Total Liabilities and Fund Balances	$62,650	$70,700	$34,132	$32,326	$25,052	$224,860	$186,749

EXAMPLE 7
Name Of Governmental Unit

Combining Statement of Revenues, Expenditures, and Changes in Fund Balances— All Special Revenue Funds

For the Fiscal Year Ended December 31, 19X2

	Parks	State Gasoline Tax	Motor Vehicle License	Parking Meter	Juvenile Rehabilitation	Totals Year Ended December 31, 19X2	Totals Year Ended December 31, 19X1
Revenues:							
Taxes	$189,300	$ —	$ —	$ —	$ —	$ 189,300	$ 168,400
Intergovernmental revenues	—	422,500	201,000	—	207,600	831,100	749,990
Charges for services	—	—	—	79,100	—	79,100	71,420
Miscellaneous revenues	70,700	—	—	600	325	71,625	63,614
Total Revenues	260,000	422,500	201,000	79,700	207,925	1,171,125	1,053,424
Expenditures:							
Public safety	—	—	199,400	80,900	199,700	480,000	414,040
Highways and streets	—	417,000	—	—	—	417,000	346,414
Culture and recreation	256,450	—	—	—	—	256,450	238,419
Total Expenditures	256,450	417,000	199,400	80,900	199,700	1,153,450	998,873
Excess of Revenues over (under) Expenditures	3,550	5,500	1,600	(1,200)	8,225	17,675	54,551
Fund Balances - January 1	32,600	49,980	28,272	28,506	11,677	151,035	96,484
Fund Balances - December 31	$ 36,150	$ 55,480	$ 29,872	$27,306	$ 19,902	$ 168,710	$ 151,035

EXAMPLE 8

Name Of Governmental Unit

Statement of Revenues, Expenditures, and Changes in Fund Balance—Budget and Actual—Parks Fund For the Fiscal Years Ended December 31, 19X2 and 19X1

	19X2			19X1		
	Budget	Actual	Variance - Favorable (Unfavorable)	Budget	Actual	Variance - Favorable (Unfavorable)
Revenues:						
Taxes:						
Current	$189,000	$188,700	$ (300)	$170,000	$168,000	$ (2,000)
Penalties and interest on delinquent taxes	500	600	100	500	400	(100)
Total Taxes	189,500	189,300	(200)	170,500	168,400	(2,100)
Miscellaneous Revenues:						
Rents and royalties	80,000	70,100	(9,900)	60,000	62,414	2,414
Interest revenue	500	600	100	500	500	—
Total Miscellaneous Revenues	80,500	70,700	(9,800)	60,500	62,914	2,414
Total Revenues	270,000	260,000	(10,000)	231,000	231,314	314
Expenditures:						
Culture and Recreation:						
Supervision of parks	20,000	19,300	700	16,500	17,200	(700)
Parkways and boulevards	32,500	30,000	2,500	26,000	28,842	(2,842)
Park areas	129,050	122,850	6,200	120,000	122,432	(2,432)
Park lighting	33,300	29,850	3,450	28,000	26,414	1,586
Park policing	20,700	20,220	480	10,000	14,219	(4,219)
Forestry and nursery	36,450	34,230	2,220	30,500	29,312	1,188
Total Expenditures	272,000	256,450	15,550	231,000	238,419	(7,419)
Excess of Revenues over (under) Expenditures	(2,000)	3,550	5,550	—	(7,105)	(7,105)
Fund Balance - January 1	32,600	32,600	—	39,705	39,705	—
Fund Balance - December 31	$ 30,600	$ 36,150	$ 5,550	$ 39,705	$ 32,600	$ (7,105)

GLOSSARY

Accounting period A period at the end of which financial statements are prepared.

Accrual basis The basis of accounting under which revenues are recorded when earned and expenditures are recorded as soon as they result in liabilities for benefits received, notwithstanding that the receipt of the revenue or the payment of the expenditure may take place, in whole or in part, in another accounting period.

Budgetary accounts The control or management of a governmental unit or enterprise in accordance with an approved budget for the purpose of keeping expenditures within the limitations of available appropriations and available revenues.

Budgetary control The control or management of a governmental unit or enterprise in accordance with an approved budget for the purpose of keeping expenditures within the limitations of available appropriations and available revenues.

Cash basis The base of accounting under which revenues are recorded when received in cash and expenditures are recorded when paid.

Depreciation (1) Expiration in the service life of fixed assets attributable to wear and tear, deterioration, action of the physical elements, inadequacy, and obsolescence. (2) The portion of the cost of a fixed asset that is charged as an expense during a particular period.

Expenditures Whenever accounts are kept on the accrual basis or the modified accrual basis, this term designates the cost of goods delivered or services rendered, whether paid or unpaid, including expenses, and capital outlays. If accounts are kept on the cash basis, the term designates only actual cash disbursements for these purposes.

Expenses Charges incurred, whether paid or unpaid, for operation, maintenance, interest and other charges that are presumed to benefit the current fiscal period.

Modified accrual basis The basis of accounting under which expenditures are recorded at the time liabilities are incurred and revenues are recorded when received in cash, except for material and/or available revenues that should be accrued, to reflect properly the taxes levied and the revenues earned.

7
Pension Systems

This chapter reviews public employee pension plan design and financing problems, their causes, and likely solutions—issues that mayors are inextricably caught up with and for which others are turning to them for leadership.[1] Its examination of the pension system makes it possible to compare and evaluate the validity of those obligations to which a city is now committed. New ideas are described and explained so that predictable and inevitable change may be planned for rather than reacted to. A nontechnical explanation of how pension plan costs are determined and the significance of actuarial assumptions are also discussed.

As most mayors are painfully aware, the cost of public employee fringe benefits in general, and pension plans in particular, is growing at an alarming rate. For example, 44 percent of pay for hours worked by "general" personnel and 48 percent of pay for hours worked by "sworn" personnel represent the expenditures for fringe benefits expected to be made for public employer fiscal years ending June 30, 1979, according to the *Fourth National Survey of Employee Benefits for Full-Time Personnel of U.S. Municipalities,* the Special Report sponsored by the Labor-Management Relations Service of the United States Conference of Mayors. Of these percentages, roughly one-third, or about 15 percent of pay for hours worked, represents the expenditures made for retirement—in the form of municipal pension and Social Security benefits—retirement funding being the largest single expenditure after salaries and wages. It is no wonder, then, that mayors are vitally concerned about the sound and economical design and financing of municipal pension plans.

Note that the word used in describing the aforementioned 15 percent of pay attributable to financing pension and Social Security benefits is "expenditures," not "costs." Expenditures do not necessarily reflect evaluation of

[1]This chapter draws heavily on John S. Perreca, "Municipal Public Employee Pension Plans: How to Create Order Out of Chaos." (©Edward H. Friend & Company, 1979). We are grateful to the author for permission to use his work. Further distribution and/or reproduction of this chapter is prohibited without the written permission of Edward H. Friend & Company.

the Social Security System, Civil Service Retirement System, and many state, county, and municipal pension plans.

In both the public and private sectors, the most commonly known pension plan is Social Security. Social Security covers virtually every working individual in the private sector and a significant number in the public sector as well.

For 1979, the tax to be paid by each of us in our capacity as employees was 6.13 percent, to be matched by an additional 6.13 percent from each of us in our capacity as employers. But *The New York Times* reported that A. Haeworth Robertson, most recently former Chief Actuary for the Social Security Administration (SSA), observed with great concern in his May 2, 1978 address to the Chamber of Commerce of the United States that the SSA's then-projected tax rate of 12 percent from each employee and 12 percent for each employer needed to avert large deficits during the first half of the next century, coupled with "the myriad of employee benefits which have grown up over the years . . . may well be developing into an unsustainable burden."

The second most commonly known public employee pension system is Civil Service. The Civil Service Retirement System covers most Federal civilian employees. Those who are not covered by Civil Service have a Federally sponsored plan of their own, for example, employees of the Foreign Service, the Central Intelligence Agency, the Tennessee Valley Authority, and a host of other smaller groups such as the Federal Judiciary, U.S.Tax Court Judges, and employees of the Board of Governors of the Federal Reserve Board.

Under Civil Service, the employee contribution rate is 7 percent of payroll, matched by an employer contribution of 7 percent. According to a recent study completed by the Civil Service System's own actuary, under the auspices of the General Accounting Office, the employer contribution should, in fact, be of the order of magnitude of 50 percent of payroll in order to keep it at a relatively controllable and level rate when expressed as a percentage of total payroll. Thus the true costs of these plans substantially exceed current expenditures.

The financial problems of municipal pension plans are probably different only in detail and degree, but what are reasonable objectives? What are the major pension plan design and financing problems facing mayors? What should be kept in mind with respect to plan provisions? How are pension costs determined and about what should a mayor be concerned with regard to their funding? What are the significant unfolding changes and trends in municipal pension plan design and financing, and how should they be dealt with? Finally, what action should be taken?

I. THREE BASIC DECISIONS ABOUT PENSION SYSTEMS

We begin with three major decisions about pension systems that can dramatically shift city costs. Many specialists will probably insist that such policies afford little leeway, but since pensions are often one of the largest single items in a city budget, the mayor should consider engaging an expert to help find some.

The Benefit Level

Pension benefits for different classes of municipal employees vary according to their age, seniority, salary, and other indicators. How do benefits for public employees compare to those for reasonably similar positions in the private sector? In other cities?[2] Consulting firms make such computations in detail; some are probably available from personnel departments, local banks, or major local employers. Benefits often vary considerably by type of employee, with police and fire personnel enjoying more generous benefits. If the mayor feels that benefits are distinctly too high or too low, this should be stressed on appropriate occasions, e.g., in collective bargaining negotiations or when setting personnel policy and overall compensation decisions.

The Funding Level

Some cities have "pay as you go" systems, which are unfunded. The logical opposite is a fully-funded system, where money has been set aside to cover all benefits granted to employees. Almost no system is fully funded, however; many are about 60 percent funded, which is generally considered adequate. Such figures are hard to compare across cities since they differ in the way they are computed, especially the actuarial tables for employee retirement. Several financial ratios can be calculated to evaluate pension systems. Unfunded liabilities are hard to compare; more meaningful for comparison are ratios such as assets/annual payments and annual receipts/annual payments. The first reflects the level of assets in the system and indicates how many years of annual payments, at current rates, are covered by existing assets. It is shown in Table 7.1 for 38 cities administering at least one of their own pension plans. For cities with more than one local system, the one with the

[2]A detailed study reporting pensions and other benefits for 12 cities is Elizabeth Dickson, Harold A. Hovey, and George E. Peterson, *Public Employee Compensation* (Washington, D.C.: The Urban Institute, 1980).

largest membership is shown. Pittsburgh's unfunded system is lowest, having no accumulated assets. At the other extreme are a few cities with assets, shown by a ratio larger than 20, to cover over 20 years of current payments. The second meaningful ratio is that of annual receipts/annual payments, a funds flow measure indicating whether annual receipts exceed annual payments; if they do, assets are being accrued for the future.There are many complications in interpreting such measures, as discussed below and in the sources cited. The Census Bureau publishes pension data annually for systems with 20 or more members, permitting computation of the measures shown in Table 7.1 for systems that do not appear in the table.[3] This information helps provide comparative benchmarks for the funding level of each city.

One Solution to Linking Funding and Benefits

The necessity to consider the "funding level" at all comes from the fact that benefits may not be directly linked to the revenues available to cover them. One solution is to link the two more tightly. Lakewood, Colorado did this in 1978 by converting its police pension system from a "defined benefit program" (found in most cities) to a "defined contribution program." This plan permits retirement at any point, rather than requiring police officers to work for 20 years before they may retire, and has the additional advantage of boosting the morale of those who remain on the job. Since life and disability coverage are insured, the bulk of the contributions may be used for retirement. This approach takes the burden off the employer of guaranteeing a given level of benefits, irrespective of the availability of funds. It also makes the employees and employer concerned with investment and management of pension funds. Policies of this sort may demand lobbying to change state regulations.

Investment Strategies

Far too little attention has been given to differences in pension investment strategies, which have become far more critical since inflation soared in the 1970s. Many cities are losing money daily by continuing investment strategies that do not yield a return higher than the inflation rate. Others have significantly increased assets by more aggressive investment.

A study of 31 public pension systems by the Government Finance Officers Association showed that in 1974-1978, the average rate of return for those investing in Treasury Bills was about 6 percent; in corporate bonds, about 9

[3]The annual source is U.S. Census, *Finances of Employee-Retirement Systems of State and Local Governments in (year)* (Washington, D.C.: U.S. Government Printing Office).

Table 7.1. Two Ratios for Pension Systems

City	System Coverage	(1) Assets / Annual Payments	(2) Annual Receipts / Annual Payments
Atlanta	General	16.9	5.37
Birmingham	General	29.3	4.7
Boston	General	4.0	1.06
Cambridge	General	4.0	1.99
Charlotte	Fire	18.8	3.2
Ft. Worth	General	18.0	3.7
Gary	Fire	0.216	1.18
Indianapolis	Police	0.032	0.97
Jackonsonville	General	1.97	1.29
Malden	General	4.18	1.35
Memphis	General	17.2	2.9
Milwaukee	General	21.0	3.2
Minneapolis	General	11.9	2.26
Newark	General	0.16	1.02
Pasadena	Police & Fire	8.45	1.5
Phoenix	General	25.0	5.0
Pittsburgh	General	0.0	0.99
St. Louis	General	15.6	3.09
St. Paul	Police	5.3	1.89
St. Petersburg	General	5.8	0.89
San Francisco	General	9.15	1.8
San Jose	General	29.3	6.6
Seattle	General	12.1	1.78
South Bend	Fire	0.20	0.92
Tampa	General	10.75	2.46
Warren	General	44.5	7.69
Waterbury	General	9.53	1.57
New York	General	11.7	2.32
Chicago	General	9.4	1.83
Los Angeles	General	15.7	2.86
Philadelphia	General	5.79	2.37
Detroit	General	12.4	2.02
Houston	General	13.1	3.56
Baltimore	General	14.1	1.92
Dallas	General	20.0	3.65
San Diego	General	12.8	2.6
San Antonio	Police & Fire	7.43	2.3
Washington, D.C.	Teachers	2.42	0.89
Average of 38 systems		$\frac{448.178}{38} = 11.79$	$\frac{96.69}{38} = 2.5$

(Source: Terry Nichols Clark and Lorna Crowley Ferguson, *City Money.* New York: Columbia University Press, 1983.)

percent; and in common stocks, about 15 percent. Since 1960, public pension systems have been shifting away from the lower-yields of Treasury bills toward common stocks. From 1960 to 1979, common stocks increased from 2.5 to 21.9 percent of the holdings of all state and local pension systems.[4]

Pension systems for private corporations have moved in the same general direction. Problems of pension fund investment are broadly similar to those for other large institutions, such as banks or insurance companies. The risk is greater in common stocks in the short term, but pension systems are primarily concerned with long-term growth. The city and its administrative employees may want to review the degree to which it prefers more security but slow growth, versus more risk but also probably more growth. Since the city as the employer is obligated to pay a certain benefit level, it is clearly in the city's interest to have pension funds invested to generate a high return. One common means is to allow each of four different teams (e.g., from investment firms, banks, etc.) manage one-fourth of the portfolio and compare the results, regularly terminating the contract of the poorest performer after reasonable periods (perhaps every two years). The mayor should ask for a table showing annual percentage changes in the city pension fund over the last 10 years and use this as the basis of a discussion with staff, and perhaps an outside expert, of alternative investment strategies.

II. OBJECTIVES FOR THE DESIGN AND FINANCING OF MUNICIPAL PENSION PLANS

The following are the most frequently identified objectives for the design and financing of municipal pension plans.

Old Age

Solve the old age problem by having a definite plan for orderly retirement, with the concomitant advantage of creating opportunities for promotion and growth among the younger ranks.

Adequate Benefits

Provide an adequate level of benefits for retirement, premature death, total and permanent disability, and resignation (or discharge).

[4]John E. Peterson and Catherine L. Spain, "Public Employee Retirement System Investment Performance and Alternative Investment Objectives," *Governmental Finance,* vol. 10, No. 2 (June, 1981), pp. 3-11. On the general risk-growth association, see Jack Francis and Stephen Archer, *Portfolio Analysis* (Englewood Cliffs, N.J.: Prentice Hall, 1971).

Plan Provisions

Provide attractive plan provisions (i.e., salient features) that are readily comprehensible to all employees.

Soundly Financed Plans

Soundly finance the pension plan by having predictable costs that can be expected to remain relatively level when expressed as a percentage of total covered payroll.

Economical Administrative Expense

Ensure economical financing with a high level of investment performance and a low level of administrative expense.

Clear and Simple Plan Provisions

Design plan provisions that are as simple and comprehensible as possible to promote the understanding and sense of security required for employee appreciation, industry, and goodwill (rather than disappointment and distrust).

Administration Simplicity

Maintain simplicity in the administration of the plan, especially with respect to the calculation of benefits to which participants may become entitled under various circumstances.

III. MAJOR PLAN-RELATED PROBLEMS

The design and financing problems a mayor must cope with may be unique, but they probably embrace many of the following common problems, some of which persist because of popular misconceptions.

Generous Public Pension Plans

Pension benefits paid to public employees, especially when combined with primary Social Security, are being increasingly criticized as being too generous when compared with what is typically provided in the private sector. The classic argument that public employees should receive larger benefits than those enjoyed by their counterparts in the private sector because of the compensation differential is no longer valid; compensation levels in the public sector often exceed those for the same job in the private sector with the exception of the most highly paid positions. Exacerbating the problems are those instances of retiring public servants being entitled to receive a total retirement income, including primary Social Security, in an amount equal to more than 100 percent of his or her final compensation. Less understood, however, is the fact that with the earlier normal retirement ages characteristically found in the public sector (e.g., ages 50 to 60 instead of the private sector's popular age 65), the eroding effect of inflation eventually reduces the apparent "windfall" pension to an amount that prevents the retired public employee from maintaining the standard of living to which he or she had deceptively grown accustomed immediately after retirement.

Employee Contributions

Required public employee contributions have been pointed to as justification for their larger benefits by employee representatives, alleging that these payroll contributions cover a significant portion of the total plan cost. When there is significant post-retirement indexing, however, required employee contributions usually represent less than one-quarter of plan costs. It is of interest to note that in a contributory plan, employee contributions are usually recovered in the form of tax-free pension benefits at retirement within the first three years, with employer-financed pension benefits continuing for 12 to 18 years thereafter.

Political Considerations

Political considerations at the time of budget making and employee negotiations on compensation have had a significant impact. Notably, there is an inclination to promise more for later (which has no immediate cost) rather than face the immediate ire of taxpayers asked to pay a more moderate increase now (which has a current cost). This avoidance of "rocking the boat," especially in times of inflation, has contributed to significant deficits in the financing of public employee pension plans. Recently, however, many states have developed permanent legislative pension commissions that require thorough fiscal notes in all legislation proposing pension improvements. These fiscal notes require a statement not only of current costs, but also actuarial projections of future costs.

Rising Employer Contributions

Required employer (i.e., taxpayer) contributions are growing beyond manageable limits. When over half the property tax in the City of Los Angeles must be directed to finance the uniformed employees' pension plan, something has to give. Employer contributions to a pension plan should remain relatively constant when expressed as a percentage of total covered payroll.

Merging Pension Plans

Merging an adequately funded municipal pension plan into county and state retirement systems presents a new set of problems because many of the county and state retirement systems into which a municipal pension plan is merged are no better funded, and in some cases less adequately funded, than the municipal plan.

Administrative Deficiencies

Administrative deficiencies, including incomplete and inaccurate records together with careless processing of benefit requests, have sometimes resulted in benefits being paid to those without entitlement or in excess of what participants have earned. For example, as reported by *The Washington Post* (October 14, 1978), "A financial audit and management review of [one state's] $1.3 billion state and local government employee pension fund have concluded that the fund's recordkeeping and operations are a shambles." The article further states, "Three former fund employees have been convicted of theft and a dozen persons, not employees of the agency, were charged with helping them, according to the reports." The *Post* went on to state, "The reports were replete with numerous instances of shoddy management," including the fact that "until early this year, employee contributions were being refunded to employees who withdrew from the fund without verification that the contributions had in fact been made."

IV. GUIDE TO PLAN PROVISIONS

Plan provisions have developed in an almost crazy-quilt manner. Calculating the normal retirement pension benefit for a general (i.e., nonuniformed) employee covered by a well-known Southern city, for example, requires 18 separate mathematical steps, using a procedure extending over two typewritten pages, because of the complexity of the formulas and the excessive amount of detail in the city ordinances.

The following considerations should be kept in mind with respect to a plan's provisions.

Level of Pension Benefits

Although the level of pension benefits to be paid at retirement, whether in addition to or in lieu of primary Social Security, has been debated at length, it has not been conclusively determined what constitutes an "adequate and proper" level of retirement income. Reduced to its basics, it would probably be agreed that to provide a career employee (e.g., one who has worked for 30 or more years) with a total retirement income equal to 100 percent of his or her final average compensation would be excessive. An amount equal to 100 percent of the participant's *preretirement net spendable income* would be most generous, and something less than that should be adequate. Obviously, lower-paid employees will require a higher percentage of their final average compensation than a higher-paid employee.

The not uncommon occurrence of long-service public employees retiring with more than 100 percent of their final (e.g., last three years' average) compensation has been justified by those who share the view that it is necessary to pay this larger amount in order to offset the effects of inflation which, as we have all witnessed in recent years, quickly erodes the purchasing power of a fixed pension. There are better ways of hedging against the impact of inflation after retirement, however, ways that will not raise as many eyebrows among the citizenry who are responsible for underwriting the plan's ultimate cost.

Cost of Living Adjustments

Post-retirement cost-of-living-adjustment (COLA) pension increases can be provided on one of two bases, the first of which is to make periodic ad hoc increases for already retired personnel, with the city amortizing the additional cost over a period of 25 to 35 years. The advantage of this approach is that it is not automatic, thereby enabling the mayor and city council to provide COLA increases as is deemed appropriate and within the city's capacity to pay. Unfortunately, however, "ad hoc on top of ad hoc" builds a bigger and bigger debt to be amortized and can eventually lead to a cost even higher than that of the fund approach described next. If the ad hoc nature of the COLA increase is preferred because of the hope it can be eliminated when funding becomes burdensome, bear in mind that public employees have been known to both expect and demand such increases, thus making it difficult to discontinue them arbitrarily.

The second basis for providing automatic post-retirement COLA increases (these are found most frequently in public rather than private plans) places a limit or cap on the amount by which the pension benefit can be increased from year to year, or in aggregate over a period of years (usually the participant's retired lifetime). Without a limit, as the State of Maryland finally discovered and rectified during their 1979 legislative session, current and future costs can grow to entirely unmanageable proportions. Characteristically, limits on post-retirement pension benefit increases might be in the order of 3 to 5 percent, but certainly no more than 6 percent, per year, notwithstanding recent double-digit inflation.

The introduction of automatic COLA escalators mitigates the eroding effect of inflation on purchasing power. Assuming, for example, a 5-percent annual rate of inflation and a 3-percent capped COLA provision, the participant receives 82¢ on the dollar after 10 years of retirement (compared with only 61¢ where no benefit escalation arrangement exists); 91¢ with a 4-percent capped COLA; and full retention of purchasing power where the COLA cap is at 5 or 6 percent (see Table 7.2).

Table 7.2. Portion of One Dollar's Purchasing Power Which Remains After Retirement Under Various Inflation Scenarios and Benefit Escalation Arrangements

Benefit Escalation Arrangement	Number Of Years After Retirement	If Annual Rate of Inflation Is					
		5%	6%	7%	8%	9%	10%
None (level benefits)	5	78¢	75¢	71¢	68¢	65¢	62¢
	10	61	56	51	46	42	39
	15	48	42	36	32	27	24
	20	38	31	26	21	18	15
	25	30	23	18	15	12	9
3% per annum	5	91¢	86¢	82¢	78¢	75¢	71¢
	10	82	74	68	61	56	51
	15	74	64	56	48	42	36
	20	67	55	46	38	31	26
	25	61	48	38	30	23	18
4% per annum	5	95¢	91¢	86¢	82¢	78¢	75¢
	10	91	82	74	68	61	56
	15	86	74	64	56	48	42
	20	82	67	55	46	38	31
	25	78	61	48	38	30	23
5% per annum	5	Full	95¢	91¢	86¢	82¢	78¢
	10	Full	91	82	74	68	61
	15	Full	86	74	64	56	48
	20	Full	82	67	55	46	38
	25	Full	78	61	48	38	30
6% per annum	5	Full	Full	95¢	91¢	86¢	82¢
	10	Full	Full	91	82	74	68
	15	Full	Full	86	74	64	56
	20	Full	Full	82	67	55	46
	25	Full	Full	78	61	48	38

Social Security Coverage

Social Security coverage is, and will likely remain, an integral part of public employee retirement systems as it has been in the private sector. Although some cities have opted out of Social Security, there is little evidence that a city or any other plan sponsor can provide the benefits available from the Social Security program at an expenditure less than or even the same as that represented by the employer and employee tax. After studying the termination of Social Security coverage by the City of San Jose, California, former Social Security Administration Chief Actuary and now independent consultant, Robert J. Myers, stated in his opening summary of findings, "[It] has been widely asserted that both the employees and the City of San Jose profited significantly by terminating Social Security coverage and then liberalizing the previously existing complementary retirement system. [But] the facts do not bear out these assertions." Keep in mind that the Social Security System is not a funded system in the same manner in which private pension plans are required to be by law. Social Security is simply an "exchange" system (intergenerational transfer system) where the active workers pay for the retired workers.

What, then, if opting out of Social Security is not cost-effective? A city should coordinate with Social Security, using it as a base on which the municipal pension benefit is superimposed. The combined benefits should be responsive to a plan's objectives at an affordable cost. True, most municipal pension plans covering police officers and fire fighters do not include Social Security benefits. Nevertheless, most of these uniformed employees have earned, are earning, or will earn Social Security pension and other benefits through prior employment, during possible military service, through current moonlight employment, or in the future through employment to which they will likely be committed upon retiring from their present position. Referring to the aforementioned inflation-caused deterioration of the purchasing power of municipal pension benefits (Social Security pensions do have an unlimited cost of living adjustment), uniformed personnel will not be able to afford to exist on pension benefits alone and will therefore reenter the job market and automatically accrue Social Security benefit credits.

Employee Contributions

Employee contributions, long unpopular in private sector plans, continue to be popular among public employee plans. This persistence is often attributable to the continuation, or introduction, of more liberal pension plan provisions such as the introduction of post-retirement COLA increases, a reduction in the normal retirement age, and provision of early retirement benefits that are not proportionately (i.e., actuarially) reduced to reflect the likely longer payout period.

In many cases, a municipal pension plan conceivably could more effectively serve the needs and interests of both the city and its employees by not requiring employee contributions. This is not necessarily a benevolent measure, private sector employers whose pension plans do not require employee contributions are not ordinarily know for their benevolence. The change is warranted because it reduces administrative expense and avoids current income taxes. For instance, for an employee to contribute one dollar to a pension plan, he or she must be paid more than one dollar for that contribution. Because required employee contributions are paid from net income after taxes, the employer can provide a larger pension benefit value by not having these dollars first pass through the employee's pocketbook.

All of the above notwithstanding, there appears to be an emerging trend to regard employee contributions as the solution to budget squeezes when public jurisdictions realize that they are having difficulty financing the *real* cost of their pension plans. There are three advantages to be obtained:

1. Costs for the sponsoring jurisdiction are dampened.
2. Employee demands for benefit liberalizations are curtailed when it becomes apparent that they must share in the cost.
3. Target replacement income is reduced since the working employee takes home less and therefore needs less in retirement.

Voluntary employee contributions can be an effective compensation tool under certain circumstances. Those made after taxes will allow investment earnings to accrue and be deferred until distribution at a time when the participant will be in a lower tax bracket. The participant is then taxed only on the accrued investment earnings, the principal contributions having previously been made net after taxes were returned tax free. This presumes that the investment performance realized on the fund is higher than that which the participant might realize net after taxes by merely accumulating money through individual savings and investments.

Retirement Age

The normal retirement age, characteristically 65 in private plans, is ordinarily 5 to 10 years earlier in public employee plans and even earlier among public plans covering uniformed personnel (e.g., as low as age 40 or 45 in some instances).

Municipal employees, especially uniformed personnel, often lobby for a younger normal retirement age. The cost of granting such requests is high. It is possible for a pension plan's costs to increase by as much as 40 percent if the normal retirement age is reduced by 5 years (e.g., from age 60 to 55). Early retirement can be impractical for the employee as well, if for no other reason than the incessant erosion of purchasing power attributable to inflation. This is one reason why most police officers and fire fighters enter new careers after "retiring" from public service.

Postponing Retirement

Postponing retirement will become popular because of Public Law 95-256, The Age Discrimination in Employment Act Amendments of 1978, extending the mandatory age to 70 for both public and private sector plans. Demographic studies indicate that the "graying of America" is leading to an advance in the average age with the result that a larger percentage of our population will have to remain gainfully employed in order to support those who have retired or are otherwise dependent.

Early Retirement

Early retirement has its place, especially where employees prematurely experience the physiological infirmities of advancing age over which they cannot exercise direct control. Early retirement for a reason other than this (or for total and permanent disablement), however, is difficult for either the employee or employer to justify. Contrary to popular opinion, a growing number of active employees in both the private and public sector choose not to retire early not ony because they feel not able to afford to, but because they want to be active, needed, and contributing to their personal welfare and that of their family, community, and country. Related to this trend is the emerging appearance of a direct relationship between life expectancy and employment longevity; persons who retire early for reasons other than disability do not seem to live as long as those who remain more active.

Disability Retirement

Disability retirement, notably that occasioned by total and permanent disablement, is a vexing problem, especially among uniformed personnel. Although short-term (e.g., less than 3 or 6 months) disablements are ordinarily attended to by income continuation plans under existing personnel policies and benefit plans, the problems associated with total and permanent disability are more profound. Wherever medical boards partial to such findings are in charge, public employees, especially among the uniformed group, are sometimes inclined to take advantage of flexible administrative procedures by opting for total and permanent disability pensions. Such an award ordinarily not only provides a larger percentage of pay than early retirement benefits but is income-tax free. Although no one would deny any employee the right to receive a substantial and entirely tax-free lifetime pension because of total and permanent disability, one should question, and take steps to correct, the occasional abuses. According to a National Conference of State Legislatures report, *A Legislator's Guide to Public Pensions,* "83% of the District of Columbia's retired police and firemen receive disability pensions. The Chief of Police retired on disability for a knee injury. His nontaxable pension is more than $30,000."

If an employee benefit plan provides preretirement disability benefits through the vehicle of insurance (such long-term disability, or LTD, plans ordinarily provide benefits only to age 65), a city can defer the commencement date of the disability benefit from the pension plan until the aforementioned LTD benefit stops and make the disability pension larger thereafter. Doing so will accomplish two things. First, prenormal retirement age disability income will not be so great as to promote malingering, a risk that is taken when spendable income from disability benefits are significantly greater than direct compensation from gainful employment. Second, the disabled employee will not be faced with an abrupt reduction in income at the age when the LTD insurance benefits cease and the participant is left to cope with the smaller (but earlier paid) pension plan disability benefit together with Social Security, if eligible.

Identifying the most cost-effective manner of providing preretirement total and permanent disability benefits is beyond the scope of this chapter. It can be demonstrated, however, that commercial LTD insurance is not often an economical way of providing this protection because LTD plans characteristically offset the insured benefit with Social Security benefits, workers' compensation benefits, and sometimes even pension plan disability benefits. The result is that lower-paid municipal personnel stand to receive no benefit at all from the LTD coverage because the formula benefit (e.g., 50 or 60 percent of pay) is already provided from the sources used for the offset.

Furthermore, if employees are required to share in the cost of the LTD coverage (a popular procedure, especially when the benefit is initially sold), what can be expected of lower-paid disabled employees when they hear that they are entitled to nothing from that which they have helped to finance?

It is possible to introduce an income replacement program covering both total and partial, and permanent and temporary, disablements under a payroll system for a period of 3 or 6 months, with the benefits that are paid thereafter financed through the pension plan or a self-funded hospitalization and medical benefit program. No less flexibility will be available from such a program than that provided by established, but not necessarily logical and cost-effective, methods, and significant savings may accrue to the city as well.

Vesting

Vesting upon termination of service is characteristically less liberal among public pension plans, but it is moving in the direction of that now required by the Employee Retirement Income Security Act of 1974 for the private sector. ERISA is a Federal law establishing minimum requirements covering all aspects of private pension systems. The objective is to guarantee benefits to members participating in these systems. Among the most conservative (i.e., least generous) vesting formulas allowed by ERISA is no vesting until the attainment of age 40 and the accumulation of 10 years of service, with 100 percent vesting beginning when both of these requirements have been satisfied. Liberal vesting provisions have not been found in public plans principally because of expectations that the public employee would remain at least until he or she was entitled to begin receiving pension benefits —usually at a fairly young age (e.g., 55 for nonuniformed personnel and 50 for uniformed personnel).

V. DETERMINATIONS OF PLAN COSTS

The mystique of how pension plan costs are calculated is not easily displaced, but the fundamentals on which they rest are not difficult to understand and manage. The term "funding method" refers to the actuarial (i.e. mathematical) basis by which pension and related future benefit costs are calculated. The funding method most frequently used in calculating the costs of public sector pension plans are those traditionally used for private sector plans with only a few, if significant, exceptions. Important to each of these methods is how projected costs are expressed as a percentage of the unfolding total covered payroll. As previously identified, most mayors and council members prefer (as do executives and their accountants in the private sector) to have unfolding costs remain relatively constant (or even go down) when expressed as a percentage of total covered payroll and not increase beyond their control and capacity to finance. How then, in the most basic way, are pension plan costs determined?

Actual Costs

Actual costs, as distinct from calculated costs, can be determined only after the fact. The formula is quite simple. Actual costs equal the benefits actually paid out plus expenses actually incurred, less the total net (after investment-related expenses) investment performance actually realized on the accumulated funds before disbursement (Cost = benefits + expenses − investment return). Because the benefits to be paid are determined by formula, the only two, but enormously important, variables over which control can be exerted are expenses and investment performance (i.e., total investment return including interest, dividends, gains, and losses). Unfortunately, because administrative expenses are more easily identified than net investment performance, many mayors and members of council have directed more attention to the former than the latter, notwithstanding the fact that investment performance is much more significant than administrative expense. For example, if the total cost of administration does not exceed 5 percent of the contributions being made to the pension fund (this level of expense would be for a small fund) and the net investment performance can be increased by one quarter of 1 percent (e.g., the 0.25% difference between 8.75% and 9.00%), the entire cost of administration can be offset.

Calculated Costs

Calculated costs, on the other hand, are those for which an actuary is responsible. His calculations are made on the basis of at least the following assumptions (suggested by him but approved by his client, recognizing that the plan sponsor is ultimately responsible for adequately funding every pension plan):

- Investment performance
- Wage and salary increase projections
- Cost-of-living adjustments after retirement
- Social security benefits and offsets
- Average age of employee retirement
- Employee turnover among nonvested participants
- Life expectancy before and after retirement
- Rate and duration of disability
- Administrative expenses

Although it is the responsibility of the actuary to estimate how much of the pension cost is apt to be based on a realistic combination of actuarial assumptions, he has the option—subject to the city's preference—of using "implicit" or "explicit" actuarial assumptions.

Under the "implicit" approach, long popular in the costing of public employee pension plans, actuarial assumptions are to be realistic *in the aggregate,* but individual assumptions may not necessarily be realistic. If the "explicit" approach is used, *each actuarial assumption* is set realistically. Singularly important among these assumptions is that of investment performance. Note that it is ranked first on the preceding list, with administrative expenses ranked last.

It is interesting to note, for example, that if the owner of a 30-year 8-percent coupon bond were to reinvest the coupons at only 4 percent, the rate of return over the 30-year period deteriorates to an average of only 5.8 percent.

Because of ERISA, there is an accelerating trend toward using "explicit" actuarial assumptions in the private sector. All public sector plans exempt from ERISA, however, can continue to use "implicit" actuarial assumptions and run the risk that their actuary's calculated costs are understated, overstated, or right on target because of the cumulative effect of individual assumptions' offsetting each other's inaccuracy.

What kind of problems might be encountered if the actuary's assumptions are not on target? Consider the provision of a plan that calculates pension benefits based on the arithmetic average of the highest consecutive five years' compensation immediately preceding retirement. If a 45-year-old employee, earning $20,000 annual salary, receives a 6-percent per year increase over the 20 years remaining before he retires, $54,037 will be the compensation on which his pension benefit is calculated (see Fig. 7.1). The actuary, in this instance, would presumably be assuming a 6 percent per year "salary scale" in order to anticipate in advance what will be a significantly larger pension benefit and cost compared with what would be determined using the $20,000 salary today. A pension plan that provides benefits based on final average compensation must use a salary and wage scale reflecting what the compensation increases are apt to be, based on the city's payroll practices in its actuarial computations. Erroneously assuming future compensation increases at significantly lower rates than those that are likely to be realized will result in a serious underfunding of the pension program.

The investment performance assumption used in cost calculations should be compared with the history of net investment performance that the fund has realized over the most recent five years. The assumed rate of investment performance should normally not be higher than that actually being realized.

The use of implicit actuarial assumptions can deceptively simplify these projections. The actuary may report that, although the salary projection

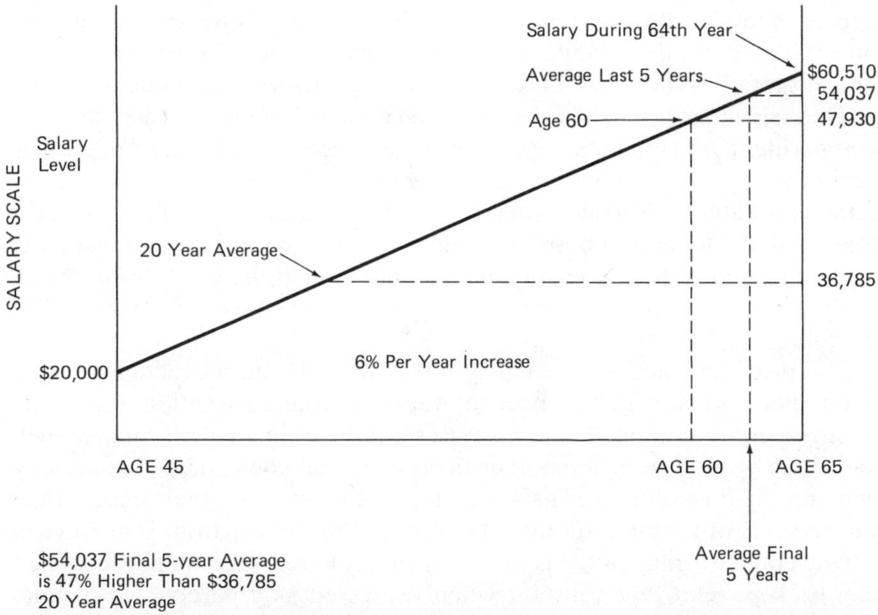

Fig. 7.1. Calculation of pension benefits based on average of highest consecutive five years' compensation preceding retirement.

assumption he has made is lower than that of actual experience, the actual investment performance has been better than that which he has assumed (that is, the understatement of future salary increases may be offset by the understatement of anticipated investment performance). In other words, the "actuarial loss" on understating future compensation increases may be balanced out by the "actuarial gain" reflected by actual investment performance greater than that which has been assumed.

For example, with respect to the preretirement period, if the actuary assumed a 3.0-percent salary and wage increase together with a 4.5-percent total net investment return, but the actual average salary and wage increase was 6.0 percent and the actual total net investment return was 7.5 percent, there will be no problem. Why? Because the difference between the paired assumptions remained at 1.5 percent. The understatement of each of the two assumptions was consistently different, with the result that the understatement of each offset the impact of the other. Similarly, if 7.0 percent was the average compensation increase and 8.5 percent was the actual net rate of investment performance, the consistent 1.5-percent difference would not require an adjustment in calculated costs. On the other hand, if the 7.0-

percent compensation increase was matched with a net investment return of only 6.0 percent, the change in difference from 1.5 to −1.0 percent (or 2.5 percent total) would result in a marked understatement of calculated costs.

Thus care must be taken in selecting and monitoring actuarial assumptions, comparing them with actual experience each time an actuarial valuation is performed (usually annually) to make sure that calculated costs realistically reflect probable true costs. Otherwise it is possible to unknowingly be party to an understatement of costs, leading to deficits that will have to made up. The end result of the understatement would be that the cost of supporting the plan will no longer be the relatively level percentage of total covered payroll.

This problem is not as grave it may appear to be. It must be recognized that actual performance with respect to every actuarial assumption, especially with respect to compensation increases and investment performance, will vary from year to year. To counter these expected aberrations, the actuary will identify these actuarial gains and losses and amortize their impact over future years of funding, thereby dampening their effect from year to year. This averaging arrangement is what helps a city have a pension plan cost that can be kept relatively constant when expressed as a percentage of total covered payroll. If in fact there are consistent and significant differences between what has been assumed and what has occurred, however, then contributions to the plan will have to be gradually increased or decreased as unfolding experience becomes unfavorable or favorable.

VI. SUMMARY OF RECOMMENDATIONS

Instead of focusing on the mechanics of pension funding, which confuse the means of achieving an objective with the objective itself, mayors should consider adopting the following perspective.

Identify Goals and Objectives

Public officals cannot delegate accountability and, therefore, must properly retain policysetting responsibility. A consultant and actuary can help articulate, reevaluate, and restate retirement goals, objectives, and priorities, committing these to paper so they can be examined, discussed, refined, and organized in such a way that they can be acted upon.

Demand Simple English

The tendency to focus on the mechanics of pension funding is a common problem because pension funding is a difficult subject for an actuary to explain clearly, and the public officials responsible for the management of a retirement system may therefore often find themselves uncomfortable when trying to understand what is being proposed. Under these circumstances, the initiative often shifts, almost indiscernibly, from the public officials to the actuary even though the public officials still retain full accountability for the results of any policy adopted. When this occurs, the clear position that all parties concerned wish to have the retirement system "properly funded" is replaced by the less understandable position that the retirement system must be "actuarially sound." Thus, a mere change of wording has excluded practically everyone except actuaries from participating in the establishment of an operating policy to guide the funding of the system. After all, who else can pronounce upon the "actuarial soundness" of any decision but an actuary? Then, whenever two parties disagree on any decision concerning funding, they do not discuss the issue carefully with whatever professional advice is required, but instead each retains an actuary, and it is the *actuaries* who debate the issue, with a high probability that the debate will rapidly focus on mechanics rather than on meeting objectives.

Use Consultants and Actuaries Wisely

The actuary's role is exactly the same as that of a lawyer. He is the best qualified person to offer independent advice in a very technical field, but he cannot set policy for a client. A mayor can augment his growing body of knowledge by attending and participating in specialty conferences sponsored by independent professional and educational organizations that focus upon public employee pension matters. If he cannot attend such meetings, he should read articles and texts on the subject that are written for the nontechnician.

Take Action Now

Procrastination will not solve the problem, reduce its severity, or redress the implications of management decisions not made. As every entrepreneur knows, no business can endure if its disbursements exceed its receipts for very long. Some public employee pension plans will have to be made less generous, at least with respect to employees not yet hired, if they are not to run the real risk of failure. No government can indefinitely assure pension costs that require larger and larger proportions of a city's revenues.

A responsible mayor must reject a short-term policy that promises immediate results for something that will bring dividends over a longer period of time.

8
Mayor's Financial Management Checklist

The purpose of this chapter is to provide mayors with an easy-to-use tool for financial management. The tool consists of a series of financial warning signals that provide a way of spotting a financial problem that already exists or heading off others before they start. Accompanying each signal is an explanation of the condition it indicates and a set of recommended actions. Some or all of the actions should be taken immediately in a crisis or periodically to insure sound financial management on a continuing basis.

This chapter can be reviewed to get a general sense of trouble areas or used as a more systematic guide if you supplement it with specific data for your city using the Mayor's Fact Sheet in Chap. 11.

I. OVERALL REVENUE AND EXPENDITURE POSITION

It is important initially to assess the overall fiscal position of the city. How fiscally strained is it? How heavy is the tax burden? Such inquiries point to factors that are hard to change rapidly but can be slowly changed over time.

Signal/Measure	Recommended Action
A. Heavy reliance on one revenue source, especially property taxes	• Consider alternative revenue sources, especially user charges, fees, sales tax • If state law is restrictive, lobby with other cities to change law • Review nearby cities for possible alternatives • Multiyear revenue projections

DISCUSSION: Proposition 13 of California and related tax and expenditure limits elsewhere sensitized citizens to the property tax. To assess the city's revenue and expenditure position, it is useful to compile basic financial indicators. Specific examples are suggested in the Mayor's Fact Sheet. The first items on the Checklist relate to these fiscal facts.

Signal/Measure	**Recommended Action**
B. Heavy reliance on intergovernmental revenue	• Seek out intergovernmental programs consistent with local policy preferences • Trim those programs with least local support • Propose specific alternatives to citizens when cutbacks are proposed, e.g., continuing service with user charges

DISCUSSION: How dependent is the city on intergovernmental revenues compared to other cities? Do citizens and staff prefer to seek out funds for new programs, or does the mayor prefer to stress sound management of local revenues? Are there any additional grant programs consistent with the mayor's policy perspective that might be applied? Who provides information to the mayor and staff on such programs? Are there other sources that can be used? Has the mayor used the U.S. Conference of Mayors? Which programs are ready to be trimmed? Which justify continuation with local funding? Are these options reviewed as part of the normal budget process?

Signal/Measure	**Recommended Action**
C. High and growing expenditures and debt	• Consider citizen preferences and how expenditure changes accord with them • Consider cutting back expenditures if citizens press for this • See section on cutback management in Chap. 3 • Use newer types of debt instruments if they can reduce borrowing costs • Consider productivity improvement approaches to gain con-

(Continued)

	Recommended Action
	trol of expenditure growth while services expand efficiently or are held level to meet community needs. See section on productivity improvement in Chap. 3

DISCUSSION: About half of U.S. cities have been trimming expenditures in some areas since 1974, often in response to taxpayers' pressure. How does the city's level and rate of growth compare to those of other cities? If there hasn't been a downturn in recent years, can the mayor be convinced that there is strong citizen support for growth? Patterns of debt finance have changed dramatically in recent years (see Chap. 5). Is the national trend toward revenue bonds and away from general obligation bonds being followed? Why or why not? What proportion of the mayor's budget is for interest on debt? Could the city borrow more inexpensively?

Signal/Measure	**Recommended Action**
D. High tax burden	• Publicize how little the city government is responsible for total tax burden • Work with officials in other overlapping governments to develop consistent policy, eliminating duplicated programs, etc. • Stress the quality of services that are provided and ask citizens and firms if it justifies the costs • Compare with that of other communities; check their service levels

DISCUSSION: The municipal contribution is usually far less than half the total tax burden on citizens and firms from state and local taxes. But mayors get much of the blame. The mayor should publicize the low percentage for which the city is responsible and any changes that are being made.

Signal/Measure	**Recommended Action**
E. Deteriorating capital infrastructure	• Assess the condition systematically • Focus on aspects of the problem that the mayor wants to develop • Develop multiyear capital budget to prioritize and evaluate projects

DISCUSSION: Maintaining capital infrastructure became a major issue only in the 1970s; hence, few cities have adequate systems to monitor and plan maintenance of capital facilities. There are many possibilities that the mayor can use for innovations and technical solutions as well as for publicizing them.

Signal/Measure	**Recommended Action**
F. Little contracting	• Try contracting out a few services where there are problems; if nothing else, the mayor can show citizens and city staff that he/she is looking for solutions • Call for bids for contracting out in several other areas. Even if they are not implemented, a baseline can be found for comparison • Impose user charges creatively, as discussed in Chap. 3

DISCUSSION: Many cities are increasingly contracting out for services and activities that can be performed better or cheaper by another government or a private firm, especially for expensive or difficult services. The mayor's staff should review contracting possibilities. A review of user charges can be made to see how fully they cover costs. If full-cost recovery is adopted as a general principle, deviations from it must be justified.

II. MUNICIPAL EMPLOYEES AND SERVICES

Cities vary dramatically in how they use their staffs. Some pay higher salaries for small staffs; other pay lower salaries for larger staffs. The mayor should consider where his or her city should appear in this continuum. Is the city's current position consistent with policy priorities? The types of new employees hired can be changed rapidly. Compensation in some cities has grown higher than in many private jobs. Certain types of staff may be underpaid (e.g., computer programmers), however, and experience high turnover problems.

Signal/Measure	**Recommended Action**
A. High staffing levels	• Document high staffing in areas that are planned for reduction, and prepare selective cutback strategies • Assess problems of hiring freeze, across-board cuts, or transfers compared to alternatives

DISCUSSION: There are options available for reducing staff levels. Some are easier on staff but cause service disruptions (e.g., hiring freezes and across-the-board cuts) whereas others may satisfy service recipients but cause staff dissatisfaction (layoffs in overstaffed departments and contracting out poorly provided services).

Signal/Measure	**Recommended Action**
B. High compensation levels	• Publicize high compensation levels to staff, and develop performance measures that make sure they justify their salaries • If compensation is high for a few but low for others, make selective adjustments

DISCUSSION: The mayor might prefer to pay high salaries to ensure an excellent staff. But the mayor and administrative staff should both be aware of their distinctive benefits; corresponding performance should be expected. Compensation often varies more by position in the private sector than in cities; the city may be underpaying legal secretaries but overpaying basic typists, for example. If civil service or unions constrain the city to pay too much or too little, the mayor should consider contracting out or starting a nonprofit corporation to permit the salary structure desired (as in San Diego for data processing).

Signal/Measure	Recommended Action
C. Low workload and high benefits for employees	• Find out how different types of employees fare • Publicize the dollar value of the benefits, such as on payroll checks or year-end earnings statements.

DISCUSSION: A table of working hours, holidays, sick leave, overtime, health insurance, pensions, and related job characteristics for major classes of municipal employees can be prepared. One mayor has used a large sheet reviewing such information for his and nearby cities to help establish his collective bargaining strategy. There are often major variations across departments. Again, the mayor may or may not want to change these but should at least have them recognized for their full dollar value.

III. HELPFUL BUDGET TOOLS

After the mayor has identified the problem areas and tried various solutions in different departments, feedback is needed to help assess their impact. Monitoring basic service areas with performance measures can be complemented by special studies.

Signal/Measure	Recommended Action
A. Citizens are dissatisfied	• Meet with staff in areas that rank low • Isolate specific problems generating dissatisfaction • Indication of mayoral concern may itself lead service recipients and staff to improved relations • Monitor the service with performance measures and review again in a year or so if it does not improve • Maintain file of complaints and responses to them

DISCUSSION: Citizen surveys may be useful to identify problems but must be structured carefully to be useful. Detailed discussion of the service area with a few service recipients and staff is important to fill in the specifics and shows the mayor's concern. See Chap. 2.

Signal/Measure	Recommended Action
B. How many of the following budget tools do you have: 1. A general budgetary policy 2. Revenue forecasts 3. Expenditure forecasts 4. Line-item budget 5. Program budget 6. Performance indicators 7. Program objectives 8. Integrated presentation of revenues, including debt 9. Measures of service demand 10. Workload measures 11. Efficiency measures 12. Effectiveness measures 13. Several years of data displayed 14. Textual rationale for program and proposed changes 15. Line-item format for personnel and basic services 16. Distinction between categories of employees 17. Audit of performance measures 18. Periodic simplification of the budget document	• Review your budgetary process with another mayor or outsider to assess which of these could be most useful • Identify from discussions with staff what they feel to be gaps in the budgetary process, which these tools or others could fill • Try out some of these tools selectively in a few departments

DISCUSSION: These are the basic items discussed in Chap. 3. Few cities use more than half of them but should consider whether they might be useful.

Signal/Measure	Recommended Action
C. Which strategies are you using to improve productivity and to confront retrenchment or control growth of costs? 1. New revenue sources 2. User charges 3. Visible efforts to improve productivity and fiscal management 4. Privatization 5. Volunteers 6. Contracting out	• Remember that you cannot change everything simultaneously; consider which strategies make special sense in terms of your more general policies • Try a few strategies on an experimental basis that have been little used in the city • Make changes in recognized problem areas

DISCUSSION: These strategies are discussed in Chap. 3 and have been increasingly adopted in cities in recent years.

IV. BUDGET/FUND BALANCE

If a local government's budget is out of balance or its funds show a negative balance, the financial well-being of the government is threatened. In some localities, it is illegal for the government to have an unbalanced budget or to maintain a negative fund balance. At any rate, budget and fund-balance problems are indicative of a failure to maintain sound financial practices in the light of changing internal or external circumstances.

Signal/Measure	Recommended Action
A. Decline in fund balance over the last three years	• Increase taxes or cut expenditures to a point where the multiyear financial forecast shows a surplus of between 0.5 and 1.0 percent • Do not appropriate all surplus on an annual basis

DISCUSSION: Repeated declines in fund balance indicate repeated budget deficits—expenditures exceeding revenues. If this situation is allowed to continue, it may lead the government into a negative balance.

Although a surplus may be used in any given year to supplement revenues, it should never be the financial policy of a government to spend more than it takes in.

Signal/Measure	**Recommended Action**
B. Deficiency of "natural" revenue growth as compared to inflationary impact	• Seek changes in taxing power that shift from property-based taxes to sales or income levies that increase with inflation • Index wage settlements only if this represents a "maximum" • Reassess properties annually to capture inflationary increases • Examine potential of user charges

DISCUSSION: Some forms of revenue do not grow with inflation as a matter of course. On the other hand, a government may expect its spending requirements to expand with the general price level. For example, property taxes will not rise with inflation unless reassessment of property values occurs annually on a city-wide basis—an unusual procedure. Therefore, a major source of local revenues will not keep pace with inflation. If this "decay" in revenue continues, major financial problems may result. Therefore, alternative revenue sources that rise with inflation, such as wage-related taxes, should be examined.

Signal/Measure	**Recommended Action**
C. Presence of unfunded deficit in any fund	• Eliminate deficit with increased taxes or charges and cut back levels of service to bring expenditures into line • Abolish and consolidate the fund, if possible

DISCUSSION: If a particular fund shows a deficit, with no plan to bring it back into balance, the local government is maintaining a financial position that is untenable and unsafe. The government's credit worthiness and financial stability may be called into question. It is necessary that the unfunded deficit be eliminated.

Signal/Measure	Recommended Action
D. Lack of capital budget	• Institute multiyear capital program with first year representing the capital budget • Specify funding sources for all expenditures • Set definitive policy on what can be financed over what period

DISCUSSION: A capital budget provides a planning document for long-range projects. Necessary preparations for capital activity, such as land acquisition and contracting activities, should be foreseen, and plans for debt issuance and other funding laid. Advance planning provides the opportunity for cost savings.

Signal/Measure	Recommended Action
E. Use of capital funds for operating purposes	• Eliminate jobs and equipment with short useful lives from the capital budget • Payback should match useful life • Substitute operating funds • Consider refunding to stretch out debt

DISCUSSION: Capital funds, when supported by debt, are repaid by future debt-service payments. These, in turn, are supported by future taxpayer revenues. To use such funds for operating purposes is unfairly to shift the obligation for services provided now to future taxpayers who will not receive the benefit of the services. When capital funds are being used, it should be assured that the benefits will be enjoyed by future taxpayers. If not, then the present taxpayers should pay for the services, and operating funds should be used.

Signal/Measure	Recommended Action
F. Wide variance between estimated and actual revenue and expenditure estimates	• Revise budget system and revenue forecasting procedure • Build in conservative estimates of revenue and liberal estimates of expenditures

DISCUSSION: Herein lies the basis of all budget and fund balance difficulties, providing a government doesn't *plan* to run deficits. The information used to construct a budget and the method of construction are essential to good financial management

Signal/Measure	Recommended Action
G. Lack of ability to measure performance or productivity	• Revise budget and cost control system • Use performance budgeting that measures output and level of service per unit of input • Institute a productivity measurement and job satisfaction program

DISCUSSION: If services are not being provided in an efficient manner, then additional resources will be required in order to achieve the desired level of services. This problem can only be detected if information is being collected that will provide a measure of productivity or performance. Performance measurement can be instituted as a feature of the budget process, as a feature of labor contracts or negotiations, or as an element of managerial review.

V. CASH FLOW

A key factor in municipal financial management is not only to have *enough* money, but to have the cash when it is needed. A balanced budget may still be unbalanced as to cash requirements if payments come due before revenues are received. Therefore, it is essential that cash flow—the monitoring and planning of cash receipts and disbursements—be given close attention.

Signal/Measure	Recommended Action
A. All revenue received late in the year	• Change dates on tax payments to insure continuous flow • Change fiscal year • Offer incentives for early payment • Negotiate prefunding or funding on the basis of estimates

DISCUSSION: The potential problem being raised here is not simply that revenue is received late, but that it is being received later than when it is needed. Solutions that rely on changing the payment timing or the fiscal year can only be performed once. If payments are accelerated by six months, any attempt to revert back to the old schedule will require the city to operate for 18 months with 12 months' cash. If borrowing costs are not prohibitive, tax anticipation notes may be issued by a city to produce the needed cash prior to the actual revenue collection, without requiring any changes in payment schedule or the fiscal year.

Signal/Measure	Recommended Action
B. No way to predict arrival	• Review arrival schedule from previous years • Establish expected arrival calendar • Set policy on due dates and communicate policy to all taxpayers • Use "cycle" billing with staggered dates to assure more continuous flow • Request state and Federal agencies to supply revenue availability estimates • Centralize billing and collection activity in a single office for all functions • If receipt is not central, notify all personnel that monies must come to some central point immediately upon receipt

DISCUSSION: Many local government revenue collection systems leave the choice of payment date to the taxpayers or other revenue suppliers. This situation can lead to inadequate cash budgeting and may require "emergency" borrowing at a high cost. The elimination of this problem entails reviewing past collection history and using that information to set a policy with regard to desired dates for revenue receipts. Billing activities, as well as other appropriate collection activities, can be adjusted as needed.

Signal/Measure	**Recommended Action**
C. Wide variance from budgeted revenue amounts	• Revise revenue forecasting techniques • Further disaggregate revenue sources • Attempt to establish a committee to discuss nature of shortfalls • Ask state and Federal agencies for exact estimates in writing prior to the preparation of the budget • Revise the budget often to reflect changes in actual and estimated receipts

DISCUSSION: Budget variances reflect either a problem in the estimation process or a problem in execution of the budget plan. The sources and methods for collecting revenue data and making projections should be reviewed to insure accuracy. Where outside estimates are depended upon, these estimates should be documented.

Signal/Measure	**Recommended Action**
D. Shortfalls caused by delinquency	• Review interest and penalty charges • Itemize real estate payments due from individuals, not by property • Begin personalized collection efforts • Arrange installment payment programs • Publish names of major delinquent taxpayers • Revise legal requirements for foreclosure and tax sale • Speed administrative process for foreclosure and tax sale

DISCUSSION: Delinquent taxpayers are essentially borrowing money from the government. These taxpayers rely on two factors: Either the interest and penalty charges on the tax are lower than bank borrowing rates (so that they benefit by not paying) or they believe that their delinquency will never be detected or payment required. In order to lower delinquencies, these factors must be addressed.

Signal/Measure	Recommended Action
E. Slow billing	• Review billing procedures to determine where delays occur • Attempt to bill in advance of services rendered • Establish billing calendar, including target dates • Stagger billing to cut down administrative work load • Centralize responsibility for billing a single office

DISCUSSION: The failure to bill on a timely basis for services rendered requires the government to use its own cash to pay for those services until the revenue is received. If the receipts match the service expenditures on a timely basis, the need for cash by the governmental unit will be eliminated. New billing procedures may have to be instituted to guarantee this result.

Signal/Measure	Recommended Action
F. Slow third-party payment	• Attempt to get payment in advance of services rendered • Bill on the basis of estimates, with adjusted bills submitted following audits • Establish a payment-liaison function that is tied both to collection responsibility and to intergovernmental relations • Charge interest and penalties when payments are late

DISCUSSION: Many grant payments are made on a reimbursement basis. Cash is paid only for cash spent. The more quickly the bills can be submitted by the government, or the more willing the third party is to accept estimates (and they will be willing only if the local government can show consistent and reliable estimates), the better position the locality will be in to collect the money sooner.

Signal/Measure	Recommended Action
G. Heavy early-year or prior-year commitments	• Change fiscal year • Consider refunding debt • Stagger debt service dates when issuing new bonds • Halt acceptance of requests to encumber funds at a particular date or for a particular period • Review contract requirements to stagger payment dates • Postpone delivery dates • Attempt to change date for commitment of pension contributions

DISCUSSION: This signal represents the expenditure side of Signal V. A, where cash payments are required before revenues are available to meet them. In order to address this situation, the local government can seek to halt or delay payments. In some cases, this step requires careful negotiation. The implications of the action should be understood clearly before payments are delayed.

Signal/Measure	Recommended Action
H. Erractic pattern of judgments or other unplanned-for expenditures	• Review planning system to get better information • Require monthly reports on status of legal cases • Prefund a certain portion of expense either with long-term debt or from operating revenue

DISCUSSION: Any expender of funds, governmental unit or not, will be forced at times to meet unplanned expenses. By their very nature, the specific timing, nature, and amount of these items cannot be anticipated. However, the fact that such items do occur can in effect be planned for by receiving better information about what might happen and putting money aside in anticipation of such events. In other words, any budget should contain a reasonable amount to be reserved for contingencies.

Signal/Measure	Recommended Action
I. Wide variances from budgeted expenditure amounts	• Revise budget process; insist on more detail

Signal/Measure	Recommended Action
	• Use allotment or allocation system • Trace flow of expenditure procedures and seek to eliminate bottlenecks

DISCUSSION: This signal corresponds to the similar revenue-related Signal V. C. Again, the problem usually can be traced to either budget planning or budget execution. Thus, expenditure information used in budget planning, and the steps that allow an expenditure to be made, should be reviewed and analyzed to guarantee a greater degree of accuracy and compliance.

Signal/Measure	Recommended Action
J. Lack of cash consolidation indicated by an excessive number of funds or an excessive number of accounts	• Eliminate all but a few operating funds and one capital fund • Use as few bank accounts as possible • Establish a single "Cash Concentration Account" • Instruct depositories to transfer all cash to concentration account

DISCUSSION: Every so often, a story appears in a newspaper about a city that had maintained in a bank somewhere a checking account with a balance of one hundred thousand dollars for years, without being aware it even had the money! This problem can occur when each department or fund handles its own cash in its own bank account. *Cash can get lost.* If cash accounts are consolidated, a cash deficit in one fund can be made up by a cash surplus in another fund, eliminating the need for borrowing. Moreover, financial officers will know where all of the government's money is.

Signal/Measure	Recommended Action
K. Investment of less than 95 percent of cash holdings	• Analyze recent 30-day period to determine actual cash in the bank • Divide amount invested by cash; ratio should be at least 95 percent

(Continued)

Signal/Measure	Recommended Action
	• Establish "Automatic Investment" or zero-balance specifications • Negotiate or bid banking services contract

DISCUSSION: If a local government has excess cash on hand, it should be earning interest through investments. Analysis of cash balances should be undertaken to determine the government's cash position, and investments should be undertaken that will return interest and free the cash for expenditure purposes as needed.

Signal/Measure	Recommended Action
L. Earnings per available dollar less than Treasury bill rate	• Revise investment policy • Analyze bank statements or use of funds • Seek longer or short term investments • Seek changes in legal structure to allow expanded investment capability

DISCUSSION: Once the cash is invested, it should be invested to maximize the return to the government. New investment vehicles continue to be developed (see Chap. 5).

VI. CONTROL

The road to financial problems is paved with good intentions when control is not exerted over the operations of a government.

Signal/Measure	Recommended Action
A. Modified accrual basis of accounting not being used	• Adopt modified accrual • Bring accounting system into conformance with GAAFR

DISCUSSION: The modified accrual basis of accounting is best suited to measure the financial operation of government. (See Chap. 2.)

Signal/Measure	Recommended Action
B. Inability to get operating results quickly	• Revise management information system • Integrate budget and accounting systems • Use on-line systems wherever appropriate

DISCUSSION: A system that collects any or every needed piece of information is useless if the managers that need that information don't receive it on a timely basis. It is necessary that attention be given to the process by which information is transmitted and the interactions between systems and departments in order to ensure that managers will receive useful information on a timely basis.

Signal/Measure	Recommended Action
C. Overly complicated or inaccurate reports	• Simplify reporting process • Institute "pyramid" reports • Establish criteria for reports to top management

DISCUSSION: Financial information may be collected *and* transmitted, but it can still be useless if the form of the reports is unnecessarily complicated or confusing. Ideally, each person who receives financial reports should receive just that level of detail that he or she requires to fulfill his or her duties. Thus, persons with more general responsibilities for oversight should receive summary reports, and persons dealing at lower levels should receive the detailed information. This is a "pyramid" reporting process. A local government confronted by this danger signal should reevaluate the information needs and corresponding reporting structure of its personnel.

Signal/Measure	Recommended Action
D. Lack of GFOA Conformance Certificate	• Review steps in getting certificate • Consider annual outside audit

DISCUSSION: The GFOA Certificate, discussed in Chap. 6, evidences a local government unit's excellence in financial accounting and reporting. Lack of the certificate is not necessarily indicative of pending financial disaster, but a financial reporting system that is awarded the certificate can be confident of its accuracy and acceptance.

Signal/Measure	Recommended Action
E. No enterprise accounting system	• Review GAAP • Install system

DISCUSSION: Certain governmental activities are managed in a nearly identical way to private sector endeavors. For instance, a municipal water system bills its customers, accounts for expenses (such as depreciation), and is not dependent on other governmental revenues to meet expenses. Such operations should be accounted for under a method similar to commercial accounting, unlike governmental accounting. An enterprise accounting system is more naturally suited to provide the financial information required to manage a governmental enterprise activity.

VII. DELINQUENCY

Delinquency in the collection of revenues impinges directly on cash flow. (See Section V.) Such problems are indicative of flaws in the legal basis for the collection activity (such as interest and penalty rates, mandated collection procedures, etc.) or in the organizational aspect of collections.

Signal/Measure	Recommended Action
A. Property tax collection rate of less than 90 percent within the year of levy or less than 95 percent within two years	• (See Signal V. D)

DISCUSSION: It is to be expected that some portion of property taxes will be uncollectible. When the uncollectibles approach 10 percent over the first collection year, however, and 5 percent over a two-year period, indications of a breakdown in the collection activity exist.

Signal/Measure	Recommended Action
B. Cumulative delinquencies exceeding 5 percent of current roll	• (See Signal V. D)

DISCUSSION: This situation, too, indicates that insufficient impetus exists to motivate taxpayers to pay taxes. It may be a result of low penalties and interest charges or inefficient collection procedures.

Signal/Measure	Recommended Action
C. Lack of adequate interest and penalty provisions	• (See Signal V. D)

DISCUSSION: "Adequate" interest and penalty provisions can be pinpointed either by the mere fact of high delinquency or by comparison to the general level of interest rates. If the interest and penalty provisions together result in a charge to taxpayers lower than that of commercial lending rates, taxpayers who require cash will prefer not to pay taxes and incur the penalties for delinquency rather than borrowing.

Signal/Measure	Recommended Action
D. No control of third-party payers, especially intergovernmental payers	• (See Signal V. D)

DISCUSSION: A government may find itself waiting a long time for money promised by state or Federal governments or other third-party payers. The surest way to address this difficulty is to request firm commitments as to when this revenue will be received. The commitment may be for a date later than desired, but it will provide a basis for planning and action.

VIII. DEBT

Debt, both short-term and long-term, plays a distinctive role in governmental financing. Short-term debt may provide a means of easing cash flow and revenue timing problems; long-term debt allows a government to extend the financial burden of long-term prospects into the future and onto taxpayers who will benefit from the projects. (For further discussion of debt, see Chap. 4.) The abuse or overuse of debt can lead to financial difficulties, however, if not disaster.

Signal/Measure	Recommended Action
A. Funding prior year's deficits with short-term debt	• Do not allow any obligations for cash flow financing to have maturities beyond one year • Eliminate cause of deficits

DISCUSSION: A government cannot hide its budget problems by issuing debt to make up deficits. This process simply hurts the governmental unit and the taxpayers in the long run by incurring interest charges and by postponing the inevitable need to trace and eliminate the source of deficits.

Signal/Measure	Recommended Action
B. Excessive use of BANs that cannot be rolled over or may have to be funded in a higher interest rate market	• Initiate long-term debt program to fund debt quickly • Eliminate BANs for cash flow purposes

DISCUSSION: A BAN (Bond Anticipation Note) is issued so that the governmental unit may have the cash needed to get a capital project started prior to the issuance of long-term debt. The BAN is usually repaid by either issue of more BANs or with funds available from the eventual long-term debt issuance. In periods of rising interest rates or tight market conditions, however, a government will face higher costs and, perhaps, inability to roll over the debt as time passes. These potential difficulties can be detected only by keeping a close watch on the market. Once sighted, however, the steps indicated above should be taken to limit the cost of difficulties to the government.

Signal/Measure	Recommended Action
C. Note rating less than MIG-2	• Review note rating and criteria • Discuss note rating with Moody's

DISCUSSION: Rating agencies will rate government debt as to credit worthiness. These ratings will have an effect on the interest rate the issuer must pay to attract investors. Thus, when a rating is low, the rating agencies have identified certain financial factors that cause doubt about the government's ability to repay the debt. The source of this doubt should be identified by taking the above steps and corrective action should then be taken.

Signal/Measure	Recommended Action
D. Payment across more than one fiscal year	• Set all maturities less than 12 months • Do not roll over RANs or TANs

DISCUSSION: Payment across more than one fiscal year unfairly shifts the financial burden to taxpayers who have not benefited from the original debt issuance. This activity threatens the financial safety of the governmental unit as the next year's budget is effectively cut by requiring payments for the year's expenditures. Therefore, all efforts should be taken to assure that the use and payment of short-term debt is limited to the current fiscal year.

Signal/Measure	**Recommended Action**
E. Dramatic per-capita increases caused either by stable debt and declining population or debt increasing even faster than population	• Measure trends in per capita debt • Analyze cause of increases • Relate to future capital programming needs

DISCUSSION: The amount of debt that a government can presently expect to be able to carry and repay is related to that government's capacity to collect revenues for the purpose of repayment. The greater the population of a community, the greater the potential that exists for revenue. As debt increases, or population declines, the amount of debt each taxpayer supports with his taxes increases. A trend of increasing debt or decreasing population may threaten future repayment.

Signal/Measure	**Recommended Action**
F. Moody's rating of less than Baa-1 or Standard & Poor's rating of less than A-	• Review rating reports and criteria • Discuss rating with rating agencies

DISCUSSION: As with short-term debt, the credit rating for long-term debt will affect interest costs. Therefore, as discussed above, the root causes of low credit ratings should be identified and addressed.

Signal/Measure	**Recommended Action**
G. Issuance to fund equipment purchases without matching useful life to maturities	• Establish debt policies • Do not fund equipment with less than five-year life by means of debt

DISCUSSION: One potential use of long-term debt is to finance the acquisition of equipment with extended useful lives. The equipment will provide service for a certain expected number of years. Taxpayers who will receive the benefit of that service should be expected to carry the burden of repaying the debt. Thus, the debt issued should have maturities corresponding to the life of the equipment. Equipment with a short life should not be funded by long-term debt.

Signal/Measure	**Recommended Action**
H. Wide variance in market acceptance between one city's debt and that of similarly rated jurisdiction	• Analyze results of bonds as compared to *The Bond Buyer Index* • Analyze results of bond sales as compared to other similarly rated jurisdictions

DISCUSSION: All other factors being equal, one can expect that debt issued by two jurisdictions of similar credit ratings will attract similar interest in the market. This assumption should be verified by comparing market acceptance (ease of placement and interest rates) with that of similarly rated jurisdictions. If the assumption is not realized, then further analysis should be undertaken to determine the reasons therefor.

Signal/Measure	**Recommended Action**
I. Need to issue large amounts in a short period of time	• Set up debt issuance calendar • Check issuance plans of neighboring cities or states

DISCUSSION: Sudden, large issuances of debt are looked upon by the market with some trepidation. Slow, steady borrowing of smaller amounts seem to indicate careful and complete planning of projects and debt issuance, inspiring investor confidence. A debt issuance calendar, designed to correspond to capital projects and other long-term needs, should be set up and adhered to.

Signal/Measure	**Recommended Action**
J. Growing burden of debt service as a percentage of total budget	• Analyze trends of debt service as a percentage of total general fund budget • Analyze trends of debt service as a percentage of revenues from own sources • Slow pace of capital spending and debt issuance if ratios are too high

DISCUSSION: If debt service becomes too large a portion of the total governmental budget, insufficient funds may exist to provide for operating services. Such a trend may indicate that the government is now paying the price for earlier year's overuse of debt to finance operating activities if clear danger to the government's budget or financial well-being is evident, steps should be taken to limit the use of long-term debt in the present and future, and additional revenues may be required until the situation stabilizes.

IX. PENSIONS

As indicated in Chap. 7, pensions, pension contributions, and all corresponding functions and responsibilities are a growing part of current government financial management. As much attention should be given to financial management for these responsibilities for the other "mainstream" financial activities.

Signal/Measure	Recommended Action
A. Lack of actuarial study within the last three years	• Retain actuary • Set policies • Undertake study

DISCUSSION: An actuarial study provides a government with information about its present and expected future pension obligations. The study will indicate, given certain levels of staffing and pension benefits, how much can be expected to be paid to pension recipients. With this information, management can plan for future obligations by setting aside money at the present. In this way, the embarrassment and hardship resulting from future pension obligations not being met can be avoided.

Signal/Measure	Recommended Action
B. Existence of an accrued unfunded liability of more than 50 percent of total liability	• Establish plan to amortize accrued liability • Fund increased contribution

DISCUSSION: An unfunded liability is a future pension obligation for which no money has been put aside. Most pensions, because of previous years' neglect of the importance of sound pension planning, have some unfunded pension liability. Sound financial management requires that the unfunded liability be addressed, however, and provision must be made to put additional funds aside until the unfunded liability has been met.

Signal/Measure	Recommended Action
C. Failure to pay current normal costs of future benefits	• Pay normal costs • Reduce or stabilize benefits

DISCUSSION: A governmental employee is compensated for his services not only by salary, but also by additional benefits such as a pension. Compensation for current services in the form of payments put aside today that will be paid to employees in the future is the current normal cost of a pension. The current normal cost should be met on a current basis; the taxpayers benefiting from the employees' service should pay *all* of the compensation now. Failure to do so is to create an unfunded liability and to obligate future taxpayers to pay for current services, endangering the government's future financial position.

Signal/Measure	**Recommended Action**
D. Investment yielding less than actuarial rate	• Revise investment policy • Consider swaps

DISCUSSION: In determining how much money needs to be put aside today to meet future pension payments, the actuarial study assumes that currently invested money will earn a certain return. If that return isn't achieved, insufficient funds will exist when the time comes to pay out the pension liability. Thus, if investments are falling behind the target, alternative investments and investment strategies should be considered.

Signal/Measure	**Recommended Action**
E. Poor investment performance relative to appropriate indices	• Revise investment policy • Get new investment advisors

DISCUSSION: The problem of investments not performing as well as market indicators would seem to indicate they should be (even if the return is greater than the actuarial rate) is similar to the preceding problem. The only way the actuarial rate can be met is for investments to perform as well as the market as a whole during strong investment periods so as to offset the inevitable poor market periods. Failure to do so may threaten the future ability of the government to meet its pension obligations.

Signal/Measure	**Recommended Action**
F. Failure to amortize accrued unfunded liability	• Set plan to amortize accrued liability • Fund increased contribution

DISCUSSION: As discussed in Signal IX. B, the existence of an accrued unfunded liability must be addressed immediately. Failure to put aside the added amounts needed is certain to bring about future financial problems.

Signal/Measure	Recommended Action
G. Failure to recognize cost of pension benefits when engaging in collective bargaining	• Develop mechanism for costing pension benefits • Cost all benefits before negotiation

DISCUSSION: Because pensions aren't paid until some time in the future, it is a temptation to offer compensation to employees in the form of pensions rather than direct salaries. However, great care should be taken when addressing the situation. Prudent pension management requires that funds be set aside for every fiscal period in preparation for the future. At some point, it is all too conceivable that the required pension contributions could exceed any additional expenditure that salary increases might have caused. Therefore, the present cost of a future pension benefit should be identified *before* bargaining commences so as to equitably compare the cost of present versus future benefits.

9
System Swap Highlights: Learning from Other Cities

This *Handbook* has concentrated on identifying financial management problems and discussing conceptual approaches to dealing with them. Although a few specific examples of systems that have been implemented in various cities have been described, the emphasis on concepts and techniques has made general discussions more appropriate. In this chapter, however, successful systems that have been installed in cities of all sizes across the country will be described, with the objectives of stimulating thinking about related innovations in other cities and identifying potential sources of information, technical assistance, and system transfers.

I. FORECASTING

In the past, cities have recognized the importance of accurate projections and new revenue sources in relation to estimated future economic conditions. This section examines four cities of varied sizes and their approaches toward multiyear revenue and expenditure forecasting practices.

Oak Brook, Illinois (population 5,280) is a small village whose Board of Trustees sets goals and objectives on a broad range incorporating four basic planning tools: (1) comprehensive physical development, (2) long-range work program, (3) capital improvement program, and (4) long-term fiscal policy. Within the parameters set forth in the comprehensive plan, each department decides on its specific objectives in relation to future manpower, equipment, and material needs as well as estimation of capital expenditures, revenue sources, and types of financing available. At the outset, the Trustees revised this comprehensive program every ten years. It has since been revised every five years, and today is updated every two years. This long-range financial plan not only provides insight into how the village's fiscal condition can be expected to change in the future (such as whether the budget will withstand the hiring of new personnel) but also prevents any overlap of responsibilities or the duplication of services by different departments.

South Lake Tahoe, California (population 13,000) depends heavily on the tourist industry. One one-day minieconomic conference has been instituted per year to develop the best financial forecasts possible for local, regional, and national trends over a 12- to 15-month period. These conferences consist of city officials working with area employers and leaders of the banking community, the latter providing financial information developed by their own forecasting staffs with regard to regional and national trends. This consultation enables the city to use the expertise of the private sector to supplement its own and helps it anticipate changes in employment and mortgage rates as well as generate community support for city goals and objectives.

Vancouver, Washington (population 42,834) recently instituted a five-year forecast of revenues and expenses, which is updated annually. A separate committee was established to determine the procedures and methodology to be used. The forecasts are derived from historical trends of revenues and expenses, assuming no clear evidence to the contrary. As a result, past data have to undergo careful scrutiny, and adjustments are then made to insure compatibility with present figures, that is, allowances for organizational changes, rate changes, new revenue sources, deletion of old ones, etc. The statistical method was found to be more accurate than other methods as it accounted for factors such as inflation that rise at an accelerated rate. A percentage was established to depict the change between the present year and five years thereafter as obtained from the logarithmic curve of the corresponding historical data. If the calculations appear unreasonable (too high or too low), the curves are adjusted accordingly by city staff judgment. Vancouver has found this forecasting methodology to be helpful in establishing the parameters for developing the city budget.

New Orleans has (564,561) developed a computer program incorporating econometrics that enables people other than economists and statisticians to calculate revenue and expenditure projections. This forecasting is done annually for six-year budget-projection periods. All present value costs are inflated for possible wage increases as well as projected increases in the appropriate nonlabor components of the Consumer Price Index. The use of a computer program permits the testing of a wide variety of assumptions and variables under the guidance of expert judgment. The model parameters involve the interrelationship between explanatory variables (income, population, and price) and revenue equations.

Instructions for the model aggregate the revenue sources into large categories of 1 percent or more of the total budget. Estimates are then composed for these categories relative to income, price, and population. These new values are then related to other values of personal property and real estate and also to income, population, and price. Finally, personal income of the city is projected as a function of U.S. personal income. In using this econometric approach, one must have a clear understanding of the local economy as related to regional and national trends.

II. EVALUATING FINANCIAL CONDITIONS

Different methods have been created to help cities review their current financial condition. Dallas, Texas (population 943,848) evaluates itself by establishing financial performance criteria that are applied directly to current fiscal management. The city has defined 23 criteria that fall within three main categories of (1) operating programs, (2) capital and debt management, and (3) accounting, auditing, and financial planning. Financial management policy evolves as a result of analysis based on these criteria. Guidelines were established that promote the city's goals of preserving its financial stability and protecting its favorable bond rating. In addition, the criteria have become a source of information promoting common understanding of the city's financial policies.

In a different vein, Greensville County, Virginia (population 10,903) created a fiscal study whose ingredients were a combination of historical and current data resulting in short-term fiscal projections. These projections were then related to trends in revenues, expenditures, fund balance, and debt. The city determined four variables: (1) available revenue source, (2) percent of total revenues from local sources, (3) information on revenues originating from local, state, and Federal government, and (4) current trends in the tax base. In conjunction with these variables, a cost analysis was run on such things as schools, county administration, social services, and public safety during the preceding seven years and for the next three years. An analysis of the fund balance as a percentage of revenue was completed along with a review of capital outlays, debt obligations, and debt service requirements. The study, in effect, identified a number of financial issues while providing pertinent supporting data.

Lakewood, Colorado (population 118,498) instituted a financial policy model that identified the different facets of the city's financial planning process. It has five components, ranging from broad policy to specific day-to-day requirements. First, the financial policy statements establish city policies for short-term decisions with regard to growth management, service levels, and revenue sources. Then, long-range decisions are derived from these policy statements, such as the five-year capital improvement plan. The city also uses the fiscal impact analysis for development planning. After establishment of these long-range decisions, short-term decisions are formulated.

The mayor and council develop their goal-setting process, program performance budgeting, and the annual capital improvement budget. From these, the day-to-day responsibilities are derived for smooth implementation of city directives. Last, the system is assessed annually through citizen input, review of the current financial picture, and selected program evaluation. The city actually works with short-term decisions, implementation (day-to-day), and assessment on a regular basis. Financial policy statements and long-range decisions are activated as needed. The purpose of this combination of components is to provide the necessary mechanism to deal with both immediate and long-range developments.

Northfield, Illinois (population 5,300) established a financial committee of five "nonpublic employees" who met six times to review the town's present and past revenue history as well as assess revenue forecasts through 1983. Inflation as well as other factors was accounted for in determining the current status of town services. The committee decided that three factors limited an accurate determination of revenues and expenses. Since various levying procedures were affected by political factors, a two-year time lag was essential for establishing actual tax revenues. Second, state law for villages such as Northfield imposed cumbersome statutory constraints on creating new revenue sources. And last, legislation of the county, state, and Federal governments required extra time to handle the "red tape." The village committee thus anticipated future reductions in revenues, developed qualifications for new Federally mandated programs, and assessed new projects for village improvement.

III. FISCAL POLICY ANALYSIS

In analyzing their fiscal policy, different cities make use of different methods to establish control over their financial situation, present and future.

Dayton, Ohio (population 188,499) initiated a computer system to analyze cost factors and relate them to fluctuations in wages and fringe benefits during labor negotiations to anticipate the effects of labor settlements reached on short notice. The system thus alleviates the problem of manipulating enormous amounts of data for its calculations of these effects and has greatly improved financial decision-making capabilities.

Fairfax County, Virginia (population 596,901) developed a model to reflect the budgetary changes that will be required because of new developments. A small desk top minicomputer is programmed to focus on current revenues and expense items as these will be affected by anticipated factors. Present cost and revenue yield factors (updated annually) are multiplied by an average cost factor, revealing the estimated service increase that can be attributed to a new development. The county feels that this model puts the fiscal policy into a realistic perspective, monitoring the validity of each financial consideration.

Fairfield, California (population 58,099) created a sophisticated computer model to evaluate the budgetary impact of new developments. This cost/revenue impact system portrays the fiscal effect of community growth and land development for each city department on a ten-year projection basis. It uses three types of input: (1) data base (values of variables), (2) parameters (cost/revenue factors), and (3) development schedules (requirements of proposed developments). The end result provides a valid analysis of the fiscal effects of new developments on revenue sources, expenditures, adequacy of services, and other budgetary factors.

Holden, Massachusetts (population 14,000), on the other hand, uses a manual model to analyze the fiscal impact of proposed developments. A much less expensive method, this uses historical local data to determine a demographic multiplier. The four steps in the process involve the average number of persons per residential unit; calculation of per capita average costs from residential developments (adjusted for inflation); estimate of the cost impact of the proposed development; and finally, a projection of local and intergovernmental revenues. Although a manual technique, Holden has saved money by using it and gets reasonable estimates of how a proposed development will affect various aspects of town finances.

San Juan Capistrano, California (population 18,000) has integrated a fiscal impact analysis model into its computer system, utilizing three types of input: land use characteristics, revenue data, and cost information. Not only are annual revenue, cost summaries, and revenue-to-cost ratios calculated, but also the impact of different financing options. The city has found this model applicable for long- and short-term analysis of Proposition 13, revenue and cost forecasts in the city's five-year budget planning process, and the effect of a 114-acre industrial park and its long-range implications on the city budget, among others. The computer model has proved flexible for simple revisions or updating, as witnessed by the number of other cities that have adapted the program to accommodate their needs.

Using a different approach, Tyler, Texas (population 70,508) initiated a "fiscal note" policy for new activities, establishing cost estimates for the first five years of operations, including proposed sources of funding (taxes, etc.). The city manager is notified by each department when capital improvement projects are proposed by the preparation of a fiscal note. The fiscal note itself is divided into two separate parts: narrative and financial. The narrative section describes the proposal, its goals and objectives, and its relation to any existing programs. The fiscal part deals specifically with numbers: cost estimates of salaries, supplies, maintenance, capital outlay, etc., for the following five years. This method has been decidedly instrumental in furthering long-term policy development. As in the case of Holden, Massachusetts, the cost of implementation of this "fiscal note" concept has been nominal.

IV. BOND SALE/CAPITAL IMPROVEMENT PLANNING

Automating Bond Sales

New Brunswick, New Jersey (population 41,442) has applied the automatic method of processing common checks to bond coupons. The bearer of the coupon simply deposits the coupon as he would a check through the regular check clearing system at his bank. The coupon utilizes Magnetic Ink Character Recognition (the printed numbers on all regular checks) for identification, processing, and reconciliation of the appropriate account. This system greatly reduces paperwork, has an improved audit trail, and requires no manual inspection. Furthermore, almost every bank in the country already has the capability to process these coupons.

Capital Improvement Planning

Fairfax County, Virginia (population 596,901) integrates legal, financial, and management considerations under a five-year capital improvement program. After defining proposed developments, the city analyzes them with regard to the effect of demographics on the overall comprehensive plan. Three concerns of the plan are depicted. Policy guidelines are established, and an assessment of the impact on the budget and taxpayer is completed. Second, specific details of the proposed development are examined. And finally, appropriate regulatory standards are created for the facility. In short, this program has enabled Fairfax County to develop, within comprehensive plan specifications, capital improvement projects that are realistic both in the financial aspect as well as time constraints.

Portsmouth, Virginia (population 105,807) arranges its capital improvement projects in order of priority through an automated computer process. Department heads submit three forms consisting of (1) a request sheet (describing and justifying cost-related data in general, source of revenue, scheduling, and location), (2) a supplemental cost data sheet (identifying all specific costs), and, (3) a priority rating sheet (establishing the urgency of the project, its conformance to the comprehensive plan, its benefits to the city, and a personal judgment of its overall value). As a result of this computer process, numerous clerical tasks have been eliminated, and the status of projects can be tracked at any time.

Every February, department officials in Wauwatosa, Wisconsin (population 51,308) submit ideas to the city administrator for five-year capital improvement projects with regard to their urgency, capital costs, and operating costs. A financing plan is then created to determine their fiscal feasibility. After establishing the monies available, the projects are evaluated and ranked according to priority. This final evaluative step is analyzed by the citizens' advisory committee, which makes the final decision whether a project is acceptable in terms of city desires and financial capabilities. At the end of the year, the capital improvement program is reviewed and the process repeated. It should be noted that the citizens' committee is comprised of nongovernmental employees representing both city council members and private citizens, thus providing for a variety of perspectives.

Wichita Falls, Texas (population 94,201) established in 1973 what is termed a General Plan to allow new expenditure proposals to be scrutinized by officials and planners each year. Every January an addendum is published that compares the actual population to the projected population of the General Plan and then relates this information to the overall development goals of the city. This survey establishes a "list of needs," in which ongoing capital improvements are updated and new marginal proposals deleted, thereby creating a revised "addendum" for the ensuing year.

V. BUDGETING

Many budgeting systems have been developed, most of them falling into three broad categories: (1) automated systems, (2) program and performance systems, and (3) zero-based systems. Some, however, involve unique concepts and do not fit neatly into any general classification.

Automation in Budgeting

An important element in preparing a budget is to provide accurate, accessible information that will help officials make responsible management decisions. Because of the growth of computer technology, the size of a city is no longer a consideration as to whether it can afford to automate various functions. Wethersfield, Connecticut (population 27,000) purchased its own minicomputer after ten years of participating in a cooperative (shared) system. City officials made their decision based on recommendations that a minicomputer would increase flexibility in reporting procedures and decrease the lag time experienced with the cooperative municipal information center.

Many advantages were realized by the city. Since its software package makes use of the English language, the computer can be used by departmental clerks and other personnel who have the most complete knowledge about overall department operations however limited their computer training. The computer also alleviates administrative and program planning efforts by handling the entire budget process from beginning to end. Changes, updates, and revisions are easily made. The budget can be sorted and printed both in total and by department and the final product published for evaluation by the council and townspeople.

The City of Burbank, California (population 84,625) has implemented an automated budget and accounting information system featuring on-line updating and inquiry capabilities. Rather than develop an entirely new system, Burbank decided to adapt an already operational system. At a cost of $150,000 the city modified a software package from a vendor to meet its specific needs. This system, which takes 21 people to maintain and operate, includes budget and appropriations accounting modules to facilitate budget preparation. Other financial management activities are also automated, including encumbrances, purchase order processing, payroll, budgeting, forecasting, and the like.

An important feature of Burbank's system is its ability to integrate and interface with other city systems. The Public Service Department, for example, can direct on-line inquiries regarding utility billings to both billing and accounting files as well as perform on-line maintenance on these files. The system also provides interactive data-processing capabilities, offers up-to-the-minute information on some 5,400 accounts, eliminates duplicaton of efforts by departments, and allows city officials to obtain immediate responses in specifically structured reports.

Since 1977 Portsmouth, Virginia (population 105,807) has operated a computerized on-line budget system as part of the city's overall financial reporting system. Portsmouth uses two types of budgets in preparing its annual budget: a program budget and an automated budget-by-line item. The budget preparation begins with a print-out of detailed information in which the prior year's expenditures, extracted from the system's data base, are compared to a proposed budget for the coming year. On-line programs are then used by the finance staff to add, change, or delete data in the budget request. Once the budget has been adopted, a monthly financial report is produced that records expenditures and encumbrances as they occur.

City officials feel that the system is an immense aid in preparing the budget, not only significantly decreasing the time required for it but increasing staff productivity as well.

City officials in Garden Grove, California (population 126,340) also feel that their computerized on-line system has significantly reduced budget preparation time and effort. Because of the direct connection of all city departments to the minicomputer via 26 CRT terminals, instant inquiry, easy access to budget and financial information, and better management control are advantages that can be realized throughout the year. The system's simplification of the budget process is evidenced by the fact that it now takes the city about three weeks to do the entire job, whereas it previously took an estimated two months just to complete the various forms.

Anaheim, California (population 226,467) developed its Municipal Automated Finance Information System (MAFIS) in order to modernize its complex and antiquated batch-mode financial systems, convert to a program budget format, and be provided with appropriate cost accounting techniques. The MAFIS system, which features various on-line subsystems—e.g., general ledger, equipment rental, budget, personnel/payroll, etc.—has provided the City of Anaheim with accurate, immediate budgetary and accounting information. Sound budgetary decisions are aided by its cost-accounting information, and program managers have all the up-to-date data they need to monitor and supervise operations in an efficient manner. The city has made MAFIS available to 14 smaller cities that are members of the Municipal Data System joint powers authority.

Fort Lauderdale, Florida (population 153,755) has developed a computerized system to control expenditures in accordance with its budget. The system, called the Fort Lauderdale Overexpenditure Warning System (FLOWS), produces written warning statements whenever a city department is in danger of overexpending any one object area, e.g., salaries, supplies, or utilities. FLOWS operates in response to a table of percentages stored in the computer by object code. Each city department has its own object codes and set of percentages based on past performance. When the computer, which monitors all departments on a daily basis, has determined that a department is in danger of overexpending an object code, it will generate a memo from the director of finance.

The numerous benefits of implementing this system include continuous monitoring of available funds, sufficient safeguards to eliminate all but a few manual determinations, keeping formal budget transfers to a minimum, highlighting department problem-spending areas, and easy adaptability by any governmental unit with a computerized system.

Performance Budgeting

Because of the dollar squeeze, measurement of the effectiveness of each program or activity a city provides becomes significant. Five cities that are striving for justification of expenditures through performance budgeting are

Carbondale, Illinois (population 26,287); Rockville, Maryland (population 43,811); Downers Grove, Illinois (population 42,572); Plainfield, New Jersey (population 45,555); and Palo Alto, California (population 55,225). Since the measures taken, and the advantages realized, by these cities are similar, they will be discussed as a group.

Carbondale's approach is based on measuring unit costs for each departmental program to provide an analysis of its past and projected productivity as well as its overall goals, including its general purpose.

Rockville's "Budget-by-Program" approach crosses city organizational lines by following an output category hierarchy rather than an organizational hierarchy. It emphasizes policy and functional data as well as financial data, while ensuring financial controls and accountability throughout the fiscal year.

Downers Grove integrates a management-by-objectives/goals system with a program budget format that directly links projected expenditures with the goals and objectives to be achieved. It also includes an individual employee evaluation system.

Plainfield's unique contribution to the "Budgeting-by-Objectives" approach is to integrate community participation into the budget process by means of a citizen's budget advisory committee and citizen survey.

A component of the Palo Alto system is a semiannual performance measurement report that includes the following information: (1) expenditure and revenue forecasts, (2) major accomplishments for each department, and (3) progress in meeting performance targets.

The major advantages of implementing performance budgeting mentioned by all these cities are the increased help council and decisionmakers have in analyzing budgets, better descriptions of services provided and allocations of resources, improved productivity, and the ability to readjust the focus of programs to respond to changing circumstances. In some cases this program has reduced the size of the work force, increased coordination between departments whose programs cross departmental lines, improved staff/council relationships, and, in the case of Plainfield, community participation and satisfaction in city services.

Zero-Based Budgeting

Zero-based budgeting (ZBB) is similar to performance budgeting in that it seeks to provide information that will serve as clear justification for departmental budget requests. Its difference is that it also provides for making choices and offering alternatives for city services.

Four cities that have implemented ZBB programs are North Miami, Florida (population 42,566); Iowa City, Iowa (population 50,508); Wilmington, Delaware (population 70,195); and Garland, Texas (population 148,975).

Preparation of a "how-to" manual was the first step in North Miami's program. Training sessions were held for all personnel involved, and within a year the program was implemented citywide. All service levels were ranked according to priority by the respective department heads and this information submitted to the council for changes or approval.

Iowa City designed its system in response to the city council's request for a budget that would allow it to base decisions on programs rather than on line-item figures.

Wilmington wanted a process that would allow for making trade-offs in services and that could predict the implications of significant changes in the funding of a particular service. It implemented ZBB in 1977, and each year since the city has strived to improve its procedure to provide more specific information.

Garland formed a project team in 1974 to adapt the ZBB process to its specific needs and found that reliance on outside experts as well as internal personnel offered the most efficient approach.

The following advantages have been enjoyed by these cities from implementing ZBB:

1. Detailed information available on all city services
2. Arrangement of city services into systematic priority rankings
3. Explicit management and objectives program
4. A more meaningful role for the city council in the budget process

Walnut Creek, California (population 53,643) instituted a "Two-Year Option Budget" format that combines certain elements of program budgeting with the techniques of ZBB. It opted for a two-year program not only because the usual fiscal year did not lend itself well to some of its operations, but because a two-year program allows for more fiscal continuity and an opportunity for more thoughtful decision making. Another important element of the program that attempts to make the budget more responsive to the needs of the total community is a resident survey for public input. The survey is conducted by questionnaires regarding spending on five city services: police services, maintenance of parks and recreation facilities, streets, leisure service programs, and civic art programs. Citizens are requested to choose areas for proposed reduced spending.

Tallahassee, Florida (population 102,579) has implemented a program similar to that adopted by Walnut Creek. The Service Level Budgeting System (SLBS) is used to prepare and administer the city's operating and capital budgets; it also provides for a resident option survey. This information is used by city officials to prepare a program option budget that outlines "present" level costs (costs of continuing current programs at their present level over the next two years) and "basic" level costs (costs of continuing at 60 to 80 percent of the present level of service, but still workable).

The impact of ZBB on these cities has been a more meaningful budget evaluation and preparation process. Especially important is the shifting of the city council's involvement in the budget process from mere reaction to staff work toward overall policy-making decisions.

Other Budget Systems

In 1978, in response to the growing size of its municipal organization and the increased complexities of its budget, Pontiac, Michigan (population 76,715) had a ten-member task force develop a comprehensive *Policies and Procedures Budget Manual* to provide directions and explanations for every phase of the city budget. City officials believed that as staff members became committed to the policies and procedures outlined in the *Manual,* they would gain a better understanding of programs and performance as well as more control over expenditures. Widespread use of the *Manual* was also seen as a technique for making staff have an awareness of the total budget process, not merely a limited perspective on some isolated part. The *Manual* also serves as a clear and comprehensive guide for citizens on the allocation of public tax dollars.

VI. PERFORMANCE MEASUREMENT

Performance management techniques have provided municipalities with the means to measure the achievement of established goals as well as to measure service demand. Well developed systems can distinguish between individual and departmental performance and thus allow extraordinary efforts to be recognized and rewarded.

Lakewood, Colorado (population 118,498) developed a quarterly program performance chart to analyze various trends and problems previously encountered. Its data are measured against the originally established goals and objectives by a four-part indicator scale reflecting (1) the demand for the program, (2) the workload to be completed within the year, (3) efficiency (in terms of the cost per unit of output, referred to as a "productivity indicator"), and (4) effectiveness, or degree of public satisfaction. These indicators are combined in an analytical report to reveal the present status of projected goals. They are also used by the mayor and city council for the annual budget review.

Newark, Delaware (population 25,247) established a resident survey that samples 8 to 9 percent of the city households. This data-base information is stored in a computer in two files: "Household" (presenting information on the people actually interviewed) and "Person" (portraying selected information on all household members of those interviewed). The data base thus discloses the various trends and needs developing among residents of the city and the degree of public satisfaction with all city services.

Portland, Oregon (population 367,530) developed a performance measurement manual for its staff to use in preparing a measurement system. It includes three types of performance measures. First, the city is able to assess its own performance through the establishment of realistic goals and objectives and comparing actual accomplishments with them. Second, information on departmental objectives indicates the direction in which a department is moving. And finally, citizens are able to measure service performance through their own participation in the process of setting objectives.

Randolph, New Jersey (population 18,000) also relies on the use of a citizen survey to monitor public desires, needs, and "appraisals" of township services. Numerical ratings are given to indicate the importance of each service. The effectiveness and quality of each service are also rated. As in other cities, Randolph officials feel that such surveys (given three times in five years) are instrumental in defining problems and monitoring resident satisfaction.

Savannah, Georgia (population 145,699) instituted a "Responsive Public Services Program" that divided the city into geographical areas or neighborhoods. Each neighborhood was examined and rated according to its living conditions (cleanliness, crime rate, animal control, etc.). Four techniques were employed to gather the data. Field inspections were made to measuring each area's deficiencies (such as the amount of uncollected trash). Citizen surveys were taken to measuring public satisfaction with ongoing programs and facilities. Special studies such as land use compatibility and water and sewer adequacy were made for each area. Last, operational information was collected, such as the number of registered complaints related to municipal programs. In this way each neighborhood received a "score." The score then determined the urgency of city reaction to the deficiencies encountered. The program allows neighborhoods to be continuously evaluated and provides the city with the information it needs to structure its overall comprehensive plan in regard to fiscal capabilities.

The use of performance measure techniques has not been without problems.

The experience in Phoenix, Arizona, (population 824,230) for example, indicates the dangers of overpromising results, as well as a tendency for cumbersome reporting systems to develop.

Operating managers in San José, California, (population 659,181) had little use for its performance measurement program, finding it applicable only to the impact budget and policymaking process. What they wanted was a specific set of measurements intended for their own individual needs. An approach in instances like this one might be to develop a "core" of questions and then add others tailored to the specific aspects of the municipal service in question.

It should be remembered that performance measurements are to be used merely as indicators, not as absolutes. Los Angeles initially experienced difficulty in convincing its staff of the need for such a program, while Cincinnati assessed its accomplishment as, in reality, the result of changes in employee attitudes, not of productivity data and customer/citizen satisfaction.

Milwaukee found the costs involved in implementing performance measurement to be excessive, as did San Diego. The extra time and personnel need to maintain the performance measurement project were the major factors in the expense.

Cities that have adopted performance measures are in virtually unanimous agreement that each measurement system should be reviewed and revised regularly to ensure continuing usefulness. Phoenix, for example, greatly simplified its cumbersome reporting system in 1979-80 even as it was broadening its overall productivity improvement approach. The reduction in the reporting burden and the decentralization of analytic staff support renewed and strengthened departmental efforts at productivity improvement. A Seattle official summed up the universal rule for implementation: "You can't measure the universe without first establishing a clear idea as to what use will be made of the resultant data."

VII. SOURCES OF INFORMATION

Most of the material in this chapter was extracted from the International City Management Association's primary project on exemplary practices, part of the Capacity Sharing Program.[1] For more information about contacting the proper person in each city, contact ICMA, 1120 G Street, N. W., Washington, D. C. 20005 or call (202) 626-4600.

[1] *Current Approaches to Financial Management—A Directory of Practices,* Management Information Service, Special Report #6 (Washington, D.C.: International City Management Association, February 1980).

Sources of further cost-cutting suggestions include:

Robert W. Poole, Jr. *Cutting Back City Hall* (New York: Universe Books, 1980, 224 pp.) This paperback summarizes cost-cutting practices in service areas such as police, fire protection, etc., drawing on the experiences of many local and foreign governments.

Elizabeth K. Kellar, ed. *Managing with Less: A Book of Readings* (Washington, D. C.: International City Management Association, 1979, 150 pp.) A collection of papers, many from ICMA journals, with sections on management, building a strong organization, lessons from Prop. 13, city services, and financial management.

Illinois Department of Commerce and Community Affairs. *A Catalogue of Municipal Cost Cutting Techniques.* (Department of Commerce and Community Affairs, 222 South College Street, Springfield, Il 62706). A listing of about 200 one-page "Cost-Cutter Briefs" organized by functional areas such as data processing, fire-protection-equipment, refuse collection, etc. Many are from Illinois cities.

10
Who Can Help and How: People, Organizations, and Resources

This chapter is designed to be a reference guide that provides summaries of research, demonstrations, data sources, and technical assistance available from the Federal government, public and special interest groups, and private consultants.

The first section describes the major programs the Federal government operates for the benefit of state and local governments. The second section provides a listing of public interest groups and information about the areas of research these agencies are working on and the types of services they offer to the mayor and city officials.

A more extensive listing of public interest and special interest groups, including addresses and telephone numbers, is presented in the third section as potential assistance for the whole variety of problems faced by mayors and their staffs. The fourth section reviews the services private consultants can provide to help state or local governments with the full range of financial management problems. Finally, the fifth section identifies some key published materials.

SERVICES PROVIDED BY THE FEDERAL GOVERNMENT

Department of Housing and Urban Development

Office of Policy Development and Research (PD&R). HUD's Office of Policy Development and Research works with local and state leaders and intermediary groups to develop products and services that will improve the capacity of state and local governments to manage change. Local leaders identify major problems. PD&R then works with specialists to develop products incorporating tools and techniques used successfully by various communities to solve similar problems. Next, intermediary groups and technical assistance organizations work together to put this information into usable form and share it with local and state governments seeking ideas.

Broad areas addressed by PD&R include the following:

1. Financial management
2. Productivity improvement
3. Strategic planning for cities and counties
4. Encouraging local community partnerships
5. Alternatives for delivering services to the public
6. Managing and financing capital facilities such as roads, bridges, and water and sewer systems

A variety of resources and informational vehicles covering these areas has been assembled through a support network of existing organizations that assist local governments. A considerable range of products and services is available, as follows:

1. *Publications*—Overviews, directories of workable practices and sources of assistance, handbooks, annotated bibliographies
2. *Workshops*—Persons experienced in alternatives for delivering local services give workshops nationwide in conjunction with state associations, limited on-site assistance, and advice in response to inquiries from local officials to help examine issues and practices.
3. *Inquiry Service*—Staff in PD&R refer local officials to resource persons and publications on new initiatives and local financial management issues (e.g., evaluating local financial condition, forecasting revenues and expenditures, and productivity).
4. *Resource Center on Community Partnerships*—Case examples of public-private partnerships for solving major community problems are available on a computer network and by request from PD&R.

For further information, contact:
Office of Policy Development and Research, Room 8138
U.S. Department of Housing and Urban Development
451 Seventh Street, SW
Washington, DC 20410
(202) 755-4370.

HUD User. A research information service, HUD USER, provides constituents with timely and complete information on research supported by the Office of Policy Development and Research (PD&R). The heart of the service is a computerized data base that contains complete bibliographic information, abstracts, and a source of availability for all PD&R research reports. An inquiry, response staff handles written and telephone requests for information within PD&R's scope of research, and offers topical searches of the data base, computer-produced bibliographies with abstracts, and available publications in response to requests.

HUD USER produces a number of specialized publications including *Recent Research Results,* a current awareness bulletin that announces new PD&R research reports as they are published, and Selected Bibliographies, which are produced on various topics and contain annotations and bibliographic citations for topically pertinent PD&R reports.

An additional activity of HUD USER is the Document Dissemination Facility, which provides copies of PD&R reports in response to user requests.

To use this service, contact:

HUD USER
P.O. Box 280
Germantown, MD 20874
(301) 251-5154.

(There are charges for most of the products and services available from HUD USER.)

Bureau of the Census (Department of Commerce)

The Bureau of the Census is the largest general-purpose statistical agency in the Federal government. In addition to the decennial national census, the Bureau undertakes numerous surveys to update data and conducts many special censuses, some at the request of state, local, and other Federal agencies. It makes data available to the public in thousands of printed reports each year, on computer tape, microfilm, and through special publications.

Through its *Data User Service,* Census Bureau specialists are available to answer inquiries and provide consultation on data products and services by telephone, correspondence, personal visits, or referral to appropriate sources. They can provide assistance on such topics as the availability of data on particular subjects, data sources, data definitions and concepts, data interpretation, data reliability, use of data, and processing machine-readable products.

Education and training services offered by the Bureau include introductory workshops, seminars on accessing Federal statistical resources, various courses to assist in population estimates and using reference files, and targeted programs for state and local government planners and librarians.

State Data Centers are being established through cooperative agreements between the Bureau of the Census and participating states to improve access to and use of Census Bureau and related statistical resources.

A monthly *Data User News* reports on current Census Bureau data, and other guides to particular series are published regularly. Quarterly catalogs and a cumulative annual catalog are designed to give users a means of locating needed data. Below are the more important types of information provided by the Bureau of the Census:

1. Population
2. Median age
3. Retail sales
4. Median education level
5. Number and type of housing units

This information normally can be obtained from regional offices of the Bureau of the Census and State Data Centers.

Request further information on the range of services from

Data Users Services Division
Bureau of the Census
Washington, D.C. 20233.

General inquiries are taken by telephone at (301) 763-4100 and education and training inquiries at (301) 763-1510.

The Department of Commerce also compiles data on total and per capita personal income. This information can be obtained from the regional offices of the Department of Commerce.

Bureau of Labor Statistics (Department of Labor)

The Bureau of Labor Statistics provides estimates of employment (by economic sector), labor force, and unemployment rates for many jurisdictions. This information should be obtained from the regional offices of the Bureau of Labor Statistics.

Federal Reserve System

The Federal Reserve System compiles information on numbers of bank and savings and loan offices and on branch and total deposits from reports submitted to the Federal Deposit Insurance Corporation and the Federal Home Loan Bank Board. Such data can be obtained from regional Federal Reserve Banks.

Federal Reserve Board
1700 G Street, NW
Washington, DC 20006
(202) 289-0507

II. RESOURCES AVAILABLE FROM NATIONAL GROUPS

The nine national groups described below, representing a broad range of state and local constituencies, have worked with HUD's Office of Policy Development and Research since 1978 on identifying and solving financial management problems and needs. These groups continue, via publications and direct assistance, to help their respective memberships and clients and to provide HUD with the continuing feedback that facilitates the revision and/or development of products and services to meet contemporary financial management challenges.

A brief description of these groups, plus information on how to contact each, follows.

THE COUNCIL OF STATE COMMUNITY AFFAIRS AGENCIES (COSCAA)

COSCAA is the national organization representing the state executive branch agencies responsible for a variety of local assistance functions in housing, community development, economic development, planning, training, and technical assistance. These agencies are commonly called "Departments of Community Affairs" or "DCAs." Almost all states now have a cabinet-level department or major agency responsible for these local assistance functions. COSCAA can give specific assistance in the role of DCAs in providing local financial management assistance. For detailed information, call or write:

The Council of State and Community Affairs Agencies
Hall of States
444 North Capital Street, Suite 251
Washington, DC 20001
(202) 393-6435

THE COUNCIL ON MUNICIPAL PERFORMANCE (COMP)

COMP is a national independent, nonprofit organization founded in 1973 to improve public understanding of municipal government and promote constructive change in local government management practices. COMP has prepared two guides under HUD contract—*Local Government Auditing* (1979) and *Contracting Municipal Services* (1984). COMP has also published manuals on internal controls and communicating with the investment community.

A unique feature of COMP's activities is its focus on measurement and ranking of city services and quality of life, useful for officials seeking to compare their city to others.

COMP serves local government and municipal officials by assisting them in the development and implementation of cost-effective operations. COMP also serves the public by monitoring local government service delivery. COMP consults with localities on preparation of invitations for bid or requests for proposals. The Council also assists local government officials and the private sector by sponsoring conferences on municipal financial issues.

COMP maintains a large data base on cities, covering such factors as finances, demographic trends, health, environment, education, labor forces, and crime. This base is especially strong for the 100 largest American cities and the 130 largest cities of the world.

For further information on COMP's activities, contact:

Council on Municipal Performance
30 Irving Place, 9th Floor
New York, New York 10003
(212) 420-5950

THE GOVERNMENT FINANCE OFFICERS ASSOCIATION (GFOA)

GFOA is a professional and service organization for public officials involved in the financial management of government. Its membership includes over 8,000 budgetary and financial officers serving units of state and local government, as well as over 1,000 associate members in related fields. The Association maintains offices in Chicago, Illinois, and Washington, DC.

For most of its life, until 1984, GFOA was known as the Municipal Finance Officers Association (MFOA).

GFOA is actively involved on a national level in improving the budgeting, financial management, accounting, and auditing procedures of local governments. Through its various forms of publications, training, certification of conformance with sound financial reporting practices, a technical advisory service and research, the Association has assumed a leadership role in disseminating sound financial management information to these governmental units.

GFOA engages in or sponsors a variety of research projects concerning state and local finance and financial management. To facilitate and expand these activities, the Government Finance Research Center (GFRC) was established in 1977. Located in Washington, D.C., the Center draws upon professionals from both the Chicago and Washington, D.C., offices. The GFRC has responsibility for the management of all GFOA research contracts. For more detailed information on GFOA's current programs and publications, contact:

Government Finance Officers Association
Suite 200, 1750 K Street, NW
Washington, DC 20006
(202) 466-2014

or

180 North Michigan Avenue
Chicago, IL 60601
(312) 977-9700

THE INTERNATIONAL CITY MANAGEMENT ASSOCIATION (ICMA)

ICMA is the professional and educational association of appointed administrators in cities, counties, and councils of governments. Most of ICMA's 7,000 individual members are local government professionals in the United States, Canada, Europe, and other countries.

Since its founding in 1914, ICMA's purpose has been to enhance the proficiency of professional administrators and to strengthen the quality of urban government through professional management. Its services, programs, and publications are guided by these ICMA goals:

- To strengthen the quality of urban government through professional management
- To be the professional and educational association of appointed urban managers
- To strengthen the competence of appointed urban managers and to ensure qualified talent to meet urban government needs
- To contribute to the understanding and resolution of urban government issues

- To provide information and analysis of data, management ideas, and methods for urban government management and to stimulate and participate in the development and translation of new concepts for urban government management.

Inquiries regarding current ICMA financial management programs and publications in the field should be directed to:

Director of Financial Management
International City Management Association
1120 G Street, NW
Washington, DC 20005
(202) 626-4000

THE JOINT CENTER FOR POLITICAL STUDIES (JCPS)

JCPS is a nonprofit, nonpartisan, tax-exempt organization formed in 1970. It has three specific objectives:

1. To respond to minority group aspirations to become active participants in the political process
2. To enhance their effectiveness at every level of government
3. To keep the public apprised of the extent and impact of minority political involvement.

JCPS personnel resources include economists, journalists, educators, sociologists, political scientists, public administrators, lawyers, and urban planners. The Joint Center pursues its objectives through interlocking programs in public policy analysis, research, training and technical assistance, and information services.

JCPS has a particular expertise in addressing the financial management means of small economically distressed areas. For information on this and other ongoing JCPS programs, contact:

The Joint Center for Political Studies
1301 Pennsylvania Ave., NW
Suite 400
Washington, DC 20004
(202) 626-3500

THE NATIONAL ASSOCIATION OF COUNTIES (NACo)

NACo is the only organization representing county governments in the U.S. Its membership includes urban, suburban, and rural counties. Members share the common purpose of strengthening county government to meet the needs of all Americans.

By virtue of a county's membership, all of its elected and appointed officials become participants in NACo and seek the following goals:

- Improving county government
- Serving as a liaison between the nation's counties and other levels of government
- Achieving public understanding of the role of counties in the Federal system

NACo represents counties before Congress, analyzes Federal regulations and submits the comments of member counties, and keeps in touch with the sources of Federal grants. NACo's policy steering committees study legislation, regulations, county needs, and offer recommendations for adoption by the membership. Also, NACo has a full-time staff to help county member officials to take action in many areas including community development, criminal justice and public safety, employment, energy and environment, health and education, home rule and regional affairs, labor management relations, land use, public lands, taxation and finance, transportation, welfare, and social services. Details on NACo's array of financial management publications and other ongoing activities are available through

The National Association of Counties
440 First Street, NW
Washington, DC 20001
(202) 393-6226

THE NATIONAL LEAGUE OF CITIES (NLC)

The NLC is the national action arm of the nation's cities. Included in its membership are 48 state municipal leagues and their member cities, and, as direct members, over 750 cities; there are 15,000 member cities in all.

Through comprehensive analysis of national policies and related programs and through representation before the Congress and executive agencies, NLC officers and staff address the immediate and long-term concerns of city officials and urban citizens.

Major objectives of NLC are to aid local government policy leaders in the improvement of their individual and institutional capacity to shape sound local policies and to strengthen state municipal leagues as the vehicles through which city officials influence the development of state and national policies.

The NLC can provide a number of publications on the subject of financial management and can otherwise assist local officials. For detailed information, contact:

National League of Cities
1301 Pennsylvania Avenue, NW
Washington, DC 20004
(202) 420-3000

THE URBAN CONSORTIUM (UC) AND PUBLIC TECHNOLOGY INC. (PTI)

The UC is a cooperative of 36 jurisdictions nationwide, each representing city or urban county governments of 500,000 or more citizens. The consortium works through ten task forces to identify the common technology/system/methodological needs of its members, to establish priorities among those needs, to stimulate and share in the conduct of research on those priorities, and to make a systematic effort to disseminate and utilize the outcomes of the research.

Public Technology, Inc., serves as the secretariat to the consortium, and provides technical assistance to local governments attempting to develop and institutionalize formal revenue and expenditure forecasting systems.

Further information on PTI's programs for local government can be obtained by contacting:

Public Technology, Inc
1301 Pennsylvania Avenue, NW
Washington, DC 20004
(202) 626-2400

THE U.S. CONFERENCE OF MAYORS (USCM)

The U.S. Conference of Mayors, an organization of city governments, is the national forum through which the mayors of this nation's larger cities collectively express their concerns and work to meet the needs of our urban centers. By limiting membership and participation to the 800 cities over

30,000 population and by concentrating on the question of Federal-City relationships, the Conference has become the focus of urban leadership.

The Conference of Mayors is both a clearinghouse for ideas and a center for research and information and legislative reference, with headquarters and staff located in Washington, D.C. Its comprehensive services cover an expanding range of subjects about which a mayor must be knowledgeable if he or she is to be an effective and informed official. These services include the following:

- A twice monthly publication entitled *The Mayor*
- Frequent Federal-City reporter bulletins
- Analyses of Federal legislative proposals and actions
- Analyses of impending Federal policies and administrative action
- Selection and distribution of government documents and other special interest material
- Regular activities such as the Mayors Leadership Institute and exchanges of information and experiences between elected city officials across the country.

In addition to this book, the Conference can provide publications and direct assistance geared to the local elected executive. Detailed information can be obtained by contacting:

U.S. Conference of Mayors
1620 Eye Street, NW
Washington, DC 20006
(202) 293-7330

III. LISTING OF NATIONAL GROUPS

An extensive listing of public interest and special assistance groups is given below. Although this list is not exhaustive, it should provide a reference for most of the financial management problems encountered by mayors and their staffs. To the extent that these groups cannot satisfy a city's need for assistance, one or more of the types of private consultants to be discussed in the next section should fill in the gap.

Airport Operators Council International
1700 K. Street, N.W.
Washington, DC 20006
(202) 296-3270

American Assoc. of Airport Executives
2029 K Street, N.W., Suite 701
Washington, DC 20006
(202) 331-8994

American Assoc. of Port Authorities
1612 K Street, N.W.
Washington, DC 20006
(202) 331-1263

American Assoc. of School Administrators
1801 No. Moore Street
Arlington, VA 22209
(702) 528-0700

American College of Hospital Administrators
840 No. Lake Shore Drive
Chicago, IL 60611
(312) 943-0544

American Institute of Architects
1735 New York Avenue, N.W.
Washington, DC 20006
(202) 626-7300

American Library Association
50 East Huron Street
Chicago, IL 60611
(312) 944-6780

American Planning Association
1776 Massachusetts Ave., N.W.
Washington, DC 20036
(202) 872-0611

American Public Gas Assoc.
PO Box 1426
Vienna, VA 22180
(703) 281-2910

American Public Health Assoc.
1015 15th Street, N.W.
Washington, DC 20005
(202) 789-5600

American Public Power Assoc.
2301 M Street, N.W.
Washington, DC 20037
(202) 775-8300

American Public Transit Assoc.
1225 Connecticut Ave., N.W.
Washington, DC 20036
(202) 828-2800

American Public Welfare Assoc.
1125 15th St., N.W.
Washington, DC 20005
(202) 293-7550

American Public Assoc.
1313 East 60th Street
Chicago, IL 60637
(312) 667-2200

American Society for Public Administration
1120 G Street, N.W.
Suite 500
Washington, DC 20036
(202) 393-7878

American Water Works Assoc., Inc.
6666 West Quincy Avenue
Denver, CO 80235
(303) 794-7711

Assoc. of Public Safety Communications Officers, Inc.
P.O. Box 669
New Smyrna Beach, FL 32069
(904) 427-3461

Bldg. Officials and Code Administrators International
17926 South Halsted
Homewood, IL 60430
(312) 799-2300

Canadian Assoc. of Municipal Administrators
1318-112 Kent St.
Ottawa, Ontario K 1P 5P9, Canada
(613) 237-5221

Council on Municipal Performance
30 Irving Place
New York, NY 10003
(212) 420-5950

Council of State Community Affairs Agencies
444 North Capitol Street, Suite 251
Washington, DC 20001
(202) 393-6435

Council of State Governments
Iron Works Pike
P.O. Box 11910
Lexington, Kentucky 40578
(606) 252-2291

Federation of Canadian Municipalities
1318-112 Kent Street
Ottawa, Ontario K 1P 5P9, Canada
(613) 237-5221

Government Finance Officers Assoc.
180 North Michigan Ave., Suite 800
Chicago, IL 60601
(312) 977-9700

Government Finance Officers Assoc.
1750 K St., N.W., Suite 200
Washington, DC 20006
(202) 466-2473

Institute of Internal Auditors, Inc.
International Headquarters
249 Maitland Avenue
Altamonte Springs, FL 32701
(305) 830-7600

Institute of Transportation Engineers
525 School Street, S.W.
Suite 410
Washington, DC 20024
(202) 554-8050

International Assoc. of Assessing Officers
1313 East 60th Street
Chicago, IL 60637
(312) 947-2069

International Assoc. of Auditorium Managers
500 N. Michigan, Suite 1400
Chicago, IL 60611
(312) 661-1700

International Assoc. of Chiefs of Police
13 Firstfield Road
Gaithersburg, MD 20878
(301) 948-0922

International Assoc. of Fire Chiefs
1329 18th Street, N.W.
Washington, DC 20036
(202) 833-3420

International City Management Assoc.
1120 G Street, N.W.
Washington, DC 20005
(202) 626-4600

International Conference of Bldg. Officials
5360 South Workman Mill Road
Whittier, CA 90601
(213) 699-0541

International Institute of Municipal Clerks
160 North Altadena Drive
Pasadena, CA 91107
(213) 795-6153

International Personnel Management Assoc.
1850 K Street, N.W.
Suite 870
Washington, DC 20006
(202) 833-5860

League of Women Voters of the United States
1730 M Street, N.W.
Washington, DC 20036
(202) 296-1770

National Assoc. for State Information Systems
Iron Works Pike
P.O. Box 11910
Lexington, KY 40578
(606) 252-2291

National Association of Counties
440 First Street, N.W.
Washington, DC 20001
(202) 393-6226

National Association of Housing and Redevelopment Officials
2600 Virginia Avenue, N.W.
Washington, DC 30037
(202) 333-2020

National Assoc. of Regional Councils
1700 K Street, N.W.
Washington, DC 20006
(202) 457-0710

National Assoc. of Schools of Public Affairs and Administration
1120 G Street, N.W.
Suite 520
Washington, DC 20005
(202) 628-8965

National Assoc. of Towns and Townships
1522 K St., N.W.
Washington, DC 20005
(202) 737-5200

National Conference of State Legislatures
1125 17th Street
Suite 1500
Denver, CO 80202
(303) 292-6600

National Council for Urban Economic Development
1730 K Street, N.W.
Washington, DC 20006
(202) 223-4735

National Environmental Health Association
1200 Lincoln Street
Suite 704
Denver, CO 80203
(303) 861-9090

National Governors' Assoc.
Hall of the States
444 North Capital Street, N.W.
Washington, DC 20001
(202) 624-5300

National Housing Conference
1126 16th Street, N.W.
Suite 211
Washington, DC 20036
(202) 223-4844

National Institute of Governmental Purchasing
115 Hillwood Ave.
Suite 201
Falls Church, VA 22046
(703) 533-7300

National Institute of Municipal Law Officers
1000 Connecticut Avenue, N.W.
Suite 800
Washington, DC 20036
(202) 466-5424

National League of Cities
1301 Pennsylvania Avenue, N.W.
Washington, DC 20004
(202) 626-3000

National Municipal League, Inc.
55 W 44th Street
New York, NY 10036
(212) 730-7930

National Public Employer Labor Relations Assoc.
1620 Eye St., N.W.
4th Floor
Washington, D.C. 20006
(202) 296-2230

National Recreation and Park Assoc.
3101 Park Center Drive
Alexandria, VA 22302
(702) 820-4940

National School Boards Assoc.
1680 Duke Street
Alexandria, VA 22314
(703) 838-6722

Town Affiliation Assoc. of the United States
1625 Eye Street, N.W.
Suite 424-26
Washington, DC 20006
(202) 293-5504

Public Administration Service
1497 Chain Bridge Road
Suite 202
McLean, VA 22101
(703) 734-8970

Public Technology, Inc.
1301 Pennsylvania Avenue, N.W.
Suite 800
Washington, DC 20004
(202) 626-2400

United States Conference of Mayors
1620 Eye Street, N.W.
Washington, DC 20006
(202) 293-7330

The Urban Institute
2100 M Street, N.W.
Washington, DC 20037
(202) 223-1950

Water Pollution Control Federation
2626 Pennsylvania Avenue, N.W.
Washington, DC 20037
(202) 337-2500

IV. PRIVATE CONSULTANTS

Municipal governments have used private consultants with increasing frequency as the range of services they provide and the complexity of their operations have grown. Some municipalities use consultants much more effectively than others; there also are wide variations in the types of situations in which consultants are used. The purpose of this section is to provide guidelines concerning when and how consultants should be used.

When to Use a Consultant

Some municipalities, especially those faced with severe budgetary constraints, have lean professional staff that are intended only to maintain ongoing operations. Others have more extensive staffs that can handle many of the specialized problems that occur from time to time. Although consultants would be used more frequently in the former situation, there are times in both cases when consultants could be used to advantage.

A municipality could complement or support its in-house staff for a number of reasons. Consultants are commonly used when a problem is so specialized or large that outside resources are necessary to address it adequately.

Even when a city's staff has the available resources and technical capability to deal with a problem, there are instances when consultants will be used instead. For example, if a complex system is to be automated, it often is less expensive to acquire an existing software package and have it modified to meet the city's specific requirements than to develop a new system from scratch. In some cases, consultants will be used even if internal staff could do a job as capably and economically because the political benefits of having a recognized and objective outside expert recommend a solution to a problem overcomes bureaucratic rigidities and jurisdictional disputes that would preclude the implementation of an internally generated solution.

In the situations described above, a consultant would be called in to address a defined problem. Often, however, a municipality will see only the symptoms of an underlying problem and will use a consultant to identify and define the problem as well as to analyze it and recommend a solution.

Consulting organizations also vary widely in the range of services they provide. Some concentrate on specific technical areas (such as real estate appraising, personnel, transportation, data processing, performance measurement, etc.) whereas others provide a broad range of both general and specific services. Large accounting firms provide data processing, actuarial, personnel, systems analysis, productivity and performance measurement, and other general services as well as the more traditional accounting and auditing functions.

Many consulting firms provide a broad range of services within a particular functional area. For example, a firm may specialize in personnel matters, offering services in developing job descriptions and organizational structures, performance evaluations, pay scales, benefit and compensation plans, pension plans, and actuarial studies. Other firms may specialize in developing and implementing data processing applications in different municipal operations.

Commercial banks and, to a lesser extent, thrift institutions (mutual savings banks and savings and loan associations) can provide a number of financial services to a city. Cash management services relating to the collection, disbursement and investment of cash resources are an obvious example. Many of them also engage in economic analysis and forecasting services that could be helpful to a city in projecting revenues and planning economic strategies. Banks with trust departments can manage or advise on the investment of pension fund assets.

Dept issuance by municipal governments is an activity that virtually always requires a number of different consulting services. The two primary functions are performed by the underwriter and the bond counsel. The underwriter serves as a link between the municipal borrower and the capital markets and ensures that the desired bonds are available on schedule. The bond counsel verifies the powers of the issuing government and the specific authorization for the bond issue and affirms the validity of all terms and conditions attendant to the issue. (The roles of the underwriter and bond counsel are discussed in more detail in Chap. 4.)

In the final analysis, both the underwriter and the bond counsel represent the bond holders professionally and legally. Moreover, the risks borne by the underwriter provide a strong incentive to make the issue as attractive and marketable as possible. Recognizing that it is not reasonable to expect either of these parties to represent their interests fully, while also acknowledging that they are disadvantaged by being infrequent market participants, more and more municipalities have engaged independent financial advisors to represent them in debt issuance negotiations. In addition to representing the municipal issuer in matters before the underwriter, rating agencies and bankers, a financial advisor can assist in the preparation of the official statement, analyze the financial condition of the issuer and make recommendations, and act as a consultant in matters relating to budget, finance and planning.

In a revenue bond issue, additional services are required to attest to the economic and technological viability of the project to be financed. This can require the use of accounting, engineering, architectural, and economic analysis firms.

How to Select a Consultant

The decision to employ a consultant should be based on a clear determination of the objective(s) to be achieved. This, in turn, should help define an overall strategy and the role of the consultant.

In most cases, a consultant will work in conjunction with the city's staff. Usually the consultant has ultimate responsibility for the project and the local staff provides support and participates in the work, although in some cases the consultant will simply augment the city's staff. At the other extreme, the consultant will provide all the resources for a project and will turn over a finished product to the client at the end of the work program. This is often called a "turnkey" approach and should be used only when the final product can be specified in detail and staff participation is not necessary for a usable end product to be developed.

Local procedures often require that consultants be selected through a formal bid process. When more flexibility is permitted, several alternative approaches can be used. When a unique requirement and a consultant's unique qualifications justify it, sole source selection can be used. When there are several consultants that could do the job, selection can be based on a process of negotiation that strives to achieve maximum benefits at least cost.

When the problem is more complex and less is known about the qualifications of prospective consultants, a request for proposals (RFP) can be prepared and circulated. Such a request solicits responses from several prospective consultants concerning their approach to the project. Occasionally a selection can be made based on a review of the proposals, but typically the submitters of the best proposals will be invited to make oral presentations, and then a selection will be made or negotiations will be held with a small number of this final group.

For especially large and complex projects, the solicitation process may require a two-stage process. The first stage would consist of issuing a formal request for qualifications (RFQ) that would outline the scope of the project and describe the skills and experience that a consultant would have to bring to it. After reviewing the qualifications submitted by various consultants, the best qualified would be issued an RFP. This second state then would proceed as described above.

Comprehensive advice on the contracting process may be found in John Tepper Marlin, ed., *Contracting Municipal Services* (New York: John Wiley & Sons, 1984).

Types of Consultants

There are many types of financial consultants. They vary as to the kinds of services provided and in the nature of the relationship with their municipal client. The size of consulting organizations can range from large international firms with fully staffed offices in many major cities to college faculty members who do consulting part-time and individuals who operate out of the back room of their home. The former generally can commit greater resources to a project, but the latter operate with substantially less overhead and can produce a quality product at a reasonable price. Of course, individuals and small firms should be used carefully, and references should be requested and checked.

V. RESOURCES

This section on resources lists studies and documents of several sorts. Some are budget documents, audits, and other reports by city governments that are particularly interesting in some respect. Others are summaries of innovative practices in different cities. Still others are "how-to-do-it" manuals in particular areas. The more general studies include strategies for managing problems such as productivity and cutback management.

Economic Development

Birch, David, 1981. "Who Creates Jobs?" *The Public Interest* 65 (Fall, 1981), pp. 3-14.

A summary paper by Birch, who documents the importance of small service firms for economic growth.

Burchall, Robert W., and Listokin, David. 1978. *The Fiscal Impact Guidebook: Estimating Local Costs and Revenue of Land Development.* New Brunswick, N.J.: Rutgers University Center for Urban Policy Research, 617 pp. Also available in an abbreviated version.

Presents procedures for conducting cost/benefit analyses of urban projects such as shopping centers. Indicates technical assistance sources.

Clark, Terry Nichols, ed. 1981. *Community Development.* Symposium Issue of *Urban Affairs Papers,* vol. 3, No. 2 (Spring 1981), 71 pp.

Reviews strategies used by cities to promote economic development and how they relate to fiscal policy. Papers on urban decline, Federal grant formulas, public capital investment, and municipal retrenchment by Anthony Downs, Richard Nathan, George Peterson, and others.

National Council for Urban Economic Development. 1979. *Economic Development Bibliography, 1974-1979.* Washington, D.C.: National Council for Urban Economic Development, 30 pp.

A detailed bibliography.

Vaughan, Roger J. 1979. *State Taxation and Economic Development.* Washington, D.C.: Council of State Planning Agencies, 158 pp.

Overview of research on the sources of movement of jobs, suggesting that tax incentives may have been oversold but outlining alternative strategies to encourage job growth.

Citizen Policy Preferences

Blair, Louis H., and Schwartz, Alfred I. 1972. *How Clean is Our City?* Washington, D.C.: The Urban Institute, 67 pp.

Outlines procedures for measuring cleanliness of streets and public areas using surveys of citizens, photographs, and other procedures.

Clark, Terry Nichols, ed. 1976. *Citizen Preferences and Urban Public Policy.* Beverly Hills and London: Sage, 142 pp.

Reports on surveys of citizens in St. Louis, Los Angeles, Boston, and the ten Urban Observatory cities. Several methodological papers compare results using different types of questions, including budget pies. Interpretative papers assess citizen surveys critically compared to citizen participation, referenda, and election of representatives, making explicit when and when not to use surveys.

Epstein, Paul D. 1984. *Using Performance Measurement in Local Government: A Guide to Improving Decisions, Performance, and Accountability.* New York: Van Nostrand Reinhold.

Three important perspectives on *how to use* performance measurement for improvement are provided, as well as implementation tips, guidelines for using consultants, and case examples of actual uses of performance measurement in large and small cities and counties contributed by 21 local officials from across the country. Mayor Dianne Feinstein of San Francisco wrote the Foreword.

Hatry, Harry P., et al. 1977. *How Effective Are Your Community Services?* Procedures for Monitoring the Effectiveness of Municipal Services. Washington, D.C.: The Urban Institute and the International City Management Association, 318 pp.

This guidebook contains the most comprehensive compilation of existing effectiveness measures and measurement techniques, covering nine local services including solid waste collection, solid waste disposal, general transportation and mass transit, recreation, library, crime control, fire protection, water supply, and handling citizen complaints and requests. Specific procedures such as citizen surveys and trained observer techniques are discussed in detail, and illustrative questionnaires and implementation suggestions are included.

Fowler, Floyd J. 1974. *Citizen Attitudes Toward Local Government, Services, and Taxes.* Cambridge, Massachusetts: Ballinger, 242 pp.

An overview of the Urban Observatory surveys in ten cities with detailed results by city. Contains an excellent questionnaire in the appendix that is excellent for replication in other cities. Results of individual city surveys can be compared with the following ten cities: Albuquerque, Atlanta, Baltimore, Boston, Denver, Kansas City, Kansas, Kansas City, Missouri, Milwaukee, Nashville, and San Diego.

Webb, Kenneth, and Hatry, Harry P. 1973. *Obtaining Citizen Feedback: The Application of Citizen Surveys to Local Government.* Washington, D.C.: The Urban Institute.

Handbook widely used by local government officials. Provides an overview of how to conduct and use surveys in the local government setting.

Budgeting

Ayres, Douglas W. 1977. *Integrative Budgeting System: A New Approach from Old Failures.* Long Beach, CA: California State University, Center for Public Policy and Administration.

A review of current governmental budget systems and their relationship to financial management systems that may be inadequate to determine how public monies were spent.

Clark, Terry Nichols, and Ferguson, Lorna Crowley. 1983. *City Money: Political Processes, Fiscal Strain, and Retrenchment.* New York: Columbia University Press, 440 pp.

Places budgeting in a explicitly political context in chapters on political leaders, white ethnics and black power, municipal employees, and the taxpayers' revolt. Shows how political cultures of Democrats, Republicans, ethnic politicians, and "New Fiscal Populists" (e.g. Jimmy Carter) define different rules of the game. Different council members often represent these political cultures, and mayors must mediate to establish operational rules of the game as well as specific policies. Also computes numerous fiscal strain indicators for 62 U.S. cities and analyzes them from 1960 to the early 1980s. Reviews policy options that do and do not solve fiscal strain, with examples from specific cities.

Evans, Richard D. 1975. *Municipal Capital Programming.* Boston, MA: Dept. of Community Affairs.

Manual designed to assist state and local officials in developing a capital improvement program. It provides detailed explanations of the purposes of capital expenditures and the process involved in setting up a program, including selection, scheduling, and financing.

Fitts, Hartley C., and Black, Harold. 1981. *Annotated Bibliography.* Financial Management Capacity Sharing Program. Washington, D.C.: Department of Housing and Urban Development, 33 pp.

An annotated bibliography of many of the most important recent studies concerning financial management. For obtaining publications and other documents from HUD studies, contact HUD USER, P.O. Box 280, Germantown, MD 20767.

Griesemer, James R. 1980. *Budgeting for Results in Local Government.* Downers Grove, IL: City of Downers Grove, 148 pp.

Stresses actual use of performance measures and related tools as part of a functioning budgeting system. Many illustrative tables and examples from experience of Downers Grove, but prepared for more general use.

Hayes, Frederick O'R.; Grossman, David A.; Mechling, Jerry E.; Thomas, John S.; and Rosenbloom, Steven J. 1980. *Linkages: Integrating Financial Management in Local Government.* Washington, D.C.: Office of Policy Development and Research, Department of Housing and Urban Development, 204 pp.

Stresses integration of budgeting, auditing, accounting, and performance management as mutually reinforcing aspects of a total financial management system.

Jamison, Conny. 1978. *An Improved Approach to Evaluating Future Costs and Revenues,* San Diego, CA: City of San Diego Financial Management Department.

A comprehensive review of the financing options and theoretical tools that can be used by local decison makers in comparing future costs and revenues. Focuses on the impact of inflation.

Madere, L. E. 1977. *Municipal Budget Projections: Econometric Revenue Forecasting,* New Orleans, LA: City of New Orleans, Office of Economic Analysis.

Presents the budget projection system currently used by New Orleans, abstracts from their experience, general guidelines, and rules that other localities might find useful.

Moak, Lennox L., and Hillhouse, Albert M. 1975. *Concepts and Practices in Local Government Finance.* Chicago, IL: Municipal Finance Officers Association of the United States and Canada.

A valuable reference volume providing general practical information on local government finance. Generally accepted principles and methods are addressed and evaluated along with evaluations of new approaches to investment policy, performance measurement, and policymaking.

Moak, Lennox L., and Killian, Kathryn W. 1964. *A Manual of Suggested Practice for the Preparation and Adoption of Capital Programs and Capital Budgets by Local Governments.* Chicago, IL: Municipal Finance Officers Association, 152 pp.

Municipal Finance Officers Association. 1978. *A Guidebook to Improved Financial Management for Small Cities and Other Governmental Units.* Chicago, IL: Municipal Finance Officers Association of the United States and Canada (now GFOA).

Municipal Finance Officers Association. 1978. "Forecasting: More Than 'Last-Year-Plus-A-Bit'" in *Government Finance,* vol. 7, No. 4 (November 1978).

This issue looks at forecasting and related issues of concern to local government officials. Robert Cramer writes about expenditure forecasting for local government. Harvey Henderson examines revenue forecasting as it is used for the annual budget, cash flow management, and long-range planning, among other topics.

Municipal Finance Officers Association. 1977. *Implementing Effective Cash Management in Local Government: A Practical Guide.* Chicago, IL: Municipal Finance Officers Association of the United States and Canada (now GFOA).

Managing Cash Flow and Investments

Advisory Commission on Intergovernmental Relations. 1977. *Understanding State and Local Cash Management,* Washington, DC: ACIR, 70 pp.

Reviews field of cash management and describes current and innovative practices with a view toward helping state and local governments become more efficient cash managers.

DePalma, John G.; Spector, Quentin B.; and Benway, Bruce E. 1977. *Cash Management for Small Communities.* Orono, ME: University of Maine.

A booklet designed to assist persons not specifically trained in cash management to develop an investment program for their municipality

Haskins and Sells Government Services Group. 1977. *Implementing Effective Cash Management in Local Government: A Practical Guide.* Chicago, IL: Municipal Finance Officers Association of the United States and Canada (now GFOA).

Jones, John A., and Kenneth, Howard S. 1973. *Investment of Idle Funds by Local Government: A Primer.* Chicago, IL: Municipal Finance Officers Association of the United States and Canada (now GFOA).

Details procedures for establishing an effective cash management program for local governments, including policies and procedures to produce effective and efficient investment programs and techniques for evaluating the success of the program once it is established.

Municipal Finance Officers Association. 1978. *A Treasury Management Handbook for Small Cities and Other Governmental Units.* Chicago, IL: MFOA (now GFOA).

Patitucci, Frank M., and Lichtenstein, Michael H. 1977. *Improving Cash Management in Local Government: A Comprehensive Approach.* Chicago, IL: Municipal Finance Officers Association of the United States and Canada.

A comprehensive treatment of cash management in a local government, written particularly for medium to large governmental units and those with more complex cash management environments.

Steinberg, Harold, I. 1975. "Cash Management for Local Government" in *Governmental Finance,* No. 4.

Discusses four primary elements to be considered in a cash management system: bank relations, collections, cash flow planning, and management and investment policy practices.

Financial Information Systems

Harrell, Rhett D. 1980. *Developing a Financial Management Information System for Local Government: The Key Issues.* Washington, D.C.: Government Finance Research Center, Municipal Finance Officers Association, (now GFOA), 42 pp.

Brief summary of major issues for the nonspecialist government official. Reviews basic issues on the basis of acquisition phase, implementation phase, and operational phase. Deals mainly with large integrated accounting systems.

Massachusetts Executive Office of Communities and Development. 1980. *Municipal Electronic Data Processing: A Primer for Local Government Officials.* Washington,

D.C.: Office of Policy Development and Research, Department of Housing and Urban Development, 37 pp.

Includes list of about 100 specific activities that can be automated—such as land use inventory, voter registration records, and consumer inquiries—and are currently used in one or more Massachusetts local governments. Most can be automated separately or as part of a larger integrated system. Bibliography.

Performance Standards and Auditing

Marlin, John Tepper, ed., *Contracting Municipal Services: A Guide for Purchase from the Private Sector* (New York: John Wiley & Sons, 1984). Although directed to the municipal official reviewing the potential of contracting services to a private provider, the book's chapter on "Developing Service Specifications" provides general advice on developing performance standards. Examples are provided for 65 service areas.

Report on the Performance Audit of the Parks Division of Parks and Recreation. 1980. Lincoln, Nebraska: City Budget Office, City of Lincoln, 53 pp.

Summarizes performance audit completed by city staff that audit different agencies each year. Lists 22 recommended changes, such as shifting snow removal to areas of greater public use, transferring equipment maintenance to Public Works, and reducing crew size from three to two for High Ranger tree trimming. Documents each recommendation with a detailed discussion of work procedures and potential for improvement. (One of several performance audits in Lincoln.)

Productivity

Epstein, Paul D. 1984. *Using Performance Measurement in Local Government: A Guide to Improving Decisions, Performance and Accountability.* New York: Van Nostrand Reinhold.

Aims to help local officials and others interested in local government understand performance measurement and its value to them and the community. Its main emphasis is on the many ways local officials can *use* measurement for the benefit of the government and the community. The heart of the book is three chapters that look at the uses of performance measurement from three different perspectives.

Practical Ideas for the Government that Has Everything—Including Productivity Problems. 1979. Washington, D.C.: Office of Policy Development and Research, Department of Housing and Urban Development, HUD—PDR-433, 34 pp.

Brief summaries of productivity improvement programs such as designing record-keeping systems, quality control in park maintenance, and streamlining permit application and licensing.

Washnis, George J., ed. 1980. *Productivity Improvement Handbook for State and Local Government.* New York: John Wiley & Sons, 1500 pp.

Major work with 50 chapters by national experts on organizing productivity systems, measures of productivity, use of computers, personnel relations, public works, finance, etc. Most chapters summarize the state of the art in leading cities, review problems in the area, and include a bibliography. Comprehensive but still written for the nonspecialist. An excellent reference work.

Hatry, Harry P., et al. 1978. *Efficiency Measurement for Local Government Services: Some Initial Suggestions.* Washington, D.C.: The Urban Institute, 208 pp.

A specific discussion of efficiency measures that stresses the necessity to measure demands and other factors affecting the service as well as the service itself. Helpful examples of questions and uses.

Cutback Management

Confronted with the necessity of cutbacks, some cities have completed major reviews of city services and outlined criteria for trimming. Often these have involved groups of leading citizens, as in the Cambridge study listed.

City of Boulder. 1981. *Colorado's Local Revenues.* Boulder, CO: City of Boulder.

Detailed listing of specific fees and user charges, rates, receipts generated, state and local legislation covering each, and possible limits. Indicates where specific fees could be increased.

City of Tampa. 1981. *Service Level Analysis.* Tampa, FL: Mayor's Office, Administration, Revenue and Finance, vol. 1, approx. 150 pp.

A detailed analysis of costs of services considered in relation to the advisability of contracting out. Includes careful discussion of bidding procedures, such as number of documents issued to prepare for bid, number of bids received, amounts of awards, etc. Contracting by this method is important for Tampa as the city contracts for numerous goods and services. Assembles information on bidding and contracting for all departments, suggests changes in some that have not worked well, and documents how others are important in cost saving.

Detroit Recreation Gifts Catalog "Partners." 1980. Detroit: City of Detroit. Department of Public Information, Project Pride, Inc., 31 pp.

A creatively presented "Christmas catalogue" with items like picnic tables for $120, maple tree for $100, van for $12,000. Most items illustrated with photographs of people using them. Introduction makes clear that parks and recreation programs cannot continue without private contributions. Used by volunteers who call on small businesses and neighborhood groups for contributions, which came from 88 groups in 1980.

Levine, Charles H., ed. 1980. *Managing Fiscal Stress.* Chatham, N.J.: Chatham House, 344 pp.

A collection of papers on confronting cutbacks, improving productivity, and managing resources. Especially helpful is listing and discussion of alternative strategies by which to cut back.

Office of the Auditor and Comptroller, City of San Diego. 1981. *Report to Board of Fiscal Overseers on Cost Analysis of Transfer of Paramedic Program to Fire Department.* San Diego: Office of Auditor and Comptroller, aprox. 40 pp.

Careful and critical review of the fire departments' recommendation to take over emergency medical services from private contractor. Shows that fire department underestimated costs. Led city to renew contract with private contractor. Good example of dealing with contractors on complex issues, illustrating how they can be systematically analyzed.

Report by the 2½ Citizen's Task Force to the Hon. Mayor and City Council of Cambridge. 1981. Cambridge, Mass.: City of Cambridge, 114 pp.

Includes dozens of recommendations to increase revenue and reduce expenditures, such as charging for police assistance to private users, improving billing and collecting procedures for neighborhood health centers, reducing custodial staff in schools by one-third, etc.

Debt Management

Advisory Commission on Intergovernmental Relations. 1976. *Understanding the Market For State and Local Debt.* Washington, D.C.: ACIR.

A study designed to assist in understanding various aspects of the market for state and local debt.

Lamb, Robert, and Rappaport, Stephen P. 1980. *Municipal Bonds: The Comprehensive Review of Tax-Exempt Securities and Public Finance.* New York: McGraw-Hill Book Company.

A good deal of background material on various types of debt instruments and issues of concern to investors in the tax-exempt market.

Moak, Lennox. 1970. *Administration of Local Government Debt.* Chicago, IL: Municipal Finance Officers Association of the United States and Canada.

This volume is designed as an introduction to various aspects of local government debt. It provides an overview of some important aspects of the municipal bond market and information on the planning and marketing of municipal bond issues and the administration of debt once issued.

Moody's Investors Service, Inc. 1977. *Pitfalls In Issuing Municipal Bonds.* New York: Moody's Investors Service Inc.

Prepared by the rating agency, this serves as a guidebook for municipalities contemplating a debt program.

Municipal Finance Officers Association. 1978. *A Debt Management Handbook for Small Cities and Other Governmental Units.* Chicago, IL: MFOA (now GFOA).

Long-term debt is a significant issue for a local jurisdiction because it establishes a fixed obligation for many years into the future. This is a step-by-step handbook describing procedures and techniques that can be used by local governments to plan for, issue, and administer debt. It addresses the role of specialized bond consultants, designing the bond issue, marketing the bonds, and administering the outstanding debt.

Public Securities Association. 1981. *Fundamentals of Municipal Bonds.* New York: Public Securities Association.

Provides both technical information on municipal debt as well as background information on the municipal securities industry.

Stanford, Jay G. 1977. *A Checklist for Evaluating Local Government Debt Policy.* Austin, TX: Texas Advisory Commission on Intergovernmental Relations.

This checklist can assist local officials to evaluate policies and practices for using long-term debt.

The Twentieth Century Fund. 1974. *The Rating Game.* Report of the Twentieth Century Fund Task Force on Municipal Credit Ratings (background paper by John E. Petersen). New York: The Twentieth Century Fund, Inc.

Critical analysis of the process and variables involved in rating municipal bonds with recommendations for changes to strengthen systems.

Accounting

American Institute of Certificate Public Accountants. 1974. Committee on Governmental Accounting and Auditing. *Audits of State and Local Governmental Units.* New York: AICPA.

Aronson, J. Richard, and Schwartz, Eli, eds. 1975. *Management Policies in Local Government Finance.* Washington, D.C.: International City Management Association.

Chapter 15, "Municipal Accounting Issues," includes systems design, governmental accounting systems, accrual accounting adjustments, cost accounting, and the audit function.

Comptroller General of the United States. 1972. *Standards for Audit of Government Organizations, Programs, Activities, and Functions.* Washington, D.C.: U.S. General Accounting Office.

Dirsmith, Mark W., and Simon, Abraham J. 1983. *Local Government Internal Controls: A Guide for Public Officials.* New York: Council on Municipal Performance. The need for evaluating and reporting on internal controls is explained, and methods are suggested. The book also includes a discussion of audit committees and their relationship to monitoring of internal controls.

Kobayashi, Richard, and Coopers & Lybrand. 1978. *The Municipal Audit: Choice and Opportunity.* Boston, MA: Dept. of Community Affairs.

A manual designed to assist local officials in understanding what an audit is and how to get one from a private firm, monitor the process, and evaluate the product.

Municipal Finance Officers Association. 1978. *An Accounting Handbook for Small Cities and Other Government Units.* Chicago, IL: MFOA (now GFOA).

A guidebook that describes policies and practices essential to the development of a sound accounting system. It covers areas such as the accounting process, accounting for cash, purchasing, financial reports, inventories, enterprise fund and grant accounting, and auditing.

National Committee on Governmental Accounting. 1968. *Governmental Accounting, Auditing, and Financial Reporting.* Chicago, IL: MFOA (now GFOA).

National Council on Governmental Accounting. 1979. *Governmental Accounting and Financial Reporting Principles.* Chicago, IL: MFOA (now GFOA).

Price Waterhouse & Co. 1976. *Understanding Local Government Financial Statements; A Citizen's Guide.* New York, NY: Price Waterhouse & Co.

Rousmaniere, Peter. 1979. *Local Government Auditing: A Manual for Public Officials.* New York, NY: Council on Municipal Performance.

Touche Ross & Company. 1977. *Public Financial Reporting by Local Governments.* New York: Touche Ross & Company.

Pensions

Advisory Commission on Intergovernmental Relations. 1979. *Information Bulletin: State and Local Government Pension Reform.* Washington, D.C.: ACIR.

Several states have acted recently to restore order to their pension systems by establishing stricter financial and supervisory standards and consolidating small, independent local plans into broader statewide systems. Based on these actions and previous commission recommendations, the ACIR has developed two pieces of model legislation—one delineating a state supervisory role and the other establishing a consolidated pension system—to help states come to grips with their pension problems. This bulletin discusses some of the issues in retirement system financing and reviews the action of several states and the ACIR policy in the field of pension reform.

Areson, Todd W., and Kossak, Shelley E. N. D. *Pension Issues for Local Policy-makers.* Washington, D.C.: National Association of Counties and National League of Cities, 46 pp.

A brief, useful overview of pension issues.

Jump, Bernard, Jr. 1976. *State and Local Employee Pension Plans: Watching for Problems.* Columbus, OH: Academy for Contemporary Problems.

Massachusetts Taxpayers Foundation. 1976. *Paying for Public Pensions: Will a Day Come When the Money Runs Out?* Boston, MA: Massachusetts Taxpayers Foundation.

Municipal Finance Officers Association. 1978. "Public Employee Retirement Systems" in *Governmental Finance,* vol. 7, No. 1. Chicago, IL: MFOA (now GFOA).

This issue focuses on public employee retirement systems as they were operating in the environment of the 1970s: Federal regulatory action, heightened citizens' interest in government financial management, and shrinking budgets resulting in economic strains.

Present, Phillip E. "Policy Decisions and the Administration of Local Government Pension Funds" in *Governmental Finance.* Chicago, IL: MFOA (now GFOA).

Winklevoss, Howard E., and McGill, Dan M. 1978. *Public Pensions Plans: Fundamentals of Design, Funding, and Reporting.* Philadelphia, PA: Winklevoss & Associates.

VI. OTHER SOURCES

There are many sources of information and assistance for local governments encountering problems in financial management, and the types of services vary widely. When seeking help from a consultant, the mayor should select one with references from colleagues who have experienced similar types of problems.

If leads or recommendations are not available, there are rosters of municipal finance consultants that one can check. A directory of consulting services is presented in *The Municipal Year Book,* published annually by the

International City Management Association. The *Directory of Municipal Bond Dealers,* published periodically by *The Bond Buyer,* contains listings of municipal finance consultants and bond attorneys as well as municipal bond dealers. The Government Finance Officers Association, through its Resource Center, maintains a list of experts who can deal with financial management problems.

11
Mayor's Fact Sheet

The Mayor's Fact Sheet includes measures of fiscal policy, municipal employees and services, socio-economic characteristics, and political processes. To help master these subjects, one person who is both loyal to the mayor's priorities and understands the city's fiscal situation is critical. Initially, this may be the mayor alone or one of the mayor's assistants or the finance director. Even if the staff is excellent, asking pointed questions will keep them on their toes. Others can help assemble data, but only the mayor can interpret the results to set priorities.

Five-year trends highlight changes. Data for the present and previous year and for five years ago can be plotted in a graph like the one drawn in Fig. 11.1 Of course, plotting each of the past five years and as many as ten years back would be a good idea if the data are available.

Primary data include the following:

1. Budgets and financial statements of the city for the past five years, including the auditor's report and letter if an outside auditor was used.
2. Bond prospectus if your city has sold bonds recently.
3. A report for your state including finances of your city and other cities in the state (excellent in some states, almost nonexistent in others).
4. *City Government Finances,* published annually by the U.S. Bureau of

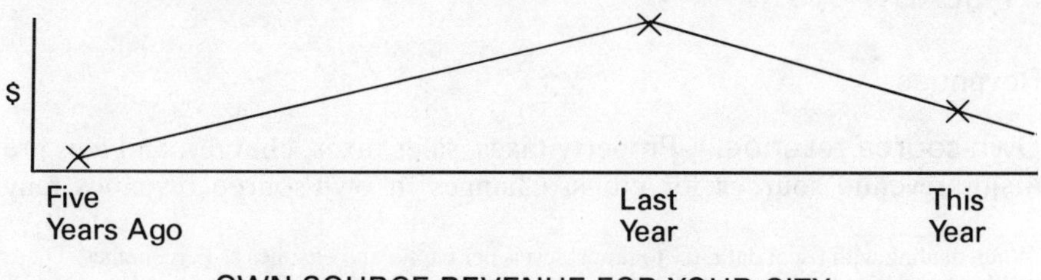

Fig. 11.1 Own-source revenue for your city.

Census, Washington, D.C. 20233, for cities with a population over 50,000.

5. *County and City Data Book* (most recent year), published about every five years by U.S. Bureau of the Census, Washington D.C. 20233; includes socio-economic data for cities with a population over 25,000.
6. If available, a report comparing finances and salaries of your city with other cities in the region (prepared by private firms or some associations of local governments).
7. *City Government Employment,* published annually by the U.S. Bureau of the Census; includes numbers of employees for several major functions for cities with a population over 50,000.

To use this Fact Sheet, you should meet with top staff, including department heads, and ask what they feel are the major problems the city confronts and what opinions they have heard. Probe them about the problems they have mentioned. Ask them for evidence and for comparisons of your city with other cities over time if possible. Watch for disparities between your ideas of your city and theirs. Use the materials here to help develop such questions but make sure to adapt them to get you through your first year. A new mayor must often work hard to determine whether current revenues will cover expenditures. The sooner you master the basic facts, the more confidence you will inspire and the more easily you can discuss serious policy options.

Don't be surprised if some facts are not readily available. Forget about them for now, but be sure to ask yourself if they are important enough to your decision making to have them collected over time.

This Fact Sheet will include many items handy for reference. Try to memorize some of its facts and cite them in discussions. You won't just sound as if you know more; you *will* know more.

I. FISCAL FACTS[1]

Revenues

Own-source revenue. Property taxes, sales taxes, charges, and fees are major revenue sources for cities. Changes in own-source revenues may

[1]When dealing with fiscal data, try to report levels per capita and changes as percentages. There will be disparities between most local reports and Census reports. The Census seeks to standardize reporting practices for comparative purposes. Watch for disparities between your results and theirs, and ask your staff to help interpret differences.

indicate changes in your city's economic conditions, population, industrial base, etc. Try to find the reasons for any major changes.

Facts to know:

1. Major sources of revenue (e.g., property taxes, sales taxes) and proportionate shares (percentage each contributes to total)
2. Current revenues from these sources
3. Revenues from each source over the past five years (ideally with rate changes in taxes or charges indicated)

Intergovernmental revenue. Revenues from Federal and state governments generally increased until the late 1970s. Has your city followed national and state trends?

Facts to know:

1. Revenue sources by major programs (e.g., General Revenue Sharing, major categorical grants) and proportionate shares
2. Current revenues from these sources
3. Revenues over the past five years

Utility revenue. By law, these revenues are usually reported separately from other revenues.

Facts to know:

1. Sources of revenue (e.g., water, public transportation)
2. Current revenues from these sources
3. Revenues over past five years

Expenditures

General expenditures. Overall expenditures should be considered as well as expenditures by function.

Facts to know:

1. General (total) expenditures per capita and for major departments or functions (e.g., general administration, police, fire, social services, education, transportation, environment, housing, parks)
2. Changes in the preceding over the past five years

Utility expenditures.

Facts to know:

1. Current expenditure levels (overall and by utility)
2. Expenditure levels over the past five years (overall and by utility)

Long-term debt. Long-term debt is incurred primarily to finance major capital projects. General obligation bonds and revenue bonds are the two main types. General obligation (GO) bonds—primarily issued to finance streets, schools, and municipal buildings—are secured by the taxing power of the issuing government. Revenue bonds finance those facilities (e.g., airports, stadiums) that are supported by user fees and service charges. Long-term debt is evaluated by investors, rating agencies, and state and Federal agencies as well as local groups and taxpayers.

Facts to know:

1. Current debt levels
2. Composition of debt (amount and type outstanding and repayment schedule)
3. Maturity dates of bonds
4. Debt levels over the past ten years
5. Comparison to other cities

Short-term debt. Short-term is often used to finance early stages of a project before long-term bonds are sold (bond anticipation notes, known as BANs) or to meet expenditure deadlines occurring prior to receipt of anticipated revenues (tax or revenue anticipation notes, known as TANs and RANs). Accounting reports should follow generally recommended accounting practices and indicate whether short-term debt is being handled appropriately. Be sure to ask your staff for a frank interpretation of past short-term debt practices.

Facts to know:

1. Current debt levels
2. Composition of debt
3. Maturity dates of notes
4. Identification of note holders
5. Debt levels over the past five years

Taxes

Tax structure. Cities vary considerably in their mix of local revenues.

Facts to know:

1. Current tax structure (amount of revenue from property taxes, sales taxes, and any other taxes)
2. Current tax rates
3. Tax structure over the past five years
4. Tax rates over the past five years

Tax collection. Cities vary considerably in tax delinquency rates. Even if the county or state collects your taxes, you can press for the improvement of a poor situation.

Facts to know:

1. Methods of tax collection
2. Current collection rate
3. Collection rate over the past five years and that for similar cities

Tax Burden. The tax burden should be computed for every local government (school district, special districts, county) that overlaps with your municipality, including the state government. Doing so allows the various components to be isolated as well as the total tax burden borne by the average citizen or firm.

Facts to know:

1. Total own-source revenues (not just taxes) from all local governments and state government, per capita. (Optional: separate computation for tax revenues only)
2. Changes over the past five years (Note: If you have difficulty obtaining these data from local sources, the U.S. Census publishes them every five years in the Census of Governments. See *1977 Census of Governments,* vol. 4, No. 5, *Compendium of Government Finances,* Table 54.)
3. Comparison with other cities

Miscellaneous

Infrastructure. Maintenance of municipal facilities and land is an ongoing cost to the city, albeit sometimes neglected.

Facts to know:

1. Current value of municipal properties
2. Age, condition, and future repair schedule of important facilities, buildings, roads, etc.
3. Long-term (10- to 30-year) trend in (1) capital construction, (2) equipment purchases, and (3) maintenance expenditures to compare with recent spending levels. Has new construction or maintenance decreased? Why?

Bond rating and fire insurance rating. Municipal bonds are often rated by Moody's and Standard and Poor's.

Facts to know:

1. Current ratings
2. Ratings over last five years

Functions performed. Many functions overlap several local governments and private agencies.

Facts to know:

1. Functions performed (services provided) primarily by the city
2. Functions shared with other entities (e.g., state or county government, private organizations); relative fiscal responsibility of each. (Note: You can obtain basic data for functions performed from annual budgets or financial statements of school districts, special districts, and major private agencies. Some cities find it useful to prepare a service-oriented handbook for citizens. Check out a few facilities personally, or have your staff do so. You will probably find some duplication and areas where better communication, if not direct cooperation, among the providers could improve services to your citizens or permit cutbacks without impairing services.)

Contracting out. What percentage of your operating expenditures are for contracting out with other governments or private firms for services (e.g., for garbage collection, park maintenance)? How well is contracting working as compared to using city staff to provide the services? Do you have any cost comparisons?

II. MUNICIPAL EMPLOYEES AND SERVICES

Number of employees. Are any departments overstaffed? This is a hard question to answer, but ask for specific reasons from each department head. Ask them to compare their staffing levels to other departments and cities. Can they document their arguments convincingly?

Facts to know:

1. Number of employees per capita, by total and by function
2. Number of employees, not per capita, by function over the past ten years
3. Number of employees per capita, by function compared to similar cities
4. Optional: Compute No. 1 to No. 3 by subfunction, e.g., police patrols separate from crime lab, etc.

Extent of employee unionization. Extensive unionization may hamper your personnel policies.

Facts to know:

1. Percentage of employees unionized by function and unions they belong to.

Details of the civil service system. Employees differ in their tenure and rights. Press to learn just what powers you have over each type of employee.

Facts to know:

1. Percentage of employees, by function
2. Percentage of civil servants, by seniority and function
3. If you wish to terminate an employee for cause, must his case be reviewed by the union, civil service board, or both? How long is the review process? How much does it cost the city?

General contract information.

Facts to know:

1. Expiration dates of major contracts
2. Strike history of each major union (number, duration, issues, settlement)

3. Disparity between past demands and settlements for major groups of employees
4. Do contracts include automatic cost of living increases?
5. Do contracts include productivity clauses or other incentives rewarding performance? How well do the incentives work?
6. Are you comfortable with the tone of contract wording? Would your citizens be comfortable? Are there any points you want to publicize to remind workers of their benefits or to create a climate to help bring about change?

Labor capital tradeoffs. If labor costs increase, savings may be had by increasing relative spending on labor-saving capital items. How do your departments compare with each other and across cities?

Facts to know:

1. Ratio of personnel/capital expenditue by total and by function
2. Compute No. 1 over the past ten years
3. Compare Nos. 1 and 2 to similar cities

Compensation and benefits. You may want to pay employees more than other cities or local private employers, but you and others should be aware of doing so. Few cities have precise information on these matters for all categories and levels of employees.

Facts to know:

1. Average wage per employee, by total and by function
2. Average fringe benefits per employee, by function (including dollar value of sick days, vacation, estimated pension cost)
3. Average overtime per employee, by function
4. Average of Nos. 1 through 3 over the past five years
5. All these averages compared to those of other similar cities
6. The first four averages for different levels of employee (e.g., by seniority and expertise). Valuable for comparisons with the averages in Nos. 4 and 5 but hard to obtain precisely.

Service performance measures. Cities vary considerably in how they use performance measures. In some, dozens of measures appear in the annual budget, whereas in others they remain in departmental files unused by elected officials. It is often convenient to have a single office or staff member compile such data.

Facts to know:

1. Do you have any performance measures regularly collected and reported to you for general managerial purposes?
2. Are performance measures prepared by the departments or separate staff? Do the departmental staff trust the nondepartmental data and use it themselves? When and why do they keep separate figures?
3. How many of the following sorts of measures does your city report to the mayor?
   (a) Emergency response time for police, fire, and ambulance services
   (b) Library and park usage measures by neighborhood
   (c) Frequency of garbage collection; tons of garbage collected per employee; comparisons over time and with other cities
   (d) Number and percentage of citizens using public transportation; percentage of transportation expenditures covered by fares; contributions by Federal, state, and local governments
   (e) Some basic measures of the effectiveness of each major service provided by your city government
4. Do you have staff that regularly review specific tasks for productivity improvement purposes? How much have they saved your city in the past five years?

III. SOCIO-ECONOMIC CHARACTERISTICS

This section includes basic data that become more interesting over time or when compared to other cities. Most are collected by the U.S. Census Bureau about every five years (see primary data source No. 5 at the beginning of the chapter.)

Population Characteristics.

Facts to know:

1. Current population size
2. Population change over the last two decades
3. Percentage of population by young and old age groups, race, national

origin, income levels, median school years completed, high school, and college graduates

4. Comparative data on Nos. 1 through 3 for similar cities

Economic base.

Facts to know:

1. Median per capita income
2. Median family income over the past ten years
3. Current assessed and equalized value of taxable property—residential, industrial, and total
4. Current retail sales
5. Total number of private and public sector jobs in the city (may be available only for the county)
6. Number of jobs by major economic sector (e.g. retail sales, manufacturing)
7. Changes in Nos. 1 through 6 over the past ten years and comparative data for similar cities
8. Ten largest employers and ten largest taxpayers

Poverty and Unemployment.

Facts to know:

1. Percentage of population below federal poverty level
2. Percentage of unemployed
3. Percentage receiving public assistance (e.g., welfare, food stamps)
4. Changes in Nos. 1 through 3 over the last ten years and comparisons with similar cities

Monitoring policy impacts of services. Some socio-economic characteristics are partially related to public services. Consider monitoring those for which you have some form of related performance indicators.

Examples:

1. Crime rates, by total and by type of crime (e.g. burglary)
2. Number of fires, by season and year
3. Achievement test scores of students in public schools as compared to national average
4. Racial composition of schools
5. Percentage of students attending private/parochial schools

IV. POLITICAL PROCESSES

1. What five groups or organizations are *most active* in city government (e.g., the press, municipal employees, business groups, etc.)?

   (a) ______________________________

   (b) ______________________________

   (c) ______________________________

   (d) ______________________________

   (e) ______________________________

2. What is the position of *each of these groups* on overall government spending? Write in a score from 1 to 10 for each of the five groups.

1	2	3	4	5	6	7	8	9	10	0
Prefers *reduced* spending			Prefers *about same* spending as currently					Prefers increased spending		No position clear

   (a)________ (b)________ (c)________ (d)________ (e)________

3. What is the position of *most citizens* on spending? Write in a score from 1 to 10 here:________________.
4. What is *your* position? Write in a score from 1 to 10 here:________.
5. What is the position of the *current council?* Write in a score from 1 to 10 here:________________.
6. What was the position of the *mayor and council five years ago?* Write in a score from 1 to 10 here:________________.
7. What have been the most visible pressures from any local groups for reducing spending in your city in recent years?________________

   ____

8. What have been the most visible pressures to maintain or increase spending?________________

   ____

   ____

9. What is your position on the number of municipal employees? Circle one number.

1	2	3	4	5	6	7	8	9	10	0
There is overstaffing				About right			There is understaffing			Not sure

10. What is your position on compensation of municipal employees? Circle one number.

1	2	3	4	5	6	7	8	9	10	0
They are underpaid				About right					Overpaid	Not sure

11. Do you have a published multiyear plan for capital budgeting?
12. Do you have a multiyear plan (personal or public) for number and compensation of employees?
13. Do you have a multiyear plan (personal or public) for changes in basic services performed by the city?

At a Mayors Leadership Institute, some of these political process questions should be of the most interest when the experiences of various cities are compared. Measures of this sort are analyzed in Terry Nichols Clark and Lorna Crowley Ferguson, *City Money* (New York: Columbia University Press, 1983).

Index